OUR LADY OF EPHESUS

Our Lady of Ephesus

BERNARD F. DEUTSCH

Angelico Press

This Angelico Press edition is a reprint of the work originally published in 1965 by The Bruce Publishing Company.
Angelico Press © 2024

All rights reserved:
No part of this book may be reproduced or transmitted, in any form or by any means, without permission

For information, address:
Angelico Press, Ltd.
169 Monitor St.
Brooklyn, NY 11222
www.angelicopress.com

paperback 979-8-89280-003-7
cloth 979-8-89280-004-4

NIHIL OBSTAT:
RT. REV. CLEMENT V. BASTNAGEL, J.U.D.
Censor deputatus

IMPRIMATUR:
✠ JOSEPH CARDINAL RITTER
Archiepiscopus Sancti Ludovici
2 Februarii, 1965

The Nihil Obstat and Imprimatur represent official ecclesiastical declarations that a book is free of doctrinal or moral error. They do not, however, imply that those making the declarations agree with the contents, opinions, or statements expressed.

Cover design
by Michael Schrauzer

TO
MY MOTHERS
MARY AND MARIE

Acknowledgments

I take this occasion to express my gratitude to Templegate Publishers for their gracious permission to quote extensively from A. C. Emmerich's *The Life of the Blessed Virgin Mary* and to the American Society of Ephesus for the generous authorization to use its publications. I wish to thank the Most Rev. Joseph Descuffi, C.M., Archbishop of Smyrna, who forwarded valuable materials; Fr. Francis Allen, S.M.M., who as a resident priest at Mary's home in Ephesus patiently furnished information available from no printed or readily accessible source; and Maj. Robert F. Overman, chaplain, U.S.A.F., who introduced me to the Shrine of Our Lady of Ephesus.

Furthermore, I acknowledge my indebtedness to the many individuals who in sundry ways assisted me in the preparation of this book. No attempt will be made to list them by name, with the exception of the following couples: John and Mary Margaret Audette, Clarence and Carolyn DuClos, Paul and Elizabeth Fraser, Fred and Teresa Hawley. And to this exception I add only the name of one person, my father, Anthony B. Deutsch.

Preface

You need not feel inferior if you have never heard of Mary's home at Ephesus, where she spent her last years on earth. I myself learned of it as recently as 1957 and found practically everyone to whom I have since mentioned the shrine in complete ignorance of such a place. The basic reason anywhere for lack of knowledge of the shrine is its recent discovery and more recent restoration. In America, however, there is a more widespread ignorance than elsewhere because of the lack of pertinent and expository literature. Although works on Mary and Ephesus have appeared in many languages, extremely few have been written in English, and of those none exceeds the size of a pamphlet. With the hope of appreciably improving that situation this book was conceived.

The problem concerning *Panaya Kapulu*, Mary's home in Ephesus, can be stated simply. There are traditions, as well as historical and diversified arguments, which establish it as the dwelling place of Mary during her final years on earth, as well as the site of the Assumption. In Jerusalem, however, there is the tomb popularly supposed to be that of Mary as well as the site of her Assumption. Thus either the Ephesus or the Jerusalem tradition is false: Mary could not have spent her last years, and died perhaps, and been assumed into heaven at more than one place. Although absolute scientific certitude as to the geographical location does not seem possible, a moral certainty concerning one of the two possibilities may be enjoyed.

It is only fair that from the outset you be informed of my attitude toward the evaluation of this problem. I am, if not skeptical, altogether circumspect when it comes to most private visions, some extraordinary cures, certain pious traditions, and so on. And I am at least as wary as is the Church itself in issuing its official declarations on such matters. But once something fundamental concerning them can be established from solid factual arguments, then all the attending circumstances assume a new significance. The case for the Ephesus tradition may be said to enjoy real factual foundation plus manifold auxiliary arguments. The Jerusalem tradition, however, has apparently few of the latter and none of the former.

I have been as objective as possible in considering the evidence of the controversy and have arrived at a judgment. It is my hope, of course, that you reach the identical conclusion. The facts and arguments in the following chapters seem more than adequate to fulfill that hope. All the evidence known to me, whether for or against the Ephesus tradition, is included and generally evaluated.

Regardless of your final judgment it cannot be denied that *Panaya Kapulu* is a shrine of our Lady, and as such it has the highest ecclesiastical sanction. Mary surely dwells there today; this is evident, for instance, from the many cures. While the frequent cures do not prove the authenticity of the shrine, they would at least seem to indicate divine approval of the faith and devotion manifested there. If those cures alone could be used as proof that *Panaya Kapulu* was Mary's home at Ephesus, then nothing further would have to be said.

The decision on the authenticity of *Panaya* may and should be formed, therefore, from the collection of facts and related arguments presented prior to the treatment of apparitions and cures.

People are all fascinated in various degrees by the unknown, the mysterious, the supernatural. Elements of this nature permeate the text which follows. As this narrative proceeds you will be exposed to all of the history of Mary's home that I am capable of presenting. You will learn of the remarkable discovery of the shrine. You will marvel, it is hoped, at the many traditions, the related legends, the extensive writings, and various facts concerning it. You will acquire knowledge of the pilgrimages, cures, and innumerable other details. But it is my hope, most of all, that you will be thinking of Mary throughout this book and will thereby be in some way honoring her. Most likely she and her home at Ephesus will occasionally come to mind long after you have finished this handbook.

Preface

The term *handbook* is used in the sense that this is the most complete and up-to-date work available on Mary's home, a sort of manual on Our Lady of Ephesus. A wealth of further reading matter is indicated in the bibliography.

For several years I have wished many times for a manual wherein references and sources for all the salient points of *Panaya* could be found. This is the first attempt at one in English.

Contents

Acknowledgments vii
Preface ix
Foreword to the 2024 Angelico Press edition . . . xv

   I. Allow Me to Present 1

  II. Mary's Home — Panaya Kapulu 8

 III. Relevant Legends, Traditions, and Literature . . 25

 IV. Relevant Documents, Facts, and Studies . . 51

   V. Development of the Shrine 84

 VI. Shrine of Our Lady of Ephesus 98

Mary's House 130

Appendix 131
Notes 137
Bibliography 165

Foreword

TO THE 2024 ANGELICO PRESS EDITION

Encountering the visions of Anne Catherine Emmerich can raise the question: How is it possible that this woman, who never left the German region in which she was born, could describe in such detail the geography and topography of Palestine, along with the customs and habits of people living there, including minute details of dress and architecture? To help answer this question, Angelico Press has over recent years published exhaustive new editions of these visions, together with supplementary material regarding geographical and temporal details found in the visions, and other never before published material.

This project has benefited from the work of others who laid much groundwork. The primary contributions were two extensive works by the German priest Helmut Fahsel: *Der Wandel Jesu in Der Welt Nach den Visionen der Anna Katharina Emmerich*, Ilionverlag, 1942 (complete with numerous illustrations and 40 specially drawn-up maps of the journeys of Jesus Christ); and *Die Heiligen Drei Könige: In der Legende und Nach den Visionen der Anna Katharina Emmerich*, Ilionverlag, 1942, also with illustrations and maps. Others have undertaken research on the basis of the universe of detail in Anne Catherine's visions, the most exciting of which is the subject of the present text, which describes in absorbing detail the thrilling discovery of the location of the Virgin Mary's house in Ephesus.

In brief, a French priest, Abbé Julien Gouyet of Paris, after reading an account of Anne Catherine's visions concerning the death of the Virgin Mary near Ephesus, traveled there and searched the whole area. On October 18, 1881, guided by various particulars in her account, he discovered the ruins of a small stone building on a mountain (Bulbul Dag, "Mount Nightingale") overlooking the Aegean Sea with a view across to the remains of the ancient city of Ephesus.

Distant View of the House of Mary, by Clemens Brentano

Abbé Gouyet was convinced that this was the house described in Anne Catherine's visions as the dwelling place of the Virgin Mary during the last years of her life. He was at first ridiculed, but several years later the ruins were independently discovered again by two Lazarist missionaries who had undertaken a similar search on the basis of Anne Catherine's visions. They ascertained that the building had been a place of pilgrimage in earlier times for Christians descended from the church of Ephesus, the community referred to by St John (Rev. 2:1–7). The building had been known in those days as *Panaya Kapulu*, the House of the Blessed Virgin, and the Turkish city of Izmir determined that the foundation of the original house dated back to the first century AD. It noted that the structure of the house conformed exactly to Anne Catherine's detailed description.

The house has since been restored and is an active place of pilgrimage. At a ceremony to commemorate the hundredth anniversary of its restoration, Archbishop Bernardini made this statement: "Dear brothers and sisters, all our bishops agree that the Virgin Mary died here. September 28 and May 12 are very significant holy days for us, for on September 28, 1890, it was confirmed that the Blessed Virgin lived and died here, and on May 12, 1891, the first religious ceremony was held here in her honor. This house is the only known surviving building in which the Blessed Virgin lived."

This remarkable example demonstrates at least the partial authenticity of Anne Catherine's visions. That her visions provide spiritual

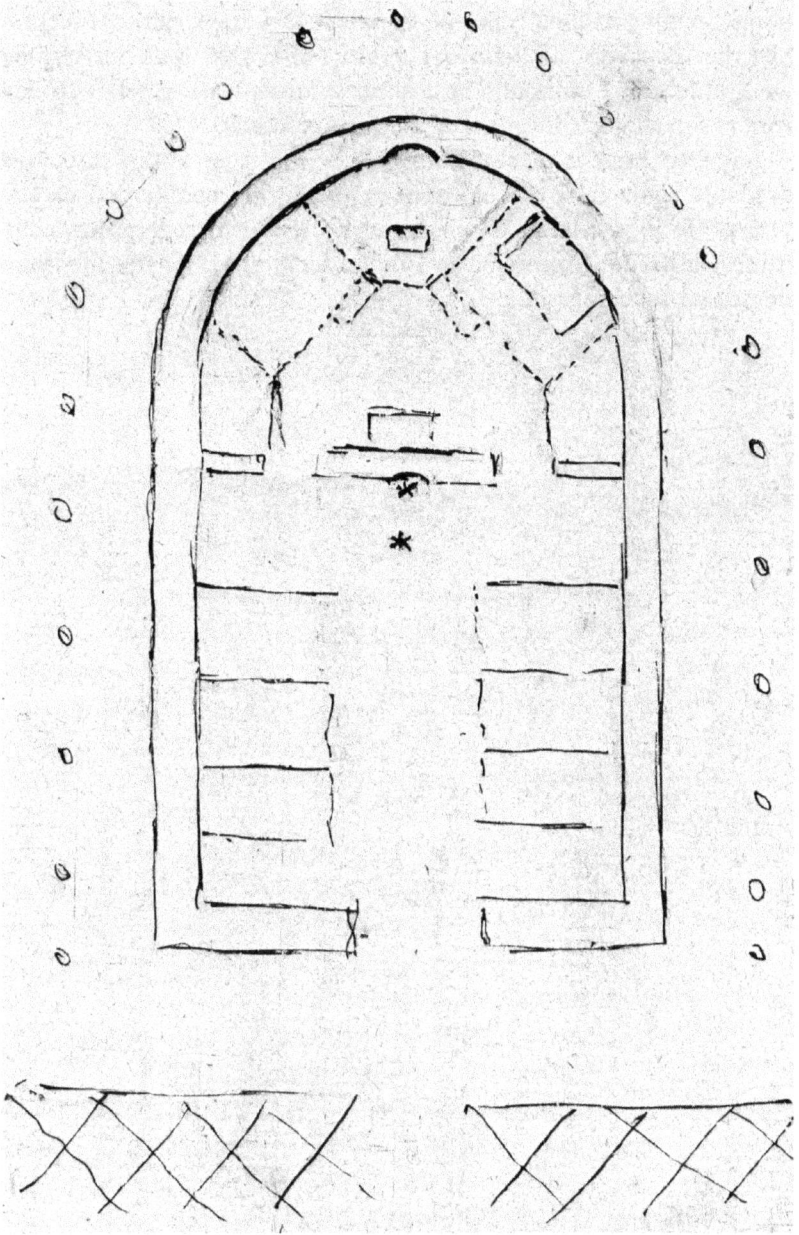

Floor Plan of House of Mary, by Clemens Brentano

nourishment had long been the experience of many spiritual seekers, but the discovery of Panaya Kapulu confirmed that her visions were objectively authentic and accessible (at least in part) to corroboration along conventional lines of research.

Angelico Press is pleased to make the full story of this discovery available again in a new edition. It is a fitting companion to our other offerings related to the remarkable contributions made by Anne Catherine Emmerich to our understanding of the life, journeys, and teachings of Our Lord Jesus Christ.

OUR LADY OF EPHESUS

CHAPTER I

Allow Me to Present...

§ 1. *Anne Catherine Emmerich (1774–1824)*

It was through Anne Catherine Emmerich that the Shrine of Our Lady of Ephesus was discovered. While it is quite true that Mary's cult was practiced in Christian Ephesus, and that one could speak of Our Lady of Ephesus in that sense, the title refers to Mary primarily as she is honored at her home in Ephesus, the house wherein she lived for the last nine years of her life, the place of her Dormition — the site of her Assumption. It is altogether proper to say that without Catherine Emmerich, Mary's home, or *Panaya Kapulu*,[1] as the local people call it, would in all probability not be known to the world today. Without her, then, this house of the Holy Virgin, where already hundreds of thousands have venerated Mary, would still be nothing but a relatively deserted ruin, known only to a few.

Catherine Emmerich was born on September 8, 1774, in the village of Flamske, near Coesfeld, in the diocese of Münster, Westphalia, Germany. A peasant, she was bound out to a farmer at the age of twelve. Six years later she was apprenticed to a dressmaker in Coesfeld, and after two years of sewing she went home and began in earnest her efforts to enter a convent, a desire she had entertained from her early teens.

> She asked to be received at the Convents of the Augustinians at Borken, of the Trappists at Darfeld, and of the Poor Clares at Münster; but her poverty, and that of these convents, always presented an insuperable obstacle to her being received.[2]

Catherine simply did not have a dowry; she would have appeared, therefore, to any poor convent as a definite liability. When twenty years were behind her, she had amassed through her sewing the vast fortune — vast to a poor peasant girl — of about ten dollars. The idea had come to her that with that money she might learn in Coesfeld how to play the organ and then, armed with such a talent, perhaps gain admittance to some convent. But once in Coesfeld, she spent so much time, and all her money, serving the poor that there was none left for learning music. She remained at Coesfeld some four years, working and spending on the poor what little she earned.

While from her youth visions were commonplace to Catherine, she told of one that was distinctly different. She was twenty-four years old and still at Coesfeld. One day about noon, while kneeling in meditation in the Jesuit church, she experienced actually and visibly the sufferings of Christ's sacred head crowned with thorns.[3]

Four more years in Coesfeld passed, all the while Catherine's desires of becoming a nun increasing and her chances decreasing. Finally the opportunity came when the parents of a young girl whom the Augustinian nuns of Dülmen wished to receive into their order refused to give their consent unless Catherine was taken at the same time. "The nuns yielded their assent, though somewhat reluctantly, on account of their extreme poverty, and on the 13th November 1802, one week before the feast of the Presentation of the Blessed Virgin, Anne Catherine entered on her novitiate."[4]

Catherine's life in the convent of Agnetenberg was not always easy, inasmuch as she was "different" from the other nuns. But she bore all things patiently and lovingly. At the age of twenty-nine, exactly one year after her admittance, she pronounced her solemn vows.

Catherine's life in the convent was accompanied by many remarkable phenomena,[5] not the least of which were her numerous visions during her illnesses. Catherine had never been the picture of health, nor in fact did she enjoy what little health was rightly hers, for she had asked God to allow her the suffering of others and He granted her desire. In 1807 Catherine began to experience pains corresponding to the wounds of Christ, and the pain in her feet often prevented her walking.

On the 3rd December 1811, the convent was suppressed [under the government of Jerome Bonaparte, King of Westphalia] and the church closed. The nuns dispersed in all directions, but Anne Catherine remained, poor and ill. A kindhearted servant belonging to the monastery attended her out of charity, and an aged emigrant priest, who said Mass in the convent, remained also with her. These three individuals, being the poorest of the Community, did not leave the convent until the spring of 1812.[6]

In the spring of that year Catherine was thirty-seven and a very sick woman. She was moved to the home of a poor widow in the neighborhood, where she had a miserable little room for a year and a half.[7] It was toward the end of December that the full stigmata of Christ's cross and crucifixion were imprinted upon her. Not only was Catherine unable to walk or rise from bed but she also soon became unable to eat.

Word of her stigmata leaked out early in 1813 and the village doctor forced her to undergo an examination. Contrary to his expectations he was convinced of the truth of the phenomena and forthwith drew up an official report.[8] He attended Catherine as physician and friend from that time until her death. Once his examination had been conducted, of course, word spread. On March 28, 1813, the Church authorities from Münster decided that an ecclesiastical investigation was desirable, and a commission which included Dean Bernard Overberg, the vicar-general, and three physicians proceeded to Dülmen. The members of the delegation found her stigmata genuine, and one of the doctors published in 1814 a detailed account of the phenomena in the *Medical Journal* of Salzburg.

On October 23, 1813, Catherine was moved again; this time she had a window overlooking a garden — a big improvement over the past year and a half. Catherine's aged mother came there from the country in 1817 to die by her side. Her father had died at home a short time earlier.

In view of what has been said of Catherine's peasant youth, it should not come as a surprise to learn that she was practically illiterate. She nonetheless believed that God wished her to leave "for the good of many souls" the many revelations with which He had blessed her. In spirit she had already visited many places and witnessed numerous events, relating especially to the lives of the saints and the feasts of the Church. And she was yet to witness, in her bedridden state, even more. In her last years (1821–1824) the visions became increasingly concentrated on the life of Christ and the saints about Him, particularly Mary. When Clemens Brentano (1778–1842), the German poet, first visited her on September 17, 1818, she recognized him as the man who was to enable her to fulfill her wish to set her visions down in writing. Although her personal conviction alone would have sufficed, she was furthermore counseled personally by Bishop Michael Sailer on October 22, 1818, to relate everything to Brentano.[9]

Catherine passed her remaining years in ecstasies and sufferings, always repeating her visions to her scribe. In 1823 she said that God would soon take her to Himself.[10] On February 9, 1824, at half-past eight in the evening, having received the Last Sacraments, she breathed her last in the presence of a priest and a few friends. She was carried to the grave the following Friday, the thirteenth, followed by the entire population of the place.

As a postscript to Catherine's life, here is an extract, printed in December, 1824, from the *Journal of Catholic Literature* of Kerz:

> About six or seven weeks after the death of Anne Catherine Emmerich, a report having got about that her body had been stolen away, the grave and coffin were opened in secret, by order of the authorities, in the presence of seven witnesses. They found with surprise not unmixed with joy that corruption had not yet begun its work on the body of the pious maiden. Her features and countenance were smiling like those of a person who is dreaming sweetly. She looked as though she had but just been placed in the coffin, nor did her body exhale any corpse-like smell. *It is good to keep the secret of the king,* says Jesus the son of Sirach; but it is also good to reveal to the world the greatness of the mercy of God.[11]

The case for Catherine's beatification was introduced in 1892 by the Bishop of Münster and is still pending. As will become clearer later on, the question of Catherine's visions, as edited by her scribe, Brentano, had hindered the process all along. A gigantic step forward occurred when Pope Pius XI (1922–1939) eliminated them from further consideration.

§ 2. Her Visions in General

The visions of Catherine Emmerich as transcribed by Brentano are not wholly perfect. But after all, when you consider the means afforded her for handing them down to posterity, this is not surprising. There are some errors, but they are practically always of little consequence — chronological, geographical, or philological. And as one expert remarked, ". . . the statements of Anne Catherine Emmerich . . . are never found to be counter to the Scriptures, nor mistaken about Jewish ritual at the time."[12]

The man ultimately responsible for the written version of Catherine's visions was something of a controversial character himself. Clemens Maria Brentano (1778–1842), part-time poet and prominent member of the Romantic School, is perhaps best known for having published *Des Knaben Wunderhorn*. He married a divorcée named Sophie Mereau, and after her death in 1806 became a drifter. A second marriage proved disastrous and he left his second wife. The year 1818 found him in Berlin and "converted" — his previous indifference to his Catholic birthright transformed into fervent devotion.

Later in 1818 he first learned of Catherine Emmerich on reading a published letter of the Count de Stolberg, which bore witness to the authenticity of the phenomena observed in the stigmatic. He afterward learned more from a friend who had visited Catherine. In September, 1818, he managed an invitation from Bishop Sailer, and obtained from Dean Overberg, the bishop's vicar-general, a letter of introduction to Catherine's doctor. His first visit with her was on September 17. Shortly after that, and for reasons already mentioned, he began to transcribe all that she told him. He passed in this manner six years, although he allowed a few deliberate interruptions. Thus he remained her servant from the moment of introduction to the end.

When Catherine died in 1824, Brentano again wandered, settling finally in Munich in 1833. From the mass of the recorded visions he extracted everything pertaining to the life of Christ and edited the very last portion, some ten years after Catherine's death, under the title *The Dolorous Passion of Our Lord*.[13] Besides the large collection on the life of Christ, he extracted another smaller collection on the life of Mary. He began printing this in 1841, but never finished it because of illness. He died on July 28, 1842. His brother, Christian, who fell heir to his papers, wished to continue printing *The Life of Our Lady*, but died in 1851 without having really accomplished anything. Christian's widow, with the aid of some friends, finally succeeded in having this and other collected writings published at Frankfurt in nine volumes (1851–1855).[14]

In editing Catherine's visions, Brentano attempted wherever possible to add footnotes from Sacred Scripture, history, tradition, and geography, to show their agreement with reality. It is probable that he may even have made some changes in the visions themselves. Then, too, the language and expressions employed by Brentano, a man of superior education, are quite likely different from Catherine's own oral report. Concerning these questions the following may be noted:

> We have no hesitation whatever in allowing the force of this argument. Most fully do we believe in the entire sincerity of M. Clement Brentano, because we both know and love him, and, besides, his exemplary piety and the retired life which he leads, secluded from a world in which it would depend but on himself to hold the highest place, are guarantees amply sufficient to satisfy any impartial mind of his sincerity. A poem such as he might publish, if he only pleased, would cause him to be ranked at once among the most eminent of the German poets, whereas the office which he has taken upon himself of secretary to a poor visionary has brought him nothing but contemptuous raillery. Nevertheless, we have no intention to assert that in giving the conversations and discourses of Sister Emmerich that order and coherency in which they were greatly wanting, and writing them down in his own way, he may not unwittingly have arranged, explained, and embellished them. But this would not have the effect of destroying the originality of the recital, or impugning either the sincerity of the nun, or that of the writer.[15]

No attempt will be made to give further details of the controversy concerning Brentano. For that the reader is referred to some of the studies already made.[16] And, as already noted, the obstacle which this question had presented to Catherine's beatification has been removed.[17] Brentano undoubtedly rephrased Catherine's simple statements, enhanced them, and added some ideas of his own; let him, therefore, bear the blame for the few errors contained, and give the little nun credit for the rest. The idea of making Brentano responsible in greater part than Catherine for the germ or basic content of the majority of visions is incredible. That the finger of God is evident in those visions, even as handed down by Brentano, cannot be denied. At all times Catherine appeared humble, simple, charitable, docile.

The visions of Catherine were, at best, private revelations. Such revelations have been the object of skepticism down through the ages, and are still such today. Visions of this nature ordinarily possess merely a relative value, and the measure of their worth may be disputed. The Catholic Church, while inflexible in dogma, permits complete liberality to the human mind in almost everything else. You may, therefore, believe private revelations or reject them, as you will. You may place credence in the visions of Catherine Emmerich and others, or you may decline to accept them and dispute their authenticity and divine origin. Even when the Church approves private revelations as written by this or that saint, it does not thereby confirm the content; it gives assurance that nothing offensive is contained. The Church would only reject and condemn revelations which contained matter contrary to faith or morals, or which were opposed to Scripture and apostolic tradition. No such fault can be found with Catherine's revelations as embodied in the ecclesiastically approved *Dolorous Passion* or the *Life of Mary*, nor can fault be found with the nun herself for she related everything in a spirit of complete submission to the Church.

Revelations such as Catherine's are edifying and, since they effectively serve to promote piety, this is sufficient reason for their existence and nominal acceptance. They read as easily as the daily newspaper, and are much more credible and captivating. They took their place in the world rapidly, once they appeared, and they hold it in many languages to this day. Their acknowledged place is, of course, that of a most impressive and singularly memorable collection of meditations, having the extraordinary power of enabling their readers to appreciate the full story behind the brief and austere gospel narratives.

CHAPTER II

Mary's Home—Panaya Kapulu[1]

§ 1. *Catherine's Description*

In practically all of the accounts on Mary's home at Ephesus the pertinent vision of Sister Emmerich and the actual discovery of the house by the Lazarists are interwoven. This is entirely acceptable. There is no reason, however, why Catherine's vision cannot be preserved as such, and be separated from the account of the actual discovery. One problem does arise by placing her vision ahead of the discovery, and that is that you know what Mary's home looks like before you learn that it has been found. But this order is not really too illogical when you consider that the Lazarists themselves used Catherine's revelations to locate Mary's home, and that Catherine herself pictured the house from afar and described it in 1821–1822, while it was not discovered until seventy years later, in 1891.

The following descriptions were made by Catherine in different years, for the most part in 1821 and 1822, generally in the middle of August just prior to the feast of the Assumption.

> After Our Lord's Ascension Mary lived for three years on Mount Sion, for three years in Bethany, and for nine years in Ephesus, whither St. John took her. . . .
> Mary did not live in Ephesus itself, but in the country near it where several women who were her close friends had settled. Mary's dwelling was on a hill to the left of the road from Jerusalem some three and a half hours from Ephesus. This hill slopes steeply towards Ephesus; the city as one approaches it from the south-east seems to lie on rising ground immediately before one, but seems to change its place as one draws nearer. Great avenues lead up to the city, and the ground under the trees is covered with yellow fruit. Narrow paths lead southwards to a hill near the top of which is an uneven plateau, some half-hour's journey in circumference, overgrown, like the hill itself, with wild trees and bushes. It was on this plateau that the Jewish settlers had made their home. It is a very lonely place, but

Mary's Home — Panaya Kapulu

has many fertile and pleasant slopes as well as rock-caves, clean and dry and surrounded by patches of sand. It is wild but not desolate, and scattered about it are a number of trees, pyramid-shaped, with big shady branches below and smooth trunks.[2]

A momentary pause in Catherine's description of the site of Mary's home seems in order. You should note at this point that she has already established the general direction of Mary's Mountain, as it is called today, as well as the walking time from Ephesus and some general features of the locale. Her vision continued as follows:

John had a house built for the Blessed Virgin before he brought her here. Several Christian families and holy women had already settled here, some in caves in the earth or in rocks, fitted out with light woodwork to make dwellings, and some in fragile huts or tents. They had come here to escape violent persecution. Their dwellings were like hermits' cells, for they used as their refuges what nature offered them. As a rule, they lived at a quarter of an hour's distance from each other. The whole settlement was like a scattered village.[3]

By Catherine's reference to a persecution you already have good reason to presume that she had in mind certain fugitive Jewish converts. Such a presumption would be correct, as is obvious from one of her earlier statements. On a prior occasion Catherine, in speaking of some of Mary's Jewish neighbors, mentioned that some Jews had come to Ephesus to escape the persecution in Jerusalem, and that a number of them lived in caves in the rocks nearby.[4] Now to continue with the vision:

Mary's house was the only one built of stone. A little way behind it was the summit of the rocky hill from which one could see over the trees and hills to Ephesus and the sea with its many islands. The place is nearer the sea than Ephesus, which must be several hours' journey distant from the coast. The district is lonely and unfrequented. Near here is a castle inhabited by a king who seems to have been deposed. John visited him often and ended by converting him. This place later became a bishop's see. Between the Blessed Virgin's dwelling and Ephesus runs a little stream which winds about in a very singular way.[5]

It is apparent that the site of Mary's home had been seen in vision as it existed while Mary lived there. The city of Ephesus was just beginning to be introduced to Christianity, and later it did become an episcopal see. The topography, of course, would remain basically the same through the course of centuries, and the house, if it remained at all, would have to be in the same place as it was when Mary used it. Just as Catherine viewed the site as it was in the first century, so also did she envision the house. She described the home in detail, as it existed with its original occupant.

> Mary's house was the only one built of stone. The front and sides of the house were square, while the back was round, as viewed from the inside, or angular, as seen from the outside.[6]

Catherine said, in other words, that the house was boxlike; more precisely, it was cruciform. The single exception to the straightness of the walls appeared at the back of the house in the form of the semicircular apse. This was round, as seen from inside the house, but angular, from the outside.

> ... the windows were high up near the flat roof. The house was divided into two compartments by the hearth in the center of it. The fireplace was on the floor opposite the door; it was sunk into the ground beside a wall which rose in steps on each side of it up to the ceiling. In the centre of this wall a deep channel, like the half of a chimney, carried the smoke up to escape by an opening in the roof. I saw a sloping copper funnel projecting above the roof over this opening.[7]

The main section of the house, approximately a modest twenty by forty feet, thus had a lovely fireplace and tapering chimney as a central room divider, or at least as an effective and substantial means of dividing that main section into two rooms. Catherine continued the description of the main section in these words:

> The front part of the house was divided from the room behind the fireplace by light movable wicker screens on each side of the hearth. In this front part, the walls of which were rather rough and also blackened by smoke, I saw little cells on both sides, shut in by wicker screens fastened together. If this front part of the house was needed as one large room, these screens, which did not nearly reach to the ceiling, were taken apart and put aside. These cells were used as bedrooms for Mary's maidservant and for other women who came to visit her. To the right and left of the hearth, doors led into the back part of the house, which was darker than the front part and ended in a semicircle or angle. It was neatly and pleasantly arranged; the walls were covered with wickerwork, and the ceiling was vaulted. Its

Mary's Home — Panaya Kapulu

beams were decorated with a mixture of panelling and wickerwork, and ornamented with a pattern of leaves. It was all simple and dignified.[8]

The description, so far, is rather clear. One point of possible confusion between the last two quotations, however, is the question of the roof. Catherine first said that the windows were high up and close to the roof, which was flat; then she said that the ceiling was vaulted. Inasmuch as both statements were made on the same occasion, Catherine cannot be accused of contradicting herself. And with no more information than she has already offered, the statements can be readily reconciled. First, the roof could have actually been completely flat. In this case the vaults, or what appeared to be vaults, were such only inside the house — they could have been either real or merely simulated by interior decoration. Second, the roof could have been both flat, at its outer extremities near the walls, and vaulted, but only beginning at some distance toward its center. Third, the roof could have been vaulted even at its extremities, the walls themselves, and flat at a point still close to the walls, and remaining flat for the greater portion of its area, rather than swelling outward into full domes.

Catherine presented a few more details about the principal two-room section, and about the back room in particular.

> The farthest corner or apse of this room was divided off by a curtain and formed Mary's oratory. In the centre of the wall was a niche in which had been placed a receptacle like a tabernacle, which could be opened and shut by pulling at a string to turn its door. In it stood a cross about the length of a man's arm in which were inserted two arms rising outwards and upwards, in the form of the letter Y, the shape in which I have always seen Christ's Cross.[9]

After spending a short time speaking of the cross and the other objects with it, Catherine continued her description of Mary's home, in particular the larger, back portion of the house, which included the tiny room at the rear right, Mary's bedroom.

> To the right of this oratory, against a niche in the wall, was the sleeping-place or cell of the Blessed Virgin. Opposite it, to the left of the oratory, was a cell where her clothes and other belongings were kept. Between these two cells a curtain was hung dividing off the

oratory. It was Mary's custom to sit in front of this curtain when she was working or reading. The sleeping-place of the Blessed Virgin was backed by a wall hung with a woven carpet; the side-walls were light screens of bark woven in different-coloured woods to make a pattern. The front wall was hung with a carpet, and had a door with two panels, opening inwards. The ceiling of this cell was also of wicker-work rising into a vault from the centre of which was suspended a lamp with several arms. Mary's couch, which was placed against the wall, was a box one and a half feet high and of the breadth and length of a narrow plank. A covering was stretched on it and fastened to a knob at each of the four corners. The sides of this box were covered with carpets reaching down to the floor and were decorated with tassels and fringes. A round cushion served as a pillow, and there was a covering of brownish material with a check pattern.[10]

This description of Mary's bedroom might possibly lead you to wonder whether it was in fact a separate room to the right of the rear main section or merely a compartment of some kind to the right of the rear main section. Any ambiguity may be eliminated by this statement, which Catherine made on another occasion:

> I came into Mary's house, some three hours' journey from Ephesus. I saw her lying on a low, very narrow couch in her little sleeping-alcove all hung with white, in the room behind and to the right of the hearth-place.[11]

The following remark may be added in still further clarification: "A little altar had been set up by the Apostles in the alcove beside the Blessed Virgin's couch."[12] If Mary's bedroom was not seen by Catherine as a separate room, there would have been no reason for an altar close to her bed — the already present larger oratory would have been within arm's reach. It is obvious, therefore, that Mary's bedroom was an individual and separate room in the house.[13]

A review of the floor plan of Mary's home at this point is a simple and rapid matter, and perhaps even advantageous. Imagine a large capital T, or a beam surmounted by a crossbar, which has fallen to the ground intact. The door to Mary's house was at the bottom of the T, or at the end of the beam which is opposite the transverse. Halfway along that main section was a fireplace in the middle of the floor. Behind that was the rear of the main section, terminating in a semicircular apse, wherein was located the large

Mary's Home — Panaya Kapulu

oratory. This room was called by Catherine simply Mary's room — it was her sitting room, obviously the most pleasant place in the house, close simultaneously to the oratory and the hearth.[14] To the right was Mary's bedroom, which also had an apse at the back; to the left was a general storeroom.

Catherine began this vision by describing the site of Mary's home; she then turned to the details of the house itself; finally she spoke once again of the site.

> The little house stood near a wood among pyramid-shaped trees with smooth trunks. It was very quiet and solitary. The dwellings of the other families were all scattered about at some distance. The whole settlement was like a village of peasants.
>
> The Blessed Virgin lived here alone, with a younger woman, her maidservant, who fetched what little food they needed. They lived very quietly and in profound peace. There was no man in the house, but sometimes they were visited by an Apostle or disciple on his travels. There was one man whom I saw more often than others going in and out of the house; I always took him to be John. . . .[15]

There remains one important object outside Mary's home for Catherine to describe, and she spoke of it on two different occasions. On one of them she said:

> Behind the house, at a little distance up the hill, the Blessed Virgin had made a kind of Way of the Cross. When she was living in Jerusalem, she had never failed, ever since Our Lord's death, to follow His path to Calvary with tears of compassion. She had paced out and measured all the distances between the Stations of that Via Crucis, and her love for her Son made her unable to live without this constant contemplation of His sufferings. Soon after her arrival at her new home I saw her every day climbing part of the way up the hill behind her house to carry out this devotion. At first she went by herself, measuring the number of paces of Our Lord's different sufferings. At each of these places she put up a stone, or, if there was already a tree there, she made a mark on it. The way led into a wood, and upon a hill in this wood she had marked the place of Calvary, and the grave of Christ in a little cave in another hill. After she had marked this Way of the Cross with twelve Stations, she went there with her maidservant in quiet meditation: at each Station they sat down and renewed the mystery of its significance in their hearts, praising the Lord for His love with tears of compassion. Afterwards she arranged the Stations better, and I saw her inscribing on the stones the meaning of each Station, the number of paces and so forth.

I saw, too, that she cleaned out the cave of the Holy Sepulchre and made it a place of prayer. At that time I saw no picture and no fixed cross to designate the Stations, nothing but plain memorial stones with inscriptions, but afterwards, as the result of constant visits and attention, I saw the place becoming increasingly beautiful and easy of approach. After the Blessed Virgin's death I saw this Way of the Cross being visited by Christians, who threw themselves down and kissed the ground.[16]

§ 2. *Actual Discovery*

In 1881 Abbé Gouyet of Paris, an admirer of Catherine Emmerich, went to Palestine to verify her descriptions of Christ's life. Very happy with the results obtained, he thought he might as well go on to Ephesus. On his arrival in Smyrna, present-day Izmir, the local ordinary, Archbishop Timoni, arranged some help for Gouyet by giving him as a companion a young man who later became a priest. And so the two of them set out to find the mountain at Ephesus; they were armed with only a little note in Greek which read: "Please spare a poor traveler, harmless and without resources."[17] They encountered no brigands. After several days at Ephesus they returned, alleging to have found what they went for. But no one, except the Archbishop, believed them.[18]

Ten years later in Smyrna, when everyone had forgotten Gouyet, Sister Marie de Mandat-Grancey, superioress of the French hospital, had the French translation of Catherine's *Life of Mary* read to her community. Toward the end of the book, when the reader came to the chapters on Mary's sojourn and death in Ephesus, Sister Superior remarked: "Ephesus is not very far from here . . . it might well be worth the effort to go there and see!"[19]

Almost simultaneously Father Eugene Poulin, C.M., superior of the Lazarist College in Smyrna, was introduced to Catherine's book. Meanwhile, in order to keep peace at the hospital, the chaplain, Father Henry Jung, C.M., was reading the copy which the Sisters of Charity had forced upon him. In short order the first expedition to Ephesus was arranged. Four persons comprised the caravan: Father Jung, head of the expedition, another Lazarist, Father Vervault, and two other men — Thomaso, a servant, and Mr. Pélécas. At Ephesus they were joined by a fifth companion, a negro Mussulman

Mary's Home — Panaya Kapulu

who knew the countryside. Thus the expedition began on July 27, 1891. The express purpose of at least two of its members was not to find something, but rather to prove once and for all that Catherine Emmerich was out of her mind, and that her visions were nice little dreams and reveries, but nothing else.[20]

In the general area of Ephesus the explorers came upon a small monastery with two monks. After the usual amenities Father Jung asked them: "Where did the Blessed Virgin die?" And they answered without hesitation: "In Jerusalem!" The two monks were well versed in the Byzantine tradition concerning Mary's tomb at Gethsemani.[21]

On July 29 the group once again set out from Ayasoluk,[22] this time with Catherine's book in hand, and began to climb the mountain which fitted her description. After eleven hours of climbing under the hot July sun the indefatigable explorers reached a small plateau, where they found some women working in a tobacco field. Hot and thirsty after the tedious climb, they asked for water. The women told them that they could find some at the monastery, not far from there, indicating the direction. They hurried that way and found the water. After having refreshed themselves they scanned the horizon — this little stream from which they had just drunk, that little stone house in ruins, this uneven plateau, that rocky hill behind the house. They looked at each other stupefied, as details from Catherine's revelations were recalled one after the other. They opened her book once again and read:

> Mary's house was the only one built of stone. A little way behind it was the summit of the rocky hill from which one could see over the trees and hills to Ephesus and the sea with its many islands.[23]

One of them ran up the hill, and back and forth they shouted: "Can you see Ephesus?" "Yes!" "And the sea?" "Yes!" "How about islands?" "Yes, yes!" By this time they were all at the top of the hill, with their fatigue completely forgotten. Exactly as the seeress had stated, there was Ephesus and the whole plain, and the sea, and Samos, which itself looked like many islands by reason of its contours. They could not believe their eyes — they had found it![24]

After their initial excitement, so as not to be deceived by first impressions, the explorers spent two days diligently examining everything — the house, its orientation, the surroundings. There was no other summit in the area, from which both Ephesus and the sea could be seen, except Ala Dagh, but that was much too far to the south. After the inspection of everything possible — each step performed with book in hand — they returned to Smyrna to announce their incredible discovery.[25]

Other expeditions and investigations followed. The Lazarist superior, Poulin, went to Ephesus with a group on August 12, 1891. After two days spent in examining Mary's home, they returned to Smyrna joyous and inspired. Poulin, Jung, and four others made an extended

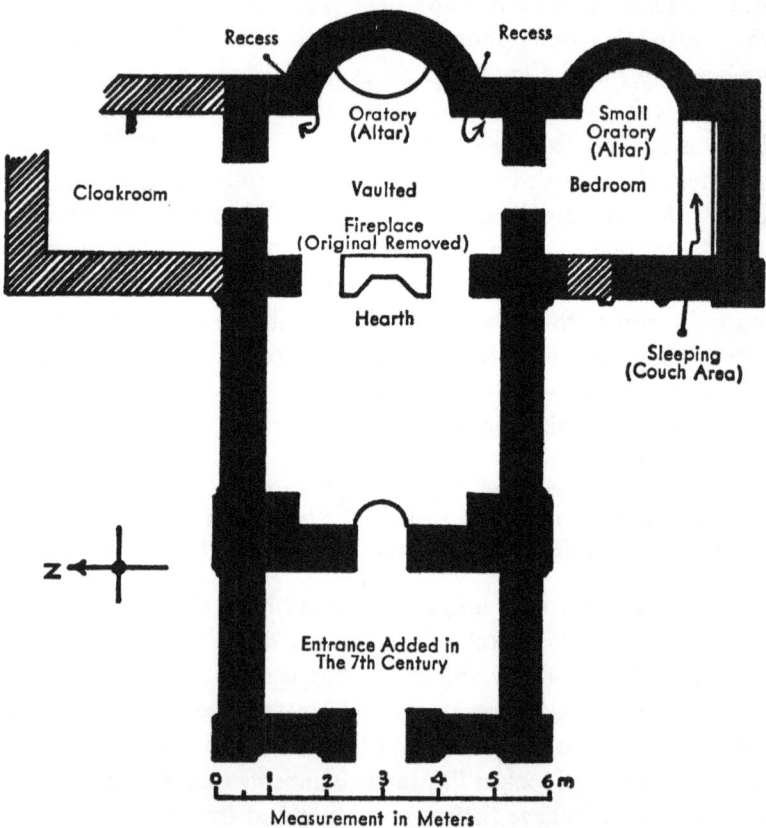

Floor Plan of "Panaya Kapulu"

Mary's Home — Panaya Kapulu

visit and a still more thorough examination from August 19 to August 25 of that same year. They returned home with maps, photographs, sketches, diagrams, and, above all, with the happy conviction that they had indeed found Mary's home.[26]

The ruins, for all the great discovery they were, did not make a pretty sight. Our Lady's house, when first discovered and for many years afterward, was far from being presentable. Only God knows how long the roof was gone. The archways had collapsed, and the walls had fallen in to a great extent. When you consider the centuries of its neglect, you probably would acknowledge that it is quite remarkable that the ruins of the house were in as good a state as they were. It is amazing how anything as isolated as that tiny building could long remain, without the help of God or man. But then, was there no aid, either divine or human? It is known, for instance, that twenty-seven years prior to its discovery by the Lazarist expedition some crude repairs had been undertaken. By whom and why is a story yet to come.[27] It is also known that on its discovery the house was nestled in a clump of high and healthy trees, which offered considerable protection.[28]

A full account of the explorers' findings, along with the results of archaeological and other studies, is presented later.[29] And to offer here even their complete report on the house in ruins would merely be to repeat Catherine's vision — the harmony between her description and the reality was phenomenal, as can be seen, for example, from the results of the subsequent official ecclesiastical inquiry.[30] As we shall see, the explorers themselves, for various reasons, did not release their report to the world until 1896. So as not to put you too far ahead of yourself, just a small portion of the substance of that announcement will be quoted here:

> ". . . the ruins found at Panaya Kapulu were of a church built in the Fourth Century over the remains of a house which, as also supported by local tradition, was the House of the Virgin Mary during the First Century A.D."[31]

The Lazarists found, in other words, a house that had been transformed into a chapel. This was to be expected. Catherine herself had said of the Apostles, after Mary's death and before their departure from her home: "They made Mary's room in the house into a church."[32] That the Christians of subsequent eras would make some changes was likewise to be expected. None of these changes, however, was of such a substantial nature as to mutilate the original floor plan and basic features of Mary's home as seen by Catherine Emmerich.[33] If there had been such a transformation, Father Poulin could not have stated:

> The marvelous conformity between the edifice discovered and the description of the visionary of Dülmen proves that she really saw it in her visions and revelations.[34]

One question is the influence of Brentano on the particular revelations of Catherine which led to the discovery of Mary's home. His overall role in her visions has already been discussed.[35] Undoubtedly Brentano exercised some influence on this vision of Mary's home, just as he did on the other revelations. But that he was responsible for its substance is sheer nonsense. It would have been impossible without God's help for him or anyone else, except for the few local people, to describe either the site or the house itself. And even those few local people could not have given all the details that Catherine did. As shall be seen later, for example, Catherine spoke of certain things, the foundations and remnants of which were not found until years after the initial discovery of the house and which were completely buried well below the surface of the ground.[36] It is necessary to conclude, therefore, that at least the substance of the revelations on Mary's home came immediately from Catherine herself and that divine assistance played an integral part.[37]

Here it is worth noting that the eminent scholar Mgr. Albert Farges (1848–1926), after stating that all the details of Mary's house corresponded to the description of Catherine, added:

> Now it is clear that the object of this vision was beyond the natural scope of the mind of a poor girl of Westphalia, without education, who had never travelled out of her province, such as was Catherine Emmerich. The transcendence is thus manifest, and hallucination admittedly impossible.[38]

Even though the supernatural element seems apparent in this vision, it should not be used as an argument for the authenticity of

Mary's Home — Panaya Kapulu 19

Mary's home. Other clairvoyants have seen the site of Mary's Dormition as Jerusalem. St. Brigit of Sweden indicated in 1371 that the Blessed Virgin appeared to her and said that she was buried in, and gloriously assumed from, the tomb in the valley of Josaphat.[39] Maria de Jesús (d. 1665), abbess of Agreda in Spain, similarly favored the Jerusalem tradition. You might compare visions and say, for instance, that those of Maria of Agreda were much more fantastic and artificial than Catherine's, but this really does not prove anything.[40] Even the fact that the Church gives its approval to certain visions in no sense means that it also thereby subscribes to their content.

While Catherine did in fact point the way to Mary's home in Ephesus, and described it so admirably well, her revelations do not prove the authenticity of the house. The house can, of course, stand on its own merits. Still, you cannot help noting the remarkable "coincidence" between her vision and the actual house, which correspondence goes unexplained, if there were no supernatural intervention. If you are reluctant to recognize such divine inspiration, as those who favor the Jerusalem tradition are, you remain faced with an inscrutable fact.

Surely you may, if you can, disregard Catherine's vision as having any probative force in the matter of the authenticity of Mary's home. In the following chapters you will be exposed to enough other arguments, both for and against the Ephesus tradition, to keep your mind occupied and to assist you in making a personal judgment. And just as Catherine's vision should not unduly influence you in one direction, neither should the inane attacks made on her and the vision influence you in the other. Some of the opponents of the Ephesus tradition revel in the few inaccuracies for which she or Brentano was responsible.[41] Such attacks on those minor discrepancies remind me of the fairy tale wherein the wolf huffed and puffed in vain at the little brick house. Not much sympathy was ever wasted on the stupid wolf.

§ 3. Inside Story

The caption "Inside Story" should not delude you into believing, that you are entering upon a confidential report on Mary's home.

Nor should it even imply the slightest notion of anything defamatory to *Panaya Kapulu*.[42] What is meant is the account, presented to you here and now, and for the first time anywhere in English, of the acquisition, loss, and recovery of ownership of *Panaya*.[43]

After the initial discovery of Mary's home and the subsequent expeditions to it, Eugene Poulin was convinced of its authenticity and thought it only proper that *Panaya* be in Catholic possession. He wanted very much to buy it, but he did not have the money. The thought came to him that Sister Marie de Mandat-Grancey, since she was of noble French lineage, just might have access to the necessary funds. He had scarcely broached the subject when she said: "The thought already came to me. Buy it!"[44] It was only after extremely laborious negotiations, which began on January 15, 1892, that the conveyance was finally signed on the following November 15. Ownership of the house and a large portion of the surrounding land was acquired in the name of Sister de Grancey.[45]

The new owner of *Panaya* was, of course, solicitous to restore Mary's home and do everything necessary to make it suitable for pilgrimages. While both restoration and pilgrimages were later initiated, they are separate stories reserved for later.[46] The owner was also aware of the need for adequate arrangements concerning succession to the property. Sister Marie, therefore, transferred the ownership and legal title to Eugene Poulin on May 11, 1910, five years before her death. She nevertheless remained responsible until her death for the expenses involved in the restoration.[47]

World War I put a stop to everything at *Panaya*, and the subsequent troubled times in Turkey kept things at a standstill for many years thereafter. In July, 1921, however, Father Joseph Euzet, C.M., and Father Paul Saint-Germain, C.M., after they had fulfilled all formalities and acquired special permission, were allowed to visit Mary's home to survey the war damage. Any plans which they and the other collaborators of *Panaya* might have had were halted by the events of 1922. They actually had little business making plans in that period when, even prior to the Conference of Lausanne (1922–1923), the new Turkey was in the process of development and organization.[48]

After 1914 the property taxes on *Panaya*, which had been paid

Mary's Home — Panaya Kapulu

regularly up to this time, were no longer sought, nor was the owner particularly anxious to pay them. And even if he were, there would have still been the question to whom they should be paid. The advice given to Poulin, and reluctantly accepted by him, was to keep to himself and forget about the mountain as much as possible. This was, of course, inconvenient for many reasons, of which one was the obvious indication or appearance of complete abandonment of the site. Poulin nevertheless refrained from visiting Mary's home. For many who were no less devoted to Panaya the troubled times and the instinct of self-preservation were sufficient causes to remain at a safe distance.

Despite those conditions, Father Euzet had little hesitation in accompanying a group of sisters to Panaya in November, 1926. After Mass had been celebrated in Mary's home, the members of that pilgrimage were of one mind to search and find the means to end as soon as possible the state of desolation and abandonment that they found at Mary's home.[49]

It was once again deemed necessary before anything else, in this process of practical recovery of the property, to provide for its succession. Originally in the name of Sister de Grancey, and later transferred to Eugene Poulin, ownership of Panaya would soon pass by escheat, if nothing were done. Although over eighty years old, Poulin obstinately refused to do anything. No one could understand his attitude, but later everyone was grateful for it. At long last, on October 23, 1926, and at the age of eighty-three, Poulin made a holographic will, in due and proper form, with Joseph Euzet instituted as heir to Panaya. After the death of Poulin in 1928, there followed one attempt after another to have the will executed. Finally, in May, 1931, all the formalities had been successfully completed, and Euzet took the train to Kuşadasi, near Ephesus, to have the title drawn up in his name.

After he arrived at Kuşadasi on May 26, Euzet went to the proper municipal office and opened his briefcase to withdraw the money to cover the delinquent taxes. But the officer of the cadastre, after perusal of his registers, asked: "How can I put in the name of J. Euzet property which no longer belongs to E. Poulin?"[50] The property was recorded as belonging, at that time, to the Treasury. This expropriation was, of course, the result of the necessary precaution whereby the owner had departed from and apparently abandoned the property. All abandoned property which belonged to belligerents reverted to the Treasury.

Euzet's only hope then was to institute a judicial process to prove illegal confiscation. Prior to presenting himself before a judge he located a dragoman, one Jacques Aboulafia, who would act as advocate, even though he was not a certified lawyer. The dragoman wanted to make sure whether the property was truly *djebel*, mountain, or *tarla*, arable land, for this was a capital point. The two of them, Euzet and his interpreter-lawyer, went to the mountain and returned late that night.

On May 28, 1931, the case was opened and at the outset the judge was petitioned to issue an injunction restraining the Treasury from alienating the property in question prior to the pronouncement of the definitive sentence. The case was pending for four months and undoubtedly caused great hardships to Euzet, such as the repeated commuting between Kuşadasi and Izmir.

In the session of July 10 the advocate for the Treasury contended that Poulin did not have the right to bequeath and devise the property in question and that, therefore, Joseph Euzet had no capacity to institute this process against the Treasury. Euzet's dragoman-advocate then requested several hours to study the Code — there was not much else he could have done. The judge granted a recess until the afternoon of the same day.

During the interval a Code was procured and an idea was conceived. The article cited in court by the counsel for the Treasury could not be found in the Swiss Code. What was the date of Poulin's will? October 23, 1926. And on what date did the Swiss Code go into force in Turkey? October 3, 1926. That meant that the will was not subject to the law of the old Code which the defense had cited. At this point you may recall Poulin's obstinacy in making his will. Had he made it when requested, the property would have been lost. There was good reason for his delay and, even though he did not know it, doubtlessly someone else did.[51]

Mary's Home — Panaya Kapulu

The greatest obstacle had been overcome. The only problem which remained was to establish that the property had not been "abandoned." You can imagine, of course, that that might not be too simple to prove, since a few years had passed without anyone even seeing the place.

A judicial inspection of the site was required. The judge, his secretary, two experts chosen by the municipality, and three acceptable witnesses chosen by the plaintiff went to Panaya and conducted the inspection. They concluded that the property had not been abandoned inasmuch as it had been planted with trees, and so on. As for any apparent abandonment, they concluded that it was due exclusively to the state of war which did not allow the owner even to go there to see the place. This on-site inspection, which followed the decree of access, took place on September 15, 1931.

The session of September 23 witnessed the final address of the lawyer for the Treasury and response of the dragoman. It was recessed to the next day in order to allow time for preparing the decision. The judgment was delivered, as anticipated and scheduled, on September 24, 1931.[52] After appeal at Dorilée (Eskisehir) on January 9, 1932, the first decision was ratified and confirmed. Yet it was not until October 23, 1932, that Euzet finally received the regular document of title of ownership from the officials at Kuşadasi.

With all the expenses involved over the period of four months, you might well wonder whether it would not have been cheaper, and much more convenient, simply to purchase the property from the Treasury and forget the lawsuit. There is no way of determining what the exact difference in costs would have been, but two things are certain: (1) there was no assurance that the Treasury would have sold the property immediately and, even if it would have, it could have offered it only at a prohibitive price; (2) Euzet himself had already thought of buying it back, but only as a last resort.

After the first decision, but prior to the futile appeal, a caretaker was found for Panaya. His name was Aziz, and he went to Mary's home with his wife and two small children in September, 1931. The isolated life at Panaya surely could not have been easy for them. Like other good Moslems, Aziz knew of Mary from the *Koran*; he also knew that he was living at a holy place. He died in May, 1951, and on his deathbed avowed: "At Panaya extraordinary things will be seen. Although I shall not see them, my children will see them. It will be like a paradise there."[53]

In 1947 there was still another threat of expropriation — from that time all forests belonged by law to the State. The indispensable official inspection of the site resulted in the declaration that there were no trees of the requisite size to constitute what could be properly called a forest. When you ponder the various successive contingencies, any of which might have effected loss of ownership of Panaya, it surely seems that the Blessed Virgin had protected her property. She undoubtedly continues that guardianship today, even though everything humanly possible has now been done to assure the future stable control of Mary's home. In 1952 Euzet transferred ownership of Panaya to a Catholic corporate body, the Dernek of Mother Mary, chartered in the previous year.[54]

That is the *inside story*; now to the stories on the outside.

> In 1896 an anonymous manifesto, bearing the approbation of André Timoni, Archbishop of Smyrna and Vicar Apostolic of Asia Minor, announced "to the Christian World" the discovery of Mary's home and place where she died on Bülbül Dagh, a mountain bordering on the ruins of Ephesus. The discovery was effected through the indications of the Westphalian visionary, Anne Catherine Emmerich.[55]

This proclamation marked the beginning of a considerable amount of literature which would be written concerning *Panaya* from that day forward. Earlier the publication of Catherine's *Life of Mary* had provoked numerous writings. But the Ephesus tradition had existed for eighteen centuries before that, so that you might expect some reference to it in Sacred Scripture, historical documents, the works of the Fathers and early historians, and even in scholarly studies on the subject. With such expectations you are prepared for the next two chapters, which consider many things — traditions, legends, ancient and more recent references, documents, related facts, studies, controversies, expert reports, activity in Rome on the subject — all of which spheres of knowledge will better acquaint you with Mary's home, and place you in an excellent position for passing judgment on it.

CHAPTER III

Relevant Legends, Traditions, and Literature

The title of this chapter makes a distinction between legend and tradition. The former refers to that which is commonly unauthentic or apocryphal. The latter applies to that which has some substance, even though handed down primarily by word of mouth. Both legends and traditions sooner or later appear in writing, and literature is generated which records and sometimes embellishes them. Quite often, too, they are already enhanced before ever appearing in written form. Only apostolic tradition is guaranteed by God.

The testimony of early historians and Fathers of the Church, which will appear in a moment, has limited value. While such testimony is usually more than mere legend, nothing can be definitely proved from it in respect to the matters presently under consideration. Where the Fathers themselves disagree, outside of matters of doctrine, for instance in the explanation of certain scriptural passages, you are free to follow whichever of their interpretations you might choose.[1]

As for Sacred Scripture itself, it serves little in establishing many aspects of the following stories. In a word, it contains too many lacunae, and thus is often used by opposite sides of a controversy, each in an attempt to prove its own point.

Once certain definite facts appear, however, then the statements of historians, Fathers, Scripture, as well as other sources, may all be advantageously applied in interpreting those facts. One problem for this and the following chapters was to decide which should be presented first — established facts or the auxiliary material. Logically it might seem better first to know a fact and later interpret it through other sources. In practice, however, a greater and more lasting impact can often be effected by the inversion, for instance, by dropping the hard rock of fact into the quiet pool of legend — the waves go on, and on, and on. For this reason among others, which will most likely become evident to you, it seemed better to give first the auxiliary material provided by legend and tradition and to follow this with the factual data.

§ 1. *Mary and John in Ephesus*

On various occasions writers have referred to Mary, or Mary together with John, or simply John in Ephesus. Those who recorded history would naturally have been more concerned with St. John the Apostle, the missionary, the public figure, than with Mary, the retiring, quiet, Mother of God, who kept to herself at home. But even when John alone was mentioned, as was the usual case with the writers of the first several centuries, Mary's presence in a place close to John's activity would seem to have been assured by reason of Christ's commission given to John from the Cross: "Behold, thy mother!" And the passage, written by John long after Mary's Assumption, confirmed the result by continuing thus: "And from that hour the disciple took her unto his own."[2]

Exegetes, both ancient and modern, have explained the phrase *unto his own* as meaning *into his house*, so that, if John's area of apostolic endeavor centered about Ephesus, Mary would have lived there too.[3]

> And (i.e., therefore, because Jesus had ordered it) *that disciple took her unto his own* (sua). Some read *sua*, "his own house," as Nonnus paraphrases it. Bede suggests, "for his own mother," or better still, "into his own charge." As St. Augustine says, "not into his own hands, but into those kind offices, which he undertook to dispense." St. John accordingly took her with him to Ephesus, and the Council of Ephesus (cap. xxvi, Synodical Epistle) says that they both for a time lived at Ephesus.[4]

The Ephesus tradition must be postulated on an early departure of John and Mary from Jerusalem. Such a tradition is not contrary to Scripture, but neither can it be proved directly from Holy Writ. There is a period of about twelve years (A.D. 37–49), beginning with the martyrdom of St. Stephen, during which John's activities and whereabouts are not mentioned. That he was in Asia during that time is an excellent theory which can be supported by many scriptural passages.[5]

Now that you have been advised of that hypothesis, it seems only fair to offer it to you in a condensed form at least.

> Some hold that St. John came to Ephesus for the first time only after the death of St. Paul in 67. But through a diligent examination of the New Testament (e.g., Gal 1:18, Acts 12:17, Gal 2:9) one may easily gather that nothing is known of John from 37 to 48. Where was that active man whom St. Paul called "a pillar of the church"? Is it conceivable that this "son of thunder" hid timidly and inactively with Mary in troubled and hostile Palestine, while other Apostles had already set out for various parts of the world? It is doubtlessly far more probable that after the Ascension John lived with Mary at Ephesus whence he made excursions through Asia.
>
> Furthermore, after the Council of Jerusalem, held about the year 50, Paul and Barnabas passing by Phrygia and Galatia were forbidden by the Holy Spirit to preach the word of God in Asia (Acts 16:6). For what reason? Because, as St. John Chrysostom writes in his Commentaries, the evangelization of Asia already belonged to John.
>
> When Paul first came to Ephesus in 53, he found faithful brethren in Phrygia and Galatia (Acts 18:23). If John had come to consular Asia later than Paul, then who could have established the seven churches mentioned in the Apocalypse? Everyone admits that, at the time John had charge of and was travelling through Asia, Paul supervised the Church at Ephesus merely for two years, after which time he never again returned.[6]

Objections to that theory will appear here and there in both this and the following section. While the Ephesus tradition is based on John's early departure for Asia, some scholars admit only a late departure, and a few even doubt any sojourn of John at Ephesus. Of the three opinions just mentioned, the first thesis seems most likely, the second less likely, and the third scarcely possible.

> Until about thirty years ago [i.e., 1875] it was not doubted, except in restricted circles, that the Apostle John had spent the closing years of his life at Ephesus. To be sure Vogel, Reuterdahl, and Lützelberger had, some time before this, expressed their doubts, but had found no support even from the Tübingen school.[7]

If all the arguments against John's sojourn at Ephesus were assembled you would see that at least they "... do not prove that the Apostle John ... did not live in Ephesus during the closing years of his life."[8] And the conclusion, at least in respect to John, if not also to Mary, may be expressed as follows:

> It is highly probable that the Virgin Mary and St. John came to Anatolia [Asia Minor] before 66 A.D. and probably between 42 and 48 A.D. There is no reference in the Holy Scriptures to the fact that St. John took Mary with him in his mission to Anatolia. The strict silence observed in the Holy Scriptures in this respect is believed to be due to the extraordinary nature of the event, and to the fear of excitement and surprise it may have caused.[9]

An investigation of the early literature on the matter results in almost universal affirmation of the sojourn in Ephesus. Tertullian (ca. 150-230) indicated that John came to Asia early.[10] And Hippolytus Portuensis (ca. 160-235) recalled that John died there.[11] A letter of the second century from Polycrates, bishop of Ephesus, to Pope St. Victor (189-199) mentioned that John was buried at Ephesus.[12] St. Irenaeus (b. ca. 150), a disciple of the Papia who was a pupil of St. John,[13] stated that John wrote his Gospel while living at Ephesus,[14] and he added, as verified and reported by Eusebius (ca. 263-339), that it was a matter of apostolic tradition that John presided over the Church of Ephesus to the time of Emperor Trajan (98-117).[15]

Clement of Alexandria (d. ca. 215) noted that John returned to Ephesus after his exile on Patmos.[16] His pupil Origen (ca. 185-253) maintained that John was in charge of Asia, that he lived there a very long time, and that he died at Ephesus.[17]

Eusebius, the great early Church historian and most eminent scholar of his day, left several pertinent texts. His first statement followed on the remark that the Jews had just begun to persecute the Christians:

> ... the holy Apostles and disciples of our Savior ... were scattered over the whole world; Thomas, as tradition holds, received Parthia; Andrew, Scythia; John, Asia, and with the people there he lived and he died in Ephesus.[18]

Eusebius noted also that after the stoning of St. Stephen (37) and the martyrdom of St. James (42) the rest of the Apostles, who had

Relevant Legends, Traditions, and Literature 29

to undergo a thousand vexations, went forth into all nations.[19] At another time he stated:

> Furthermore, there is also John, who leaned on the breast of the Lord, and was a priest wearing the breastplate, and a martyr, and teacher. This one rests at Ephesus.[20]

St. Epiphanius (ca. 315–403) wrote the following observation, the final phrase of which has been subjected to many fatuous explanations:

> And while John meanwhile left for Asia, nothing is said that he took the Blessed Virgin with him as a companion on the trip; concerning this matter Scripture is utterly silent . . . so as not to cause the minds of men to bow in greater stupefaction.[21]

Of course, as already indicated, Scripture is silent about many things. If you should wonder, supposedly along with Epiphanius, why the book of the *Acts of the Apostles* contains no mention of this journey of Mary and John to Ephesus, then you may as well worry also over its omission of Peter's first stay at Antioch, his arrival at Rome, where he later suffered martyrdom with Paul, and innumerable other events.[22]

But it is altogether possible, and even probable, that the silence of Epiphanius was motivated by reasons other than the one alleged. He was a Jewish convert, and wrote his *Panarion* against eighty current heresies. One of those affirmed, according to the example given by John and Mary, that monks could live a community life together with virgins dedicated to our Lord. The Council of Ancyra (314) had already denounced that idea, and Sts. Jerome (ca. 347–419) and John Chrysostom (ca. 347–407) later gave their orthodox views. In his turn Epiphanius also combated that repugnant proposition. St. Epiphanius, who knew Jerusalem quite well, could have simply and utterly crushed the proposition in his *Panarion* by pointing out that Mary's tomb was in Jerusalem, and that she had not been with John in Ephesus. But he did not! Here then is an argument that around the year 350 the sojourn of John and Mary at Ephesus was already discussed and that the Asiatic tradition existed.[23]

St. Jerome wrote that John founded and governed all the Churches of Asia, and that after his exile he returned to Ephesus where he was buried.[24] He also confirmed the fact that John had a little house there.[25] Jerome was an authority on Jerusalem — he lived there. It might be mentioned incidentally, though a bit prematurely, that in his book *The Hebrew Names* he virtually eliminated any tomb of Mary in Jerusalem by preterition; Epiphanius, another authority on the "souvenirs" of Jerusalem, did the very same thing.[26] As an expert on the holy places, at least on those which existed in his day, Jerome mentioned Gethsemani as a site consecrated by Christ's prayer whereon a church was built, with no indication of a "remembrance" of a tomb of Mary.[27]

At the very beginning of this section you were advised of a crucial period of twelve years when John was preaching in Asia out of his headquarters in Ephesus whither he had taken Mary. Those very years were spanned by a text of St. Gregory of Tours (538–594). After having spoken of Christ's Ascension and having fixed the date as May 14, 33, he said:

> After this the Apostles were dispersed to various regions to preach the word of God (*in the year 36*). And later, when the Blessed Virgin Mary was at the end of her days on earth and was called from this world, all the Apostles were assembled from their individual regions at her home (*in the year 48*).[28]

T. Ruinart's note, made in the mid-nineteenth century on that passage of Gregory, added that the opinion of the best scholars was that Mary died at Ephesus.[29]

St. Gregory of Tours referred to the presence of John in Ephesus, and even to a little house on a nearby mountain where he stayed while he wrote his Gospel. That house could be the home of Mary, which John used after her Assumption. The passage follows:

> In Ephesus, then, there is a place wherein this Apostle wrote the Gospel which is read under his name in the Church. At the summit of a near-by mountain of Ephesus there are four walls without a roof. John dwelled within these walls, devoting himself to prayer, assiduously beseeching the Lord for pardon of the sins of the people; and it came to pass that in that place no rain fell until he had completed his Gospel. And also even to this day it is brought about by the Lord that no violent rainstorms come near the place and no rain falls on that spot.[30]

Relevant Legends, Traditions, and Literature 31

The few apparent scriptural and traditional difficulties which do exist in relation to John's presence in Ephesus, such as Paul's preaching in Ephesus and leaving his disciple Timothy to direct the community there (1 Tm 1:3), Eusebius' calling Paul the first bishop of Ephesus (*Hist. Eccl.*, III, 4), St. Irenaeus' stating that Paul founded the Church of Ephesus (*Adv. haer.*, III, 3), and others,[31] can be easily reconciled. Most of them have already been solved by reason of the material presented in this section, and for clarification of what few may remain you are referred elsewhere.[32]

At this point you have the assurance of being familiar with almost all of the earliest literature on the sojourn of Mary and John in Ephesus. A few texts have been deliberately omitted because they are essential to matters which will be treated subsequently. There is surely no need for repetition — you have had enough of a burden in struggling through these texts, without having to read some of them twice.

While there was no serious attempt to prove anything in this section, many ideas were no doubt suggested to you. One observation, which is most obvious, is that people had spoken of John in connection with Ephesus, and Mary with him, long before Catherine Emmerich pointed the way for the great revival of devotion to them in that place. One modern scholar stated without hesitation that there was always a cult of Mary and John in Ephesus.[33] Another, who studied the early veneration of Mary in Asia Minor, concluded that in that area there was a solid Marian tradition with concreteness in Ephesus.[34] And still another scholar, Don Calmet (1672–1757), who wrote years before Catherine was born, stated simply and concisely:

> The Apostle John passed a great part of his life at Ephesus, and died there; as did the Virgin Mary and Mary Magdalen, according to tradition.[35]

§ 2. Mary's Tomb in Jerusalem

In the preceding section the problem of the death of Mary was avoided as much as possible. While that question necessarily comes under consideration in this section, inasmuch as one cannot very easily speak of Mary's tomb without suggesting also her death and burial, Mary's death is not treated *ex professo*. There is abundant material which has already done that.[36]

Since the tradition of Mary's death rests heavily and imposingly on the apocrypha, these too must be treated. The various names having relation with Mary's passing, as well as the question of Mary's age when she left this earth, may also be briefly mentioned. But the principal object of this section is the discussion of the place, the location, of Mary's passing. There are two possibilities, Ephesus or Jerusalem, but the one seems much more probable than the other.

Various terms connected with the events of Mary's last day on earth are *dormitio* (sleeping away), *transitus* (passing over), and *assumptio* (being taken up). The first two would seem to imply death, but the third not necesssarily. One scholar who wrote about the feast of the Assumption viewed those terms in this manner:

> The whole Church, Greek and Latin, celebrates nowadays the death and glorification of the Holy Virgin on August 15. The Greeks call this feast the *Dormition*, and sometimes the *Passing*, of the Holy Virgin. The Latins are also familiar with the name *Dormition*, but as a rule they give this feast the name *Assumption*.[37]

Another drew the following distinction:

> The Passing of the Blessed Mary is called by way of antonomasia the Assumption, because first she was assumed in soul and a little later, as is piously believed, she was assumed in body.[38]

There are more precise distinctions between those terms, but for present purposes they are of little use and the names may generally be used interchangeably. Since the feast has been mentioned, however, you may be interested in the following:

> In the East, evidence of a feast unmistakably connected to the dormition of Mary is not discoverable till the sixth century. It apparently made its initial appearance in the second half of that century in the Syrian Jacobite Church . . . the decisive document is the decree of Emperor Maurice (582–602) imposing August 15 for the celebration of the *koimesis* of God's Mother. . . . In the West it was Rome which first received the Byzantine feast, perhaps as late as Pope Sergius I (687–701), with the August 15 date and the original title, Dormition of the Mother of God.[39]

Relevant Legends, Traditions, and Literature

It may also be noted incidentally that when the Mass *Signum magnum* for August 15 replaced the Mass *Gaudeamus* in 1951 every vestige of reference to Mary's death had been removed. This was in keeping with the solemn definition of the dogma of the Assumption, which contained no declaration of Mary's death.[40]

In any event, and apart from the question of death, you may inquire about Mary's age at the time of the Assumption. Unfortunately, however, that age cannot be determined with any accuracy. Many writers have selected ages ranging between sixty-two and sixty-nine years.[41] In a special study one author observed that the majority of writers chose ages between fifty-seven and seventy-two, and that one went as high as one hundred and twenty-one years.[42] The final conclusion of that treatise was well put: *Ignoramus et ignorabimus* — "We do not and we will not know."[43]

It would be rash, however, to apply that same conclusion to the question of Mary's death. The matter might have been settled in the definition of the Assumption, if the Holy Father had been so inclined. But he was not. Mary's death, therefore, remains an open question. You may believe it or not, as you choose. The author is among the many who believe in Mary's death. Everyone knows that Mary, by reason of her Immaculate Conception, was not subject to death. But everyone also knows how similar to Christ she was in all things, and Christ, also not subject to death, offered up His life for mankind.

The belief that Mary died seems to have been the more common opinion through the ages, but it was never unanimous.[44] In the first centuries among those who spoke of Mary's death were Origen, St. Ephrem, St. Jerome, St. Augustine, and St. Gregory of Nyssa.[45] In later times the Fathers and other theologians mentioned the death of Mary so often that any further enumeration seems superfluous.[46] Sacred art, moreover, did not fail to reflect the tradition.

> In the numberless touching representations of the death of our Blessed Lady which medieval sculpture has left us, St. Peter and the Apostles surround her death-bed, according to legend. . . . St. John is indeed often represented as giving Holy Communion to the Mother of God, for she could receive this great sacrament of spiritual life to increase her love for her Divine Son.[47]

On the hypothesis that Mary did die, the circumstances of her death are strictly legendary. The fanciful stories describing the event come from the apocrypha — the unauthentic, noncanonical, books resembling Scripture.[48] Those of primary relevancy are the books of the *Transitus Mariae* — *Passing of Mary*.[49] They are utterly worthless as historical accounts of the Assumption.[50]

In a word, the apocrypha describe Mary's death, and imply or assert the place as Jerusalem or vicinity. They say, for example, that John while preaching at Ephesus, on the Lord's day and at the third hour, was raised on a cloud during the attending earthquake, and the cloud bore him to Mary's house.[51] That same example, quoted from the Syriac text, follows:

> John said: "To me in Ephesus the Holy Spirit announced it and said: 'The time draws nigh for the mother of your Lord to leave the world; go to Bethlehem to greet her.' And a cloud of light snatched me away, and I stood between heaven and earth, and saw the chariots of all the apostles, which were flying and coming to me."[52]

As for the date of these apocryphal narratives of Mary's death, many versions find their origin in the seventh century. The most ancient writings of the *Transitus Mariae* go back to the fifth and sixth centuries,[53] and the earliest of all could not have been written before the year 476.[54] The Gelasian Decree (ca. 496) indicated that the *Transitus* was known at the end of the fifth century. The decree specifically rejected "The apocryphal book called the *Transitus*, that is, the Assumption of Holy Mary."[55]

The belief that Mary died and was buried in Jerusalem is partially founded on these apocrypha. The Jerusalem tradition is also based on a story, to be presented momentarily, which is equally dubious. Sometimes, in an attempt to strengthen that tradition, an *ad hominem* argument is also invoked. One such follows: Mary was so attached to Jerusalem by reason of Christ's passion and death, for instance, that she could not have abandoned it. But, of course, contrary arguments of the same quality, and no less pious, are equally meritorious. No one, for example, could accuse John and Mary of lacking either man's fundamental instinct or common sense. In danger one either removes the danger or, where that is impossible,

Relevant Legends, Traditions, and Literature 35

removes himself. Mary and John, therefore, fled Jerusalem and the hostile conditions there.

The other support for the Jerusalem tradition is what may be called either the Juvenal or the Euthymian story. It is called the former because Juvenal, the bishop of Jerusalem in 451, was the principal subject of the story. It may be called the latter because St. John Damascene (ca. 675–749) quoted an unknown man named Euthymius as his source. But of the basic arguments on behalf of the Jerusalem tomb, this one is by far the oldest, easily predating those based on the apocrypha.

St. John Damascene in his second homily on the Dormition quoted the work of a certain Euthymius, which reported that Pulcheria, wife of the eastern Emperor Marcian (450–457), was building a church (*in Blachernis*) in Constantinople. She and her husband asked Juvenal of Jerusalem, who happened to be in town in connection with his trip to the Council of Chalcedon (451), for the body of the Blessed Virgin to put in their new church. Juvenal replied that he could not accommodate them because the body of Mary was in heaven, and added that there remained in Jerusalem only her winding sheets and the *loculus* — sarcophagus or bier, perhaps. Whereupon the emperor and empress requested that he send to Constantinople the cloths and the *loculus*, and when they had received them they completed their church.[56]

Whether Bishop Juvenal actually sent the *loculus* and winding sheets to the emperor is doubtful.[57] And Juvenal, whom Pope Benedict XIV (1740–1758) described as an habitual liar and forger,[58] may very well have manufactured the story of their existence. Among other things, Juvenal attempted with the aid of forged documents to escape the jurisdiction of Antioch and to acquire a patriarchal authority over Palestine, Phoenicia, and Arabia.[59]

It is obvious that the Jerusalem tradition is based on flimsy evidence. Nevertheless there are many followers of the Jerusalem theory. After all there is a church over Mary's tomb and one also over the site of the Dormition; the former edifice is in Jordan under the control of schismatics, the latter is in Israel under the administration of Benedictines. Around the year 1900 the present attractive church of the Benedictines of Beuron replaced the ancient Basilica of the Dormition.[60]

An older church, not quite so decorous, at Gethsemani, is said to be over Mary's tomb. This church dates from the Christian reign of Jerusalem. It may well have been originally the work of Emperor Maurice (582–602), who imposed by decree the fifteenth of August as the date of Mary's death.[61] Furthermore, it is possible that there was, after Juvenal (i.e., a. A.D. 450), a cult having as its object a sepulcher hewn in the base of the Mount of Olives in the Cedron or valley of Josaphat.[62]

As a matter of fact, Catherine Emmerich spoke of a "tomb" of Mary in Jerusalem. She said that a tomb was prepared, but never used. In vision she saw Mary make the journey from Ephesus to Jerusalem for a visit, while the persecution of Christians was temporarily halted. In Jerusalem Mary became quite ill and it was thought that she was dying. During that time it was announced more than once that the Blessed Virgin had died, and rumors of her death and burial spread. A tomb was prepared for Mary, but she recovered and returned to Ephesus.[63]

If all that is true, so also is the following observation:

> The sarcophagus remained in Jerusalem and was placed in a cave near the garden of Gethsemani. This could possibly be the tomb of the Virgin Mary now shown in Jerusalem.[64]

And still another simple explanation of the Jerusalem tradition is that it arose after the city of Ephesus began to deteriorate. As one author put it, "From the votaries to her tomb Ephesus flourished, until on its fall, Jerusalem acquired all the glory of this claim."[65]

At the very most, however, the Jerusalem tradition cannot possibly go back beyond 450 and Juvenal, if it actually goes that far. If you will recall for a moment the Euthymian story, an interesting facet will be revealed.

Some unknown person around the year 500 wrote several treatises wherein he posed as Dionysius the Areopagite, a convert of St. Paul. In the role of Dionysius, or Denis, he could claim to speak of Mary's burial with the authority of an eyewitness.[66] He was, of course,

Relevant Legends, Traditions, and Literature 37

a fraud and his writings are known today as the work of Pseudo-Dionysius, or simply Pseudo-Denis. From the recent excellent treatise of Gabriel Roschini, O.S.M., on Pseudo-Denis and the death of Mary, the following observations may be made:

1. It is commonly held that Pseudo-Denis wrote around the year 500, or between 480 and 530. The earliest possible date is 476.[67]

2. Pseudo-Denis had definite connection with the Euthymian story of John Damascene.[68]

3. The Euthymian story is found for the first time in the second homily of John Damascene.[69]

4. Pseudo-Denis was prior to, or contemporary with, the apocrypha.[70]

5. No tradition existed in Jerusalem in 377 (time of Epiphanius) relative to Mary's death, nor did any localization of a tomb implying her death.[71]

6. The first Marian shrine in Jerusalem was the *Kathisma*, erected after the Council of Ephesus, about 450 or later, to honor Mary's divine Maternity.[72]

7. Only in the sixth century did the *Breviary of Jerusalem* first speak of a tomb in the valley of Josaphat.[73]

8. It is evident from the Jerusalem liturgy of the year 450 for August 15, celebrating the day of Mary *Theotokos* at the *Kathisma*, that there was no knowledge of Mary's death and no mention of it.[74]

9. That very feast of August 15, celebrated at the *Kathisma* near Jerusalem, was later moved to Gethsemani, but not until the sixth century.[75]

10. The writings of the Fathers, which treated of Mary's death in Jerusalem *ex professo*, were all dependent on Pseudo-Denis.[76]

11. In the sixteenth century, under Pius V (1566–1572), the Euthymian story entered the *Roman Breviary* (II Noct., Aug. 18) and remained till the time of Pius XII (1939–1958), despite the fact that the commission established by Benedict XIV (1740–1758) for reforming the breviary had decided to suppress it because no respectable critic would accept it.[77]

It might be well to note that this spurious Euthymian story was removed from the breviary, not with the deletion of every reference to Mary's death in the Mass of the Assumption, but only with the change and suppression of the octave of the feast.[78] This story of Mary's death in Jerusalem no longer has any place in the Roman liturgy. It surely took its toll, however, in deluding the Fathers, whether in the form of the testimony of Pseudo-Denis or the Euthymian story.

It might also be well to note the final conclusions of the treatise of Roschini:[79]

1. Pseudo-Denis influenced the early Fathers and writers who treated the question of Mary's death in Jerusalem.

2. Pseudo-Denis was prior to the apocrypha on Mary's death.

3. Pseudo-Denis was prior to the counterfeit tomb of Mary at Jerusalem.

4. Pseudo-Denis was prior to the liturgical feast of the Dormition.

The author's last word was a plea that those who speak of the "death" of Mary abstain at least from calling on a nonexistent "tradition" regarding it.[80]

Roschini's work was truly a devastating blow to the Jerusalem tradition. And the remarkable part of it all is that it was struck without even having Ephesus in mind. Roschini wrote, as is obvious from his final remark and the work itself, to prove that there was no true tradition concerning Mary's death at Jerusalem. Jerusalem was merely incidentally attacked, because the author's main object was to disprove the notion of a "tradition" of Mary's death. You may or may not admit that he accomplished his purpose, but you cannot dismiss his arguments.

Since the Jerusalem tradition could not have originated before 450, the Ephesus tradition is obviously older. This has already been indicated in the preceding section and will be proved beyond doubt subsequently.[81] Even those who favor Jerusalem are forced to admit that the Ephesus tradition is earlier as, for example, the following statement shows:

> There are two traditions claiming respectively Ephesus and Jerusalem as the places of her death and burial. The tradition of Ephesus seems to be prior in time.[82]

There are many also who would not be so generous as to allow the origin of the Jerusalem tradition to be placed at such an early date as the year 500. As Jugie (1878–1954) observed:

> The existence of a tomb of the Holy Virgin at Jerusalem or in its environs is completely ignored by the tradition of the first five centuries and even up to about the year 570.[83]

Jugie argued principally against the existence of an early tradition concerning a tomb at Jerusalem. To support his view he noted these significant omissions: the silence of the *Peregrinatio Sylviae (Etheriae)*, which spoke at length of Gethsemani, but with no mention of a tomb or shrine of Mary; the silence of St. Jerome, who lived in Jerusalem and explored the holy places quite carefully, but mentioned in his books no tomb of Mary; the silence of Pope St. Leo (440–461), who wrote to Juvenal and enumerated in his letter the principal shrines of Jerusalem, but failed to include a tomb of Mary.[84] He also cited many works which did mention a tomb of Mary in Jerusalem, for example, the anonymous *Breviary of Jerusalem*, the writings of St. Andrew of Crete, St. Germain of Constantinople, Hippolytus of Thebes, St. John Damascene; to that oriental assemblage he added the occidentals, Sts. Willibald, Isidore of Seville, and Bede.[85] But in evaluating all those writings which mentioned a tomb in Jerusalem, he successfully demonstrated the unreliability of each.[86] In every case those statements were influenced by the apocrypha.[87]

It would be appropriate to offer more foundation for the Jerusalem legend but, once the apocrypha and the Juvenal or Euthymian story have been discussed, there is little more to add. The proponents of Jerusalem continue to repeat, for example: "The Holy Virgin probably died at Jerusalem, and it is unlikely that she ever came to Asia Minor."[88] Occasionally they admit, as has been seen, that the Ephesus tradition is the older, or they make some concession of the following nature:

> The "orthodox" Church, in spite of its literary and liturgical tradition which is unanimous in locating the tomb of the Virgin in Jerusalem, is beginning to shift openly in favor of Ephesus.[89]

The opponents contend, for instance, that the Jerusalem tradition is spurious, confused, and of relatively late origin.[90] Then there are a few neutrals, who can accept neither the Jerusalem nor the Ephesus tradition, because they believe that there is no definite proof for either.[91]

There is extensive modern literature on the subject of Mary's tomb in Jerusalem. But such literature has been omitted as much as possible in this section, because it does not really change the status of the question which prevailed earlier, and also because it receives mention subsequently.[92] The modern literature on *Panaya*, however, has decidedly enlivened and adorned the Ephesus tradition.[93]

One point may be noted now. In reading literature on Jerusalem which arose after the discovery of *Panaya*, I have noted that the greater volume of it was more interested in belittling the Ephesus tradition and even destroying it, if possible, than in giving solid facts to support a Jerusalem tradition. The reason seems to be obvious enough: there simply was not very much to say in favor of Jerusalem, and accordingly as much as possible was said against Ephesus. Some works, such as the diatribe of Barnabé of Alsace (Meistermann), even pretended to be concerned simply with the tomb in Jerusalem, but proved to be attempts to discredit Ephesus.[94]

As a final remark on recent literature, this peculiarity may be noted. It seems rather odd, at least to me, that the literature almost invariably compared the Jerusalem tomb with the Ephesus tomb. The strange thing about this is that there is no tomb at Ephesus; if there is, it has not as yet been found. Catherine Emmerich said that there was a tomb there, that it was covered over, and that it would someday be found.[95] But regardless of how you accept her statement, a tomb at Ephesus is not absolutely essential to the Ephesus tradition. Mary's deathbed, for example, could easily enough have been the very site of the Assumption — she may never have seen a tomb; she may never even have died. All that appears at *Panaya* today is the home where she spent her last years. Of course, once you have read Catherine's description of Mary's house, and then have actually seen it, you are inclined to believe what she said also about the tomb, or about almost anything else, for that matter.

Yet the simple distinction as just described was drawn in practically none of the literary endeavors.[96] While the advocates of the

Relevant Legends, Traditions, and Literature   41

Ephesus tradition would no doubt be delighted with the discovery of the tomb, the tradition of Mary's sojourn there, extended even to death in her home, can and does stand without a tomb. The past proponents, nevertheless, defended the ancient tradition under its fullest, and perhaps not as ancient, form and interpretation, namely, that Mary lived, died, and was buried at Ephesus. They were satisfied that there was a tomb, even though it had not yet come to light.

§ 3. Syrian Jacobites and Kirkindjites

The two traditions which will now be examined are regional, and both contend that Mary lived and died at Ephesus. That of the Syrian Jacobite Church is the more extensive by reason of the number of adherents, but also the farther removed geographically. That of the people of Kirkindje, a large village in the hills to the east of Ephesus, is quite restricted, but phenomenally specific. The two are distinct traditions and receive separate treatment, but the object of each is the same, namely, the sojourn and passing of Mary in Ephesus.

> The Syrian Jacobite Church has always followed the Ephesian tradition since the 8th century. They confirmed their belief in the 12th and 13th centuries and still continue to the present day to keep it alive.[97]

Exactly how or when the Syrian tradition began cannot be determined. Perhaps it started in the first century, for John and Mary in traveling to Ephesus along the old Roman roads would have had to pass through Syria, and thus would have been remembered.[98] St. Ignatius of Antioch (d. ca. 110), in his epistles which are recognized as genuine, wrote often of Mary; among the doubtful fragments ascribed to him there is even a letter to, and a reply from, the Blessed Virgin.[99] One of his letters indicated that Mary died and was buried at Ephesus on the Enchilos mountain.[100] That mountain was later called the Korresos, and is the site of Mary's home.[101] Perhaps the tradition began only about the time of the Council of Ephesus (431).[102] And perhaps it originated still later.

That there was such a tradition in Syria in the ninth century, however, is beyond doubt. And once it has been established that there was one at that time, then there is a logical presumption that its origin would antedate the evidence. Moses bar Kepha (813–903), philosopher and theologian, became bishop of Baruman and Beyt Kayuna in 863. A prolific writer,

> He wrote twenty-four books in one of which he refers to the death of the Virgin Mary and her tomb in Ephesus, "Saint John took the Virgin Mary with him when he left Jerusalem for Asia Minor and they settled in Ephesus where the Virgin Mary died, and her tomb is in Ephesus." This book is now the property of Hori Numan Aydin at Midyat.[103]

Later literature confirming that tradition is abundant. Dionysius bar Salibi (d. 1171), Jacobite patriarch of Tmida, wrote in his *Discourse on St. Matthew* that Mary died at Ephesus and that John and his disciples buried her.[104] Michael the Syrian (d. 1199), patriarch of Antioch, wrote in his *Chronicle*:

> John preached at Antioch and afterwards went to Ephesus and the Mother of Our Lord accompanied him. Soon afterwards, they were exiled to the isle of Patmos. On returning from exile, he preached at Ephesus and built a church. Ignatius and Polycarp assisted him; he buried the blessed Mary. He lived 73 years and died after all the apostles; he was buried at Ephesus.[105]

Abdul Faradji (1226–1286), another Jacobite patriarch, spoke of the assertions of Bar Salibi, and added that St. John buried Mary at Ephesus but kept the exact place secret.[106] And finally, Gregorius bar Hebraeus (d. 1286), the great theologian of the Syrian Jacobites, in his *Scholia on St. Matthew* repeated Michael the Syrian and the others.[107]

Beyond its antiquity, this tradition is also significant in that it endured despite the contrary, contemporary, and universal belief of the orthodox Church that Mary's tomb was in Jerusalem. Significant, moreover, is the fact that the Syrian Jacobite Church continued to celebrate the commemoration of Mary's death on August 15, contrary to the practice of the Coptic and Ethiopian Church.[108]

One final note, which may be of interest before passing on to the next story, is that the Jacobite tradition stressed corporeal interment, rather than an assumption. The menologies and other liturgical documents of the Syrian Jacobite Church spoke for the most part of the

Relevant Legends, Traditions, and Literature   43

death of the Mother of God, her passing away, and they silently ignored her Assumption, particularly as it is understood today.[109] Although the precise reason for such an attitude and tradition cannot be ascertained, its origin may perhaps lie in an erroneous interpretation of the famous relevant text of the Council of Ephesus.[110]

The second regional tradition, that of the Kirkindjites, is strictly local and full of meaning. The people of the town of Kirkindje formed the last group of known lineal descendants of the Ephesian Christians. Their ancestors lived in Ephesus until they were forced to leave, at the end of the eleventh century, as a result of the invasion of the Seldjuks, a group of Turks who soon established an empire and became a contributing cause of the Crusades.[111]

One contingent of Ephesian Christians fled to the hills and took refuge on a mountain about ten miles to the east of their old home.[112] They built a village and continued in the traditions of their forebears, preserving their Christian heritage. One of those traditions, faithfully transmitted from father to son, was to make an annual pilgrimage to *Panaya Kapula*,[113] on the Bulbul Dagh,[114] on August 15 to commemorate the Dormition of the Immaculate Virgin Mary.[115]

This would have been a relatively easy tradition and practice to observe while they lived in Ephesus, but it must have been arduous to fulfill afterward by reason of both distance and terrain. Their journey to Mary's home and back, starting from Kirkindje, required nine to ten hours; it was about a five-hour trek for them each way. On arrival at *Panaya* their priests celebrated Mass, attended devoutly by all; everyone lighted candles and prayed. They then ate and rested before returning home.[116]

That annual pilgrimage was an event which, if not recognized for what it really was, defies any other explanation. Those Christian peasants, all Greek schismatics, held to the local traditions of their forefathers despite the contradictory doctrine of the whole orthodox Church, which favored the Jerusalem tradition. They celebrated the Holy Sacrifice and commemorated Mary's Dormition at *Panaya* contrary to their own liturgical books.[117] They were thus alone in that unique belief and practice. With them it was not merely a tradition of Mary's Dormition in Ephesus, but also a belief in the same house which Catherine Emmerich had envisioned from afar, and which the Lazarists later discovered.

The village of Kirkindje, which boasted four thousand inhabitants in 1892, is no more. The town is there, but the population was entirely changed after the complete dispersion of the orthodox Christians in 1922. The new inhabitants, who came from various areas, found the place so pleasant that they called the town Serindje, which means *agreeable*. The two churches of the Kirkindjites were not destroyed, but one was transformed into a mosque.[118]

Quite fortunately, however, prior to that unhappy dispersal, all the details of the Kirkindje tradition were recorded, and the people themselves were available for interrogation for some thirty years after the discovery of *Panaya*. The Lazarists, as soon as they had been made aware of that remarkable tradition by having encountered the people during one of their annual pilgrimages, started an investigation for the purpose of determining its authenticity. The inquiry was conducted by C. Constantinidis, a lawyer and also mayor of Kirkindje, who issued on December 14, 1892, the following testimonial:

> After the crucifixion of Our Lord Jesus Christ, our blessed Virgin mother of God was in the care of St. John; and they lived at Ephesus . . . from there she moved to the mountain Bulbul Dagh . . . and it is there in her home of Kapulu that her "Dormition" took place, the feast of which is celebrated on August 15.[119]

If this curious yet wonderful tradition could have been invented (from what motives, and by whom?), it could not have been received because the neighbors of the Kirkindjites were completely ignorant of it, and the orthodox Church to which the Kirkindjites belonged followed a contrary tradition. It must have been handed down, therefore, from generation to generation and preserved in the rather isolated village. If Ephesus had been without a tradition in the sixth or seventh century, as was Jerusalem, then the city surely would have subscribed to the apocryphal movement. The fact that Ephesus resisted it with invincible firmness cannot be ignored.[120]

Aside from all the wonderment of the Kirkindje tradition, it clearly answers several other questions, for instance, the source of

Relevant Legends, Traditions, and Literature

the name *Panaya Kapulu*. This title, used by the Kirkindjites to denote Mary's home on the Mountain of Nightingales, is an idiomatic hybrid from Greek and Turkish.[121] The name is really no more of an anomaly, however, than were the Kirkindjites themselves — they were Greek schismatics, but they spoke for the most part Turkish, whence that hybrid name.[122] They may not have preserved their language, but they at least kept their Christian faith and their traditions.[123]

Another question solved by the tradition is that of the comparatively superior state of preservation of Mary's home. For more than the first ten centuries of its existence there was no problem of maintenance — the Christians living nearby and in Ephesus took care of it.[124] After 1087 the annual pilgrimage of the Kirkindjites assured at least minor and crude repairs from time to time. On investigation it was learned, for instance, that in 1864, twenty-seven years before *Panaya* was discovered, an inhabitant of Kirkindje had undertaken rather extensive repairs, one of which was doing the walls over with plaster.[125] Once *Panaya* was discovered in 1891, all efforts directed toward its subsequent preservation and restoration were well documented, but they constitute another story.[126] Prior to that time, however, the Kirkindjites can be credited not only with the preservation of the tradition of *Panaya*, but also to some degree with the preservation of *Panaya* itself.

§ 4. *Mary Magdalen and Seven Sleepers*

The legends of St. Mary Magdalen and of the Seven Sleepers are separate legends, and absolutely unessential to the tradition of Mary's sojourn. Nevertheless, the legend of Magdalen's tomb in Ephesus has some relation to Mary's sojourn there, and thus may be considered. The legend of the Seven Sleepers in included here not merely because of the topographical juxtaposition of their caves to Magdalen's tomb, but also because of the connection of the legend with Christianity and Islam, and the subsequent mention of the latter is association with Mary's home.[127]

> So the Seven Sleepers' Basilica at Ephesus, as well as the common belief, especially, in the final resurrection of the soul and body, and

> finally the cult of the Seven Sleepers, represent very important links between the Christians and Moslems. The veneration of the Seven Sleepers is the only liturgical link, while Jesus and the Blessed Virgin are the only scriptural link between the Gospel and the Koran.[128]

The tomb of Mary Magdalen lies at the entrance of the grotto of the Seven Sleepers, at the foot of Mt. Pion in Ephesus. Just as the the legend of the Seven Sleepers involved the concept of resurrection of the body and soul, so also Magdalen's life had been coincidentally or otherwise involved with that concept.

> St. Mary Magdalene was an eye-witness of the first evidence of the resurrection offered by our Lord, in the person of her brother, Lazarus. . . . She was, as we have seen, the first among all followers of Jesus to discover the empty tomb of our Lord and to bring this news to St. Peter and St. John.[129]

It is altogether possible that she lived close to Mary in Ephesus and thus in some way witnessed Mary's Assumption. The combination of the Blessed Virgin, St. John, and St. Mary Magdalen has been referred to as ". . . the second Holy Family . . . formed at the foot of the Cross."[130] The presence of Magdalen's tomb in Ephesus suggests at least a conjecture that she too traveled with Mary and John from Jerusalem to Ephesus. In fact St. Gregory of Tours (ca. 538–594) wrote:

> In Ephesus is found the place where this apostle [John] wrote the Gospel which is read under his name in the Church. . . . In that city Mary Magdalen rests, having no protection over her. . . . In it also are found the Seven Sleepers.[131]

Moreover, the Byzantine Church always favored the Ephesus legend regarding the tomb of Magdalen, and six Greek historians have confirmed the story.[132]

Echoes of that legend have been sustained through the Middle Ages to the present day.

> In his *Hodoeporicon* (cap. IX, T. Tobler, *Descriptiones*) St. Willibald, who visited Ephesus in the year 722, mentions another church, that of Maria Magdalena.[133]

The relics of Magdalen were transferred to Constantinople around the year 905, and were moved again between 1204 and 1279.[134] Such

Relevant Legends, Traditions, and Literature 47

transfers no doubt contributed to the survival of the legend. Tillemont (1637–1698) repeated that Magdalen died at Ephesus, and that it was quite natural to believe that she had accompanied the Blessed Virgin.[135] Subsequent writers stated the same thing.[136]

The identity of Magdalen's tomb in Ephesus had been lost sometime after the Middle Ages, but in 1952 it was once again identified by Louis Massignon, a singularly renowned authority on archaeology, and may be seen today.[137]

Žužić summarized in the following words the theory that Magdalen was the principal messenger of the dogma of resurrection:

> So the fact that Mary Magdalene had been buried, many, many years earlier, precisely at the entrance of that which developed to be the glorious grave and basilica of the Seven Sleepers, might have had a deep significance and be a sign given by Divine Providence. . . . There can be no doubt anymore that Divine Providence reserved for Mary Magdalene a special place not only in the mystery of penance, but also in the mystery of resurrection; and even more, a mission! Did not our Lord say to her: ". . . Go to my brethren and say to them . . ." As we have seen from the Gospel, she had been directly and personally implicated in the main manifestations of the resurrection, which God opened to the physical senses of man. We may say, where there is a sign of the resurrection, there has to be sought Magdalene, and vice-versa, where is Magdalene, there must be some evidence of the resurrection.
>
> God must have had, in His fathomless mercy, a special purpose in making His choice of a main messenger of resurrection the great sinner who became the greatest repentant. We should never forget this special sign and grace![138]

You may think what you will of that thesis, but at the very least it provides a pleasant transition to the following story.

The legend of the Seven Sleepers, which is treated in both Christian and Moslem religious literature, may be summarized as follows:

> At the time when the Roman Emperors were still pagan, under the reign of Decius (249–251), seven young princes of his imperial court, being Christians, refused publicly to offer sacrifices to idols. Afraid of the consequences of their demonstrative refusal, they took refuge in the mountain nearby (which we know as Feast Mountain) and fell asleep in a deep cavern.
>
> Some 150 to 200 years later, the young men rose from sleep and,

feeling hungry, sent one of their number to go cautiously into the town to buy something to eat. The wall had through age in the meantime collapsed. The young prince found what he wanted and offered for payment the old pagan imperial gold coin. The city of Ephesus being at that time entirely Christian found the story significant, inasmuch as at that time, the dispute whether the resurrection was of the soul and body, or only of the immortal soul, had reached its most dramatic climax.

The story came to the Imperial Court, and the Bishops and the Emperor personally came to Ephesus to look into the matter. In the meantime, the young men really died, but their bodies remained incorrupt, as if they were only sleeping. So the Church and the Emperor offered special masses for the souls of these Seven Martyrs and built a special basilica over that cavern containing their bodies.[139]

The Moslem version of that tale is substantially the same. With Islam, however, there actually is no question of a legend — the story is recorded as historical fact in the *Koran*, in Surah XVIII: "The Dwellers in the Cave."[140]

The Basilica of the Seven Sleepers in Ephesus, a shrine precious first to Christianity and later to Islam, was visited by countless pilgrims through the centuries. Documents show that the cave and the church were visited by Christian pilgrims from about the beginning of the sixth century until the end of the Middle Ages.[141] The devotion of the Moslems is apparent from the following passage:

> Having the Christian Basilica in Ephesus as a prototype, some eighteen other shrines in the entire Islamic world have been built and consecrated to the Seven Sleepers of Ephesus and their veneration, even though the Islam does not allow, under any circumstances, sanctuaries to be consecrated to mortal beings. The Prophet himself has no sanctuary of his own. The only exception, as we can see, has been the one made with the Seven Sleepers, the seven Christian martyrs. . . .[142]

On the *Armoodi*, a gold coin of the Turks, the names of the Seven Sleepers were inscribed as Jemlika, Meshilina, Mislina, Mernoos, Debbernoos, Shazzernoos, and Kephestatjoos. One more name appeared; it was Ketmehr, the dog who was trapped along with the seven princes.[143]

> These names are considered by the Turks as particularly fortunate [lucky], they are placed on buildings to prevent their being burnt, and on swords to prevent their breaking. The Mahomedans have a

Relevant Legends, Traditions, and Literature   49

> great veneration for the dog Ketmehr, and allow him a place in Paradise, with some other favorite brutes: and they have a sort of proverb which they use in speaking of a covetous person, that "he would not throw a bone to the dog of the seven sleepers": nay, it is said that they have the superstition to write his name, which they supposed to be Ketmehr, on their letters which go far, or which pass the sea, as a protection or kind of talisman to preserve them from miscarriage.
>
> The seven sleepers are held in great repute of sanctity throughout the East, and their names, engraved on gold or precious stones, are supposed to act as a powerful charm to avert evil.[144]

The names of the Seven Sleepers were listed by Christian sources as follows: Maximian, Malchus, Martinian, Denis, John, Serapion, and Constantine. The relics of these martyrs are in Rome; after a stay at the church of San Sebastiano, they were transferred to that of Santa Maria del Popolo, where they remain at present.[145] The devotion of Christians to the Seven Sleepers may be gathered from the following facts:

> In addition to the Basilica of the Seven Sleepers in Ephesus, we have among the Christians, twenty other sanctuaries consecrated to them. The most visited seems to be, at the present, the one in France. It belonged before to the seignorial properties of the family of the well-known French General and statesman, Marquis de Lafayette, who served as volunteer in the Continental army of the American Revolution. Marquis de Lafayette transferred the sanctuary to the local parish. On the feasts of St. James the Greater and St. Anne, the 25th and 26th of July each year, a great and very important worldwide Christian-Moslem pilgrimage is regularly made there.
>
> However, the most popular in the past was doubtless the shrine in Kiev, in the Ukraine, Soviet Union, where annually some 200,000 pilgrims used to come. . . .
>
> Rome, too, has a sanctuary consecrated to the Seven Sleepers, the time of construction we do not know. In 1710 Pope Clement XI restored it and used to pray there personally. It is located at the Via Porta di San Sebastiano at the beautiful property of Princess Elvina Pallavicini, which is near the sanctuary of St. John, commemorating his legendary martyrdom in Rome at the Via Porta Latina (Latin Gate).[146]

There is no point in dwelling further on either of these legends. They have little connection with the Ephesus tradition. They are recounted simply to prepare you for any future discussion of Ephesus.

I would not wish to leave you in the awkward and unenviable position of speaking of Our Lady of Ephesus with some authority, and then have a listener astound or embarrass you with a disturbing question on the tomb of Magdalen or the grotto of the Seven Sleepers.

CHAPTER IV

Relevant Documents, Facts, and Studies

§ 1. *Council of Ephesus (431)*

The Third Ecumenical Council, convoked in the year 431, summoned the bishops of the Church to the city of Ephesus. The synod convened for the purpose of dealing with Nestorianism, a heresy advanced by Nestorius, patriarch of Constantinople. A capital point of Nestorianism was the denial that Mary was the Mother of God. The heresy argued that she bore Christ as man, and hence was in no sense God's mother. Accordingly two of the dogmas defined by the council Fathers were that Christ's personality is one and divine and that Mary is, therefore, the Mother of God.[1]

The term for *Mother of God* in Latin is *Deipara*, and in Greek, transliterated, *Theotokos*. That title, which was attributed officially to Mary by the council, was not a new creation.

> The historian Sozomen reports that Origen [ca. 185–253] used the title Theotokos for Mary, although we cannot be surprised that it is not found in the wreckage of his works. This title had been employed in the School of Alexandria for a long period to express Mary's divine motherhood, when in the first half of the fifth century it was attacked and defended in the Nestorian controversies and defined in the Council of Ephesus (431).[2]

Once the title had been authoritatively approved, confirmed, and defined by the council, the dogma was clear, and Nestorianism unequivocally condemned. It is a passage of the letter of the council Fathers, which announced this condemnation to the clergy and people of Constantinople, that is of the greatest interest here. For in this letter we read that Nestorius was present in Ephesus, "*in which place John the Theologian and the Holy Virgin Mary, Mother of God*"[3] were.

These words provide documentary proof for the Ephesus tradition.

Even allowing an erroneous understanding of that phrase, Mary and John are still mentioned in some way in association with Ephesus. According to proper exegesis, and the precise interpretation, the very sojourn of Mary and John in Ephesus is definitely indicated.

A purely grammatical study, which followed all the most rigorous laws of syntax, showed the dependence of the elliptical clause on the preceding verb form modifying Nestorius, namely, *arrived* (*pervenisset*). The most precise conclusion, therefore, is that the passage truly meant that Nestorius arrived ". . . in the country of the Ephesians, at the place where John the Theologian and the Holy Virgin Mary, Mother of God, arrived."[4] Thus Mary and John did come to Ephesus and, if they *arrived*, then there is surely enough other evidence to conclude that they stayed a while or, in other words, that they lived at Ephesus.[5]

A similarly noteworthy study, made three decades earlier in Rome, explained that according to the rules of Greek grammar the imperfect tense had to be understood in the ellipsis; the letter of the Fathers was, of course, written in Greek.

> In such elliptical clauses, according to the finest of grammarians, Krüger and Kühner-Gerth, the third person *present* indicative must ordinarily be understood; but if the context excludes the present tense, then the third person *imperfect* indicative is understood.[6]

And the sense, therefore, was that John and Mary *lived* in Ephesus at some time. While that interpretation is not as precise as that of *arrived*, it is nevertheless quite correct; it expresses the true meaning, and it is thoroughly acceptable.

> Since these things are so, at the end of the related clause we must add not *are*, but *were*, and then the sense of the clause is: "in which city the *persons* of John the Theologian and the Holy Virgin Mary, Mother of God, *were*," that is, they lived there at some time.[7]

Some scholars supplied the present tense in the ellipsis, and explained that the *remains* of John and Mary are there. This is impossible, of course, for Mary was taken to heaven. Others understood that the *churches* of John and Mary are there. While that is all very true, such a meaning for the passage must be denied. Those

Relevant Documents, Facts, and Studies

who interpreted the phrase in that sense argued that the names in the passage were simply the names of the churches of John and Mary — John the Theologian Church, and Holy Virgin Mary Mother of God Church. But this is ridiculous.

First, such an interpretation cannot be sustained in view of the practice of the council Fathers, which was contrary to the use of such terms as names of the churches. In the letter of Nestorius to the Emperors Theodosius II and Valentinian III, wherein the churches of Ephesus were enumerated, the basilicas of John and Mary were mentioned, but the titles as given above did not occur.[8] When the Fathers of the council spoke of the church in which they convened, they modified it always with the simple name Mary. In the Acts of the Council there were ten occasions on which such usage occurred.[9] Thus the word church cannot be understood in the ellipsis, for it is clearly contrary to the usage of the council Fathers.[10]

Here we may note, in advance, that even if one understands church in this passage, the reference would still prove that Mary either lived or died in Ephesus. This will be explained in the following section.[11]

The principal modes, then, of completing the phrase are these: John and Mary are in Ephesus; that is, they are buried there; they died there; there were churches there dedicated to their names; they arrived, were, or lived there. While the last interpretation expresses the true meaning, all of them give evidence of a sojourn there.

Cornelius à Lapide (1567-1637) maintained that the text indicated that John and Mary lived for a time at Ephesus.[12] Tillemont (1637-1698) similarly argued that the text indicated a sojourn. He denounced the idea that the phrase understood churches, and showed that the actual practice was to use the simple name of the saint in whose honor the church was built. His auxiliary argument ad hominem was this rhetorical question: "Can you really believe that any church would bear the title 'The Holy Virgin Mary Mother of God'?"[13] He continued that such a case would be most unlikely and without example, and he had a point.

But the best argument of Tillemont against the long and unseemly name was that, if the church were really called Holy Virgin Mary

Mother of God, and if this were the ordinary usage of the faithful of Ephesus, that name would doubtlessly have entered as such into the *Acts of the Council* and have been used to considerable advantage against Nestorius.[14] But, as has been seen, it was not! And Tillemont was right. The Church is never wont to pass up such golden opportunities. To think otherwise would in this case be to consider the council Fathers stupid. They would not have failed to note the identity between the dogma they defined and the name of the church wherein they defined it, if such identity had existed.

Don Calmet (1672–1757) made the following observation: "There is a letter of the Oecumenical Council of Ephesus, importing that in the fifth century it was believed she [Mary] was buried there."[15] At the same time he indicated that Mary and John had lived and died at Ephesus.[16]

The marginal notes, which appeared in recent centuries in various editions of the *Acts of the Councils*, and which were appended to that text on Mary and John and Ephesus, read simply, for instance: "*Some* understand that they lived there at some time; *others*, that they had churches there."[17] But at any rate, as the celebrated Otto Bardenhewer, professor at the University of Munich, attested, the greatest philologists and historians of all times have seen the sojourn of Mary and John in the territory of Ephesus.[18]

There are a few scholars who have implied that the elliptical text was meaningless, or at most referred to the council church, which had a double title.[19] The first opinion is somewhat inane, because the letter made perfectly good sense both to the Fathers who wrote it and to the people to whom it was written. The second opinion, while it formerly had somewhat of an admissible basis, is nevertheless false.

The interpretation which promoted the sense of *church* is thoroughly vanquished in the next section, but here also it can be demonstrated to be false by simple argumentation. The following discussion must serve as a general example of such erroneous interpretations, their argumentation and rebuttal, because it would be neither practical nor desirable to burden you with detailed commentary on all of them.

Relevant Documents, Facts, and Studies

The particular argument and interpretation selected stated that the words *John the Theologian and the Holy Virgin Mary Theotokos* designated the two patrons and titularies of the principal church of Ephesus, wherein the council convened.[20] The author of the statement argued that the expression revealed a manner of speaking still current, for example, "I am going to Sts. Peter and Paul," and thus an Ephesian would have said, "I am going to Sts. John and Mary." In support of his contention he quoted the letter of St. Cyril in which, as noted earlier in this section, appeared the rare use of the name *Mary Theotokos* to designate the church.[21]

With a separate basilica of St. John just at the edge of town, it seems hardly credible that the Ephesians would have dedicated the city church also to John; it seems unlikely, furthermore, that St. Cyril would have been so careless in his letter as not to offer the Alexandrians the full double title, rather than simply half of it, if what he wrote was actually part of the title. This improbability is doubly confirmed by the fact that St. Cyril in two other letters, one a message to certain clergymen of Constantinople,[22] the other an apology to Emperor Theodosius II,[23] stated that the church was called *Hagia Maria* — St. Mary. Although the usage of the council Fathers has been indicated earlier, it may be noted here that in their official report to the emperors they too called the church *St. Mary*.[24]

The final argument in favor of the incorrect interpretation under consideration was the contention, after the admission that St. John's tomb was in Ephesus and that it was well known in Christendom, that certain documents were significant in that they mentioned the tomb of John at Ephesus without also mentioning the tomb of Mary. A selection from the letter of Pope St. Celestine (422–432) to the council at Ephesus was then invoked.[25] The text cited read as follows:

> I exhort you, most blessed brethren, that only that love be looked to in which we surely must abide, according to the words of the Apostle John, whose remains you venerate by carrying them in procession.[26]

In the preceding three sections of that letter, however, the Pope had been speaking of the Apostles and the proclamation of the word of God to the Ephesians.[27] There seems to be no reason why he would have had to mention also Mary. And furthermore, there was no corpse of Mary that could be carried in procession.

The next document cited was a portion of a letter of John of Antioch and companions to the senate in Constantinople.[28] That section read as follows:

> The holy churches and shrines of the invincible martyrs have been closed, so that it is not possible for those desiring to do so to pray there; those people came from even very remote places and were burning with the desire of visiting all the shrines of the holy and triumphant martyrs, especially that of St. John the theologian and evangelist (who is known to have obtained the greatest trust from, and familiarity with, Our Lord).[29]

The logic of the argument from that text, namely, that it was significant because it omitted the tomb of Mary, fails completely. The text spoke precisely of the visitors to Ephesus and their burning desire to honor all the shrines of the holy martyrs, especially that of St. John. The expression *all the shrines* confirmed the fact that there were several at Ephesus. If the Latin word *monumenta*, which was translated in the text above as "shrines," denoted tombs only, then Mary's *monumentum* would have rightfully been omitted, both because it was not in the city, but several hours distant, and because, if there ever was a tomb, she may never have been in it and certainly was not in it then. And if *monumenta*, as has been assumed, included shrines other than tombs, such as the church dedicated to Mary, the omission would have been equally meaningless. The text simply mentioned one *monument* specifically.[30] It was exactly the same thing as if you told someone that you desired to visit all the monuments in the nation's capitol, especially the Lincoln Memorial. Did you thereby exclude the Washington Monument, the Jefferson Memorial, or any others? Of course not! The argument is ludicrous.

§ 2. *Basilicas of Mary and John*

In Ephesus you may visit today the remains of two basilicas, one dedicated to Mary, the other to John. The basilica of Mary, scene of the Council of Ephesus, is sometimes called the double or twin church. Such usage is historically and archaeologically acceptable. But the notion that Mary's basilica was jointly dedicated to St. John must be rejected as false. While all these ideas receive consideration in this section, you will see also that the main objective here is to demonstrate that the mere presence in Ephesus of those early shrines consecrated to Mary and John is in itself sufficient evidence that they had lived or died there.

The basilica of St. Mary was most likely completed between the great Peace of the Church (313) and the Council of Ephesus (431). The probable date would seem to be about the year 350.[31] The church was actually a transformation of the huge building called *Museion*, which was so named because it was dedicated to all nine of the Muses, and thus probably served as a sort of university.[32] Although the exact date of completion of the church remains uncertain, it was in use at least well before the council met there. It was very likely the first basilica, and was surely the first cathedral, dedicated to Mary anywhere.[33]

When some two hundred bishops arrived at Ephesus for the council, they must have been impressed with the cathedral there.

> At the beginning of the second century when the city was still under the Roman rule, a very impressive building called "Museion" was built in the middle of the city. This building, which was 98 feet wide and 883 feet long, was either the meeting place of professors and doctors or some sort of exchange. The western part of this building was transformed into the first Christian basilica and dedicated to the Virgin Mary. When the basilica, which was supported by high columns and adorned with beautiful mosaics, was too old to be used, the eastern part of the Museion was turned into a domed church. It is for this reason that these ruins are called the Twin Churches.[34]

The reason for such terms as *twin churches* and *double church* is clear — one part of the *Museion* was used after the other.

> The greatest (471 feet) part of the Museion was immediately transformed into a church and dedicated to St. Mary, and the rest into offices and the official residence of the bishop of Ephesus and his numerous prelates. A beautiful baptistry was added on the North side of the church, with a large, deep waterpool in white marble for

baptism then by immersion. It is probably the most beautiful and also the best preserved baptistry of that kind from the early Church.

The Basilica itself had three longitudinal aisles: the central one, the nave, was very high.

The remains of ornaments and mosaics on hand today give us full evidence of the beautiful interior decoration of the church. Experts and archaeologists are unanimous in asserting that the Basilica offered a fairy-like scenery of architecture, interior decoration, and incomparable harmony of lines and colors that the primitive Christians of Ephesus and Asia Minor offered to our Lord and His Mother.[35]

The false hypothesis, which this division of the old *Museion* generated, was that the council letter referred to twin churches — one of Mary and one of John juxtaposed. As verified from archaeological evidence, there were surely two churches, but the historical evidence and explanation were ignored. Thus it happened that in the archaeological and biblical dictionaries[36] that erroneous thesis was perpetuated. The pamphlets and other works, which attacked the Ephesus tradition, all capitalized on that error in an attempt to diminish the force of the council letter, and to interpret the elliptical clause in the sense of the *churches*, rather than the *persons*, of Mary and John.

The number of incorrect interpretations of the twin churches and the council text diminished dramatically in 1930, and they appear only rarely these days. A plaque was discovered in that year, in the narthex of the basilica of Mary, whereon the Archbishop Hypatios (531-536), in the time of Justinian, clearly indicated that this was the church of St. Mary and the site of the council.[37] The name of Mary's basilica was, therefore, as already clearly shown by the usage of the council Fathers, simply St. Mary. And the council text retains all its force and confirms the sojourn of Mary in Ephesus.

Another confirmation of Mary's sojourn is the simple fact that there was a church dedicated to Mary in Ephesus. According to custom reflected in the actual canon law of that period, churches could be dedicated to the saints in those places only where they had lived or died or were buried. If this was the practice, then Mary and John had lived, or died, or were buried in Ephesus.

In the third century a constitution of Pope Felix I (269-274) established that Holy Mass was to be celebrated only over the tombs

Relevant Documents, Facts, and Studies 59

or monuments of the martyrs.³⁸ Apart from the authenticity of that enactment, however, there was undeniably in the early Church the cult of martyrs and the custom of using relics in the altars.

> The cult of the martyrs betrays its connection with the cult of the dead by the fact that it was at first exclusively associated with the grave. Antiquity hardly knew what might be called an abstract worship of the saints. As we have already noted, the graves of the martyrs were the scene of assemblies and the destination of pilgrimages. The shrines built over the tombs became veritable basilicas. This created the rather odd situation that in larger cities there were really two kinds of churches: within the city, the churches intended for community worship — what we would call parish churches — and on the outskirts of the city, the cemeterial basilicas of the martyrs.³⁹

While the tomb of St. John on the outskirts of Ephesus was a cemeterial basilica, the basilica of St. Mary, the first parish church of the city, was not.

From what has been said, perhaps the difficulty has arisen in your mind that here is a case contrary to the contemporary custom of dedicating a church to one who was not a martyr, namely, to Mary. The following words should solve that problem:

> In the early days of the Church it was established by custom that Churches or Temples could be built only in memory and under the name of the Holy Martyrs who had died fighting bravely for Christ. Under the title of martyrs are understood the Apostles, and all who are themselves actually martyrs; but the most Blessed Virgin, Mother of God, who is called by St. Jerome more than a martyr, is not excluded from this title.⁴⁰

At the time when the church of Mary in Ephesus was being constructed, a custom also prevailed which required some special connection of Mary with Ephesus for dedicating a church to her. The churches and smaller shrines (*martyria* and *memoriae*) were erected for the most part in the places where the martyrs had suffered, or where their bodies were laid to rest.⁴¹ However, the places of dwelling or property, or transferred remains of the body, were permissible substitutes for those requirements. A law was formulated just prior to the year 400, which gave official recognition to the custom that had already prevailed for years. That law read as follows:

> Canon 83: *Concerning false shrines of martyrs.* Likewise, it is our opinion that altars, which are erected here and there in the streets and out in the fields as shrines of the martyrs, in which no body or other remains can be proved to be contained, should if possible be destroyed by the bishops who preside over those places. If this cannot be brought about, however, because of popular uproar, the people must none the less be admonished not to visit those places, so that with the proper understanding they will not be considered as devoted to a superstitious practice there. And absolutely no shrine of martyrs can be laudably permitted except where the body or its remains are present, or in the place of dwelling, or property, or martyrdom as acknowledged from the most trustworthy source. And accordingly those altars, which are put up all over the place as a result of the imagination and inane simulated discoveries of all sorts of people, are wholly and altogether condemned.[42]

With all those restrictions in mind, you may easily arrive at the basis for the construction of Mary's church in Ephesus by a simple process of elimination. The place of her body or its remains is necessarily excluded. The place of martyrdom or of property (*possessio*) in Ephesus is similarly eliminated. The only remaining sufficient cause which would justify the presence of her basilica in Ephesus is that she lived there — perhaps even in the city for a while, and later at a distance on the Mountain of Nightingales rising from the city.[43]

With the basilica of St. John just outside the city of Ephesus, at the site which later developed into Ayasoluk and then the modern Seldjuk, there is scarcely any problem. John died and was buried in Ephesus, as has already been indicated.[44] A memorial was built at once over his tomb, and later on, in the fourth century, a basilica was constructed over that tomb. This was the so-called Theodosian basilica.[45] It was later remodeled, as described by the following quotation:

> The beginning of the sixth century saw a new and large Church over the tomb of the Apostle, although the old one was quite of an unusual size and beauty for that epoch. The sixth century gave the so-called Justinian Basilica, the greatest and most magnificent church of early Christendom.
> The Justinian Basilica from the sixth century had six large and high cupolas (95½ feet of height) that covered the main aisle, the nave of the Church laid down in the form of a Latin cross. Five

Relevant Documents, Facts, and Studies

other smaller cupolas covered the entrance, the so-called Narthex. This third Basilica was 428 feet long and 213 feet wide, covering the entire width, at that place, of St. John's Hill in Ephesus. If this natural topographical limit did not exist, probably the faithful Christians in their incomparable love and veneration toward the Apostle, would have made the Basilica still longer and wider.[46]

The tomb of John and the basilica erected over it were known to almost all ages. Pope St. Celestine, who convoked the Council of Ephesus, referred to St. John's tomb there.[47] A rescript of June 1, 527, from the Emperor Justinian spoke of the contemplated preservation of the venerable oratory of St. John.[48] And the other early literature on St. John's mission and death in Ephesus has already been treated.[49]

There is one composite passage which is noteworthy by reason of its indication of the pilgrimages to St. John's basilica in the Middle Ages. It reads as follows:

> Ephesus was famous in the early Middle Ages, and Western pilgrims likewise resorted thither on account of a church which is never heard of now, the church of the sepulchre of John the Evangelist, who died and was buried in Ephesus. . . .
> In the beginning of his *Hodoeporicon*, Willibald the pilgrim, just mentioned, says: "Ambulaverunt ad Sanctum Iohannem Evangelistam in loco specioso secus Ephesum." In 1102 the pilgrim Saewulf came from Patmos to Ephesus "where he [St. John] entered the sepulchre living." Sir Maundeville in the account of his journey in 1322 writes "From Patmos men go to Ephesus, a fair city and nigh to the sea. And there died St. John, and was buried in a tomb behind the high altar. And there is a fair church, for the Christians were always wont to hold the place."
> . . . We see that the interest of travellers who resorted to Ephesus in the Middle Ages was mainly centered in recollections of John the Evangelist. The legend of the manna is told by an anonymous writer in the eighth century. Concerning the fate of the Church of St. John under Turkish dominion, I have only been able to find a notice . . . "When Sultan Sason (in 1308) made Ephesus surrender from starvation, on condition of sparing the lives of the inhabitants, he carried off the valuable vessels of the Church of St. John and the immense hoard of treasure collected there."[50]

The author concluded the presentation above with the conjecture that the basilica was probably destroyed by Tamerlane in 1402.[51]

St. John's basilica is at present in the process of reconstruction, and during the necessary preparatory excavations many interesting discoveries were made.[52] But even some time prior to those excavations, some fascinating coins were unearthed in Ephesus.

> Perhaps the most interesting of the coins are those struck at Ayasalouk, bearing as they do the word "Theologos," which was the medieval name for Ayasalouk, and going far to prove that St. John's Church was erected at that place.[53]

As a final comment on this matter, it would be well to note that a common objection to the Marian tradition of Ephesus is that, while much was written about the tomb of John, nothing is known of Mary's tomb. The answer should by now be obvious. The tomb of Mary, if in reality there was one, did not contain her sacred body by reason of her Assumption, and was located in a distant and isolated place, difficult of access. Furthermore, from the earliest times until such time as the basilica of St. Mary was built, the cult of St. John in Ephesus may very well have overshadowed that of the Blessed Virgin. At any rate, the cult of Mary was slow to develop, first at Ephesus with a grand basilica dedicated to her, and then elsewhere.[54] Practically all other churches dedicated to Mary were of the fifth century or later.

> The Marian cult, in the first centuries, already on the proper path of development, was still quite far from enjoying the fullness in which we see it after its development. There were indeed few churches bearing her name at Jerusalem, at Constantinople, at Rome. What a contrast, when one thinks of the blossoming of the cathedrals dedicated to Our Lady during the Middle Ages![55]

§ 3. *Papal Attitudes*

All Christians are interested in the attitudes, opinions, and statements, both official and private, of the Popes. Even prior to the discovery of Mary's home in 1891, when the Ephesus tradition had been for centuries gaining new vigor by reason of critical studies enriched with documentary evidence,[56] the vicars of Christ did not remain silent. Perhaps the one Pope, also an outstanding scholar, who studied the matter more than all the others was Benedict XIV (1740–1758).

The pertinent statements of Benedict are found principally in two places: (1) in his treatise on Good Friday, specifically in the commentary on the third of Christ's seven last words;[57] (2) in his treatise on the Feast of the Assumption.[58] The latter composition is professedly a treatment of Mary's death and Assumption, while the former obviously is not.

In his commentary on Christ's third word from the Cross, "Woman, behold thy son . . . Behold thy mother" (Jn 19:25), Pope Benedict wrote the following:

> So that He might declare His special love for His mother, He said to her that she should love John from then on just like a son; and likewise to John, that he should take care of Blessed Mary like his mother. John amply fulfilled Christ's orders; in every way he forever cared for Mary with a sense of duty; he had her live with him while he remained in Palestine, and he took her with him when he departed for Ephesus, where the Blessed Mother at length proceeded from this life into heaven. Christ so commended Mary to John because, as the sacred interpreters argue, Joseph was no longer among the living at that time.[59]

At that point Benedict gave references to various sources and concluded his discussion of the matter. Although he made no mention of Mary's death in that passage, he clearly stated that Mary and John both went to Ephesus and that Ephesus was the site of the Assumption. Elsewhere the Pope had already stated not only that Mary died, but also that this was the opinion of the Church Universal. When he commented on the silence and consequent inference of St. Epiphanius (ca. 315–403),[60] Benedict noted the following:

> The sentiment of this otherwise extremely reliable Father is opposed to the opinion of others and, what is most important, to that of the Church Universal, which holds that she died: so that the only controversy is whether she died in Ephesus or in Jerusalem, and this controversy is brilliantly treated in the work of Tillemont. . . .[61]

In addition to stating definitely that the common opinion at that time of the Church Universal was that Mary suffered death,[62] the Holy Father also plainly betrayed his sentiments in support of the Ephesus tradition. He not only cited, but also lauded, Tillemont who had rejected the Jerusalem tradition as completely false and had demonstrated the genuineness of the Ephesus tradition.

If you were familiar with no more of Benedict's writings than the passages already quoted, you could already be certain of his attitude toward Ephesus and Jerusalem. But his treatise on Mary's Assumption covered so many notions which have received mention in this book, that all relevant passages should at least be summarized.

On the question of the age of Mary at the time of her death, the Pope mentioned the various opinions, most of which neighbored on the age of sixty-two or sixty-three, and then concluded: "Nothing at all on that point, however, can be defined as sure and certain."[63] He did interject, however, that one of his recent predecessors, Benedict XIII (1724-1730), entertained the opinion which preferred sixty-two years.[64]

The next matter which the Holy Father treated was the Jerusalem tradition. Benedict noted that the Juvenal story was based only on the authority of John Damascene's report. He mentioned several devotees of the Jerusalem tradition, namely, Canisius, Abbot Guerricus, Urban II, Burcardus, Andricomius, Petrus a Valle, and said that their opinions proved nothing because they were based on the Euthymian story, and that no one even knew who this Euthymius was, on whom John Damascene, Andrew of Crete, Nicephorus, and others relied. He added that Juvenal himself was considered by Cyril of Alexandria and Leo the Great as a felon, guilty of forgery, sedition, and a few other crimes.[65]

Benedict continued his discussion of Bishop Juvenal of Jerusalem, and agreed with the declaration of Serry that Juvenal was an habitual liar and forger. Anyone like Juvenal, he argued, who was accustomed to falsifying the documents of others, would surely have been capable of fabricating a false letter to Marcian and Pulcheria; a false letter, that is, not in the sense that it lied about its author, but because it gave testimony about a tomb of Mary at Gethsemani near Jerusalem, which tomb did not in fact exist.[66]

Toward the end of his remarks about Juvenal, the Holy Father pointed out that Juvenal was, after all, the bishop of Jerusalem and that it was easy to see, therefore, how he would be solicitous for the glory of his church, to which so much honor would come as the result of the lie that the Blessed Virgin died and was buried at

Relevant Documents, Facts, and Studies

Jerusalem. Benedict added that anyone could see this.[67] Then the Pope, a distinguished jurist himself, concluded with a presumption and noted that according to the jurisconsults with their principle, "Once a liar, always a liar," Juvenal was worthy of absolutely no credence.[68]

The Holy Father made his transition from Jerusalem to Ephesus through the following observation: "Those who reject the authority of Juvenal, and are unable to persuade themselves that the Blessed Virgin died at Jerusalem, think that she died at Ephesus."[69] And he immediately passed on to the letter of the Council of Ephesus.

In his commentary on the elliptical text Benedict noted that some proponents of Ephesus believed that *is* or *are* must be understood according to the rules and style of the Greek language. But, since John and Mary were no longer alive at the time, no other meaning could be given the passage than that their tombs were at Ephesus.[70]

As the arguments on Ephesus and Jerusalem proceeded, it became obvious that the Pope favored Ephesus, even though he cautiously framed almost everything in the third person. For instance, in his treatment of the Jerusalem tradition and its advocates, he said: "They *do not*, however, by any means *prove* this opinion."[71] But of the Ephesus advocates, of which Benedict was one, he said approvingly: "They think Mary died at Ephesus."[72] Moreover, he slipped into the plural of majesty several times, and thereby expressly gave the views as his own.[73] Furthermore, he devoted two pages to the demonstration that the Jerusalem tradition had no merit, and on a single page enumerated arguments all in favor of Ephesus.

Benedict concluded by stating his neutrality on the issues of the year and place in which Mary died. He said that he was content with having offered the various opinions and the bases on which they rested. But by that very statement be again betrayed his feelings, at least on the question of place, if not also on the problem of age. His final words, before he proceeded to the theological questions concerning the Assumption, contained a reaffirmation of Mary's death and Assumption.[74]

It is difficult to conceive that anyone could have any doubt that

Pope Benedict XIV favored the Ephesus tradition. The intrinsic evidence is apparent and, as far as an extrinsic argument is concerned, practically all subsequent writers, whether for or against Ephesus, regarded Benedict XIV as an ally of Ephesus. There was only one notorious exception.

A peculiar monk in his book *The Tomb of the Holy Virgin at Jerusalem* quoted the passage from Benedict's treatise on Good Friday, which stated that Mary came with John to Ephesus whence she was later taken to heaven. The monk then strangely attempted to devaluate this statement by citing the opinion given in Benedict's later treatise on the Assumption, wherein the Holy Father, after thoroughly studying the question, said that he wanted no part of it.[75] The monk thus made the Pope appear both unscholarly and imprudent. If anything, Benedict, in his deliberate treatment of the place of Mary's death, that is, in his treatise on the Assumption, academically left the matter open for discussion, although it was obvious from his article which side he favored. Then, in his commentary on Christ's last words, which was not an intentional treatment of Mary's passing, he flatly stated his personal belief in this matter-of-fact manner: "John took Mary with him to Ephesus whence she was assumed into heaven."[76]

Throughout the past hundred years, practically all the Popes lent support to the Ephesus tradition. While some of them were more active in this respect than others, each deserves mention. The successor of Peter at the middle of the nineteenth century was Pius IX (1846–1878). His preference for Ephesus was made manifest in several ways, one of which follows in some detail:

> It is extremely significant that Pope Pius IX adopted the theory which awakened a great deal of interest. It is significant also to note that Pope Pius reestablished the patriarchate of Jerusalem in 1847 and in recalling the past glories of the church of Jerusalem, he mentioned only that Mary had stayed there a number of years. He failed to mention either the death or the tomb of the Mother of God. To us his silence is very eloquent.[77]

This quotation refers to the *Apostolic Letter* of July 23, 1847, which restored the Latin Patriarchate of Jerusalem. The letter did recall past glories, for example, the first council of the Apostles, the monuments, such as the Holy Sepulcher, but of Mary it said only that she lived in Jerusalem with the Apostles for a while.[78] The simple fact that Pius did not mention any Marian shrine in his enumeration of the Jerusalem monuments might be insignificant in other circumstances. The fact that the Pope had mentioned Mary specifically in that context, however, and then failed to note her death or tomb, cannot be as easily dismissed.

Exactly what the time element indicated in the Pope's letter — "for a while" (diu) — means is debatable. In view of the fact that Pius IX favored the Ephesus tradition, however, he probably intimated that Mary left Jerusalem with John before the other Apostles departed. At any rate, the phrase implied that Mary did not remain long in Jerusalem. It is very likely, of course, that most of the Apostles themselves left at the earliest opportunity.

The successor of Pius IX was Leo XIII (1878–1903), and it was during his reign that *Panaya Kapulu* was discovered. It seems only natural to suppose that after the discovery of Mary's home in 1891, and after word of the discovery reached Rome, there would be some reaction at the Vatican. But the news was, in fact, slow to reach the papal chambers. It came several years after the discovery, and then in a rather accidental manner.

In 1895 Pope Leo sent to the East a commission, headed by Father Eschbach, to study the question of the Oriental rites. Eschbach was the superior of the Pontifical French Seminary in Rome. In the course of his mission he met Father Poulin in Smyrna on May 18, 1895, and at that time mentioned that he had heard of *Panaya* while in Jerusalem and that he was eager to see it. The necessary arrangements were made and on May 20 Eschbach went to Ephesus with Father Jung as his companion. He returned from Mary's home a veritable apostle of *Panaya*.[79]

On his return to Rome, Eschbach appeared before the Holy Father to give an account of his mission, and he also mentioned his delightful visit to Mary's home. Pope Leo showed the liveliest interest in the news of *Panaya*. "Do you have any pictures?" asked His Holiness. Eschbach did, and he showed them. The Pope examined them at length and conveniently forgot to return them.[80]

It was shortly after that audience that, coincidentally or otherwise, Pope Leo issued a decree whereby he transferred the indulgences, which had been previously attached to Mary's tomb at Gethsemani, to the Sanctuary of Our Lady of the Gauls, or Franks, in Jerusalem. This special brief signed by Leo on April 18, 1896, removed the plenary indulgence from Mary's tomb in Jerusalem *in perpetuum* — for all time.[81]

The Pope's true motive for removing those indulgences from the Jerusalem tomb cannot be known with certitude. The reason he proposed in the decree itself, namely, that the place was in schismatic hands and could not be visited without grave risk, was a diplomatic formula, because in fact the tomb was as easy to visit as the other shrines, if not more so. Furthermore, it almost appears that he intended his sentiments to be known because, in the sentence previous to this, he had just made provision for gaining the indulgences where a place was difficult to enter or too small for the pilgrims, so that the indulgences attached to such places could be gained without really ever entering them.[82]

Father Eschbach, who became the apostle of *Panaya* at Rome, had started something. He preached Ephesus to everyone, including the cardinals. As a result, Cardinal di Lai made the journey from Rome to *Panaya* on October 4, 1902. After he had seen everything with his own eyes, he returned quite exultant and deeply convinced.[83]

The attitude of Pope Leo toward Ephesus was explicitly manifested in 1903 when he restored the following annotation, at one time removed, in the *Diario Romano* next to the date, August 15, the feast of the Assumption: "At Ephesus . . . where according to the more probable opinion Mary died."[84]

Leo XIII had, furthermore, planned to send a pontifical commission to Ephesus in the autumn of 1904. Eschbach had launched the project to study *Panaya* with the encouragement and support of Cardinal Parrochi. The illustrious archaeologist, O. Marucchi, was commissioned to head the endeavor. But during the process of preparation, Leo died in August, 1903, and that brought the project to a halt.[85]

The interest at Rome continued to increase, however, as is evident

Relevant Documents, Facts, and Studies 69

from the letter of Cardinal di Lai to Poulin in October, 1903. Shortly after that, Pope St. Pius X (1903-1914) sent his first message to Panaya. His Holiness was fully aware of the importance of the research at Mary's home. He sent his apostolic blessing to all concerned, and encouraged the workers with a prayer that Mary herself would help them find the place of her tomb. The letter was dated April 6, 1906, and signed by Cardinal Merry del Val, Secretary of State.[86]

That letter was, for the most part, a piece of banal chancellery, and the Holy Father expressed therein little of his personal sentiment on Panaya and its authenticity. His opinion was disclosed, however, in other ways. On one occasion St. Pius privately declared himself for Panaya, and gave as the reason for his position the fact that he had been convinced by the text of St. John.[87]

St. Pius disclosed his attitude toward Panaya by the reception which he gave Sisters de Grancey and Fiévet on April 20, 1912. "Has the tomb been found?" he asked. "Not yet, Holy Father," replied Sister de Grancey. She added that she was embarrassed just then by reason of the information given by another visionary (Rosalie Putt). St. Pius then replied with a smile that one should believe the old woman (Catherine Emmerich) rather than the young girl. Sister de Grancey thereupon stated, with the boldness for which she was so well known: "Most Holy Father, I know that you believe, as did your illustrious predecessor Benedict XIV, that the Blessed Virgin died at Ephesus." St. Pius confirmed her remark, though only with a nodding smile.[88]

The final act of St. Pius in regard to Panaya was to grant the favor of a plenary indulgence to the pilgrimage there in 1914.[89] He promised that he would also grant the indulgences of the holy places to Mary's home, but he died soon afterward on the eve of World War I.[90]

During the war there was little activity concerning Mary's home anywhere, whether in Rome, or Ephesus, or elsewhere. The troubled times in Turkey continued until it became a republic in 1923. But within that period there was one letter from Rome, and one outstanding conference in Rome.

The conference was held by Father M. Hetzenauer, professor at the *Apollinaris*. On February 27, 1921, toward the end of the reign of Benedict XV (1914–1922), he delivered a well-documented lecture on Ephesus and *Panaya* at the Pontifical Roman Major Seminary, in the presence of seven cardinals and numerous prelates of the Roman Curia.[91]

The letter from Rome was the result of the presentation to the Holy Father of a small book. In 1922 Poulin forwarded to Pope Pius XI (1922–1939) his latest literary endeavor on the place of Mary's death,[92] and he received a letter from the Secretariate of State, signed by Cardinal Gasparri and dated August 13, 1922. Gasparri wrote that the Holy Father had given the brochure the warmest welcome and wished to congratulate Poulin for his contribution in this disputed question.[93]

Pope Pius XI was succeeded by Pope Pius XII (1939–1958) who, among the many things for which he will be long remembered, defined the dogma of Mary's Assumption on November 1, 1950.[94] In that definition the questions of both Mary's death and the site of the Assumption were omitted, and thus these matters are still open for discussion. But just as the discovery of *Panaya* in 1891 had generated much interest in Mary's home, and produced studies for and against Ephesus,[95] so also did the official proclamation of Mary's Assumption, and the subsequent dedication at Ephesus of the reconstructed *Panaya* in August, 1951.[96]

Meanwhile Radio Vatican became involved with *Panaya*. There is no intention of leaving the impression that Radio Vatican is an official organ of the Holy See. It is no more official than *L'Osservatore Romano*, the Vatican newspaper. It is fairly sure, however, that very little which is opposed to the views of the Holy Father and the Roman Curia would be publicized, certainly not in a favorable light, by either of these semiofficial organs. But the story of *Panaya* was broadcast to the world by Radio Vatican on a Sunday afternoon in June, 1951.[97]

In 1951 *Panaya Kapulu* was declared an official sanctuary for the pilgrims of the Catholic religion in a communication sent by Pope Pius XII to the most Rev. Joseph Descuffi, C.M., Archbishop of

Relevant Documents, Facts, and Studies 71

Smyrna.[98] In the papal decree of June 19, 1951, special privileges were granted in favor of both Mary's home and the old basilicas of John and Mary in Ephesus. Any sacerdotal pilgrim to Mary's home could celebrate there the Votive Mass of the Assumption. Similarly, the Votive Mass of the Divine Maternity at the site of Mary's basilica in Ephesus and the Votive Mass of St. John at the site of St. John's basilica at Seldjuk were permitted.[99] The question of a plenary indulgence for all pilgrims to Mary's home, under the usual conditions, was referred by Pius XII to the Sacred Penitentiary where it received favorable action.[100] Incidentally, it may be mentioned that Pius XII spoke of the Ephesus tradition with the greatest esteem in his letter of 1957 to Archbishop Descuffi, on the occasion of the latter's fiftieth anniversary in the priesthood.

The plenary indulgence granted by Pius was confirmed for all time by Pope John XXIII (1958–1963) by a decree of August 18, 1961.[101] Pope John was the only pope who had visited Ephesus; he did so in 1931, on the occasion of the fiftieth centenary of the Council of Ephesus. At that time he was the papal legate in Bulgaria and later, of course, he functioned as the delegate of the Holy See in Istanbul.[102]

While Pope John did not actually climb the mountain and visit Mary's home, but merely went to the council church down in Ephesus, one of his delegates did go to Panaya.[103]

> On July 1, 1960 His Excellency, Most Reverend Archbishop Francis Lardone, Nuncio-Internuncio to Turkey, came to the House of Our Lady. Incidentally, he is an American citizen. His Excellency celebrated a special Mass at the very place where Our Lady used to pray, and after the Mass, spent a long time in deep prayer and meditation. Afterward, he visited all houses and institutions on the grounds of the Sanctuary and openly expressed his great admiration of the work accomplished and his personal happiness in having lived a couple of hours at this holy place. It was the first time that an official delegate of the Holy Father visited the House of Our Lady in Ephesus. His Excellency also spent much time in deep prayer at the tomb of St. John the Apostle.[104]

Pope John manifested his special interest in Mary's home and Ephesus in many ways. From 1960, and through the subsequent years of his reign, he remembered *Panaya* on the feast of the Purification.

> ... the Pontiff sent a special candle to Our Lady of Panaya from among the candles he received from all parts of the world on February 2, Feast Day of Purification of the Blessed Virgin, or Candlemas Day. These candles are, after a special Apostolic benediction, sent to the most important Marian shrines in the world. His Excellency Archbishop Descuffi, in a special great ceremony, lighted the Papal candle, assisted by his clergy and some 2,000 pilgrims. In his sermon, His Excellency stated among other things, that Our Lady has now in her personal oratory burned the very light of Jesus Himself. "This candle," stated the Archbishop, "represents the very soul and heart of the Holy Father in the Meryem Ana Sanctuary...."[105]

Again Pope John remembered Ephesus in still another way when, in preparation of the Ecumenical Council, he thought of the Council of Ephesus, a shining star in the history of the Church. On February 2, 1962, after the candles were offered to Pope John in St. Peter's basilica, he said in his sermon:

> Here you have ... the *Motu proprio*, which fixes the date of the solemn opening of the Vatican Ecumenical Council II. This date is October 11th of the year 1962, already commenced: the liturgical feast of the Divine Maternity of Most Holy Mary, indeed a commemoration of the Council of Ephesus — third ecumenical — which proclaimed this Marian dogma.[106]

There can be no doubt that Pope Paul VI (1963–) is well aware of Mary's home. That is assured through his past correspondence with the Archbishop of Smyrna, and by his close association with Pius XII.[107] The story of his activity as pope in respect to *Panaya*, however, must be patiently awaited.

§ 4. Studies and Expert Opinions

Of the older studies concerning the Ephesus tradition, some of which have received mention here and there throughout this work, those of Tillemont (1637–1698) and Benedict XIV (1740–1758) were the most outstanding.[108] None of the treatises could discuss Mary's home, of course, for prior to 1891 it was unknown to the world. Once it was discovered, however, reports began to spread. Some news of it leaked out even before the official public announce-

Relevant Documents, Facts, and Studies

ment of 1896, which marked the beginning of the vast modern literature on *Panaya Kapulu*.[109] Prior to that manifesto a few articles appeared and several events transpired which are of interest and relevance.

After the discovery of Mary's home, Eugene Poulin began to work on the historical questions which were related to *Panaya*. His first thought was to obtain the opinions of experts, and thus he wrote to the historian, Louis Duchesne, on January 22, 1892. This was six months after the actual discovery and ten months before the official ecclesiastical inquiry of December, 1892.[110] Duchesne's reply, dated February 4, 1892, read as follows:

> The views of Catherine Emmerich are nothing but an abominable imposture. In what measure the alleged visionary and her associate Clemens Brentano share the honors of having compiled so many apocryphal gospels and deceitful legends, is not for me to determine and I think one could use his time more advantageously. . . . Pardon me for speaking to you in this manner, but I am a Breton and have the habit of calling a cat a cat. Moreover, my religious and moral conscience demands that I protest against the establishment of a sanctuary under such conditions. It is here that I wish I had the eloquence of St. Paul to beseech you not to go farther and not to expose your society and even the Church to exceedingly deserved criticism which will not be lacking to greet your discovery. I think you are more carried away than convinced. For the love of God, stop![111]

Duchesne was still in the mood for correspondence and, after he had written the above letter, decided to inform Poulin's superior. Thus he sent another letter the next day to P. Fiat, superior general of the Lazarists (Vincentians), wherein he called the general's attention to the discoveries at Ephesus, as well as to the attitude of his subjects there. Fiat then wrote to Poulin and, although he did not object to the continuation of research, he did advise the greatest reserve and circumspection.[112]

Those letters did not discourage Poulin. He studied the texts of the Fathers and historians, and at length drew the following conclusions:

1. There was no known real authority for the Jerusalem tradition prior to the sixth century.

2. Where the Fathers spoke of the tomb of Gethsemani, they did so only with hesitation and relied on the apocrypha.

3. The best authors of the seventeenth and eighteenth centuries favored the Ephesus tradition, and did so quite frankly.

4. The most recent historians were divided.

5. In view of all the evidence it was undeniable that the Ephesus tradition at least balanced that of Jerusalem, if it did not outweigh it.[113]

Meanwhile, as the news of the discovery was slipping out, an article by Nirschl appeared in 1894 which attacked the discovery.[114] Shortly thereafter a small book, written as a reply to that article, was published by Wegener in 1895.[115]

Once Poulin learned that the Pope, cardinals, and the Roman Curia had been informed of Mary's home through the instrumentality of Eschbach, he publicly disclosed to the world at large the discovery of *Panaya*. Out of regard for the counsel of his superior, Fiat, the manifesto appeared anonymously, but with the approbation of the Archbishop of Smyrna. Communiques were sent to the journals — *La Vérité, La Gazette de France, L'Univers, Le Bien Public, The Morning Leader, L'Italia*, and many more. And literature, both benevolent and hostile, consequently appeared in every quarter of Europe.

Poulin thought it then opportune to publish the brochure which he had prepared from his research. But from Paris came the following advice of the superior general: "Even though the matter be true, it should not be for our congregation to make this question its own affair."[116] For that reason the Lazarists completely disassociated themselves, as such, from the booklet *Panaghia-Capouli* which appeared in 1896, and they left total responsibility with the Archbishop of Smyrna, André Timoni.[117]

Thus the publication appeared anonymously — disassociated from the Congregation of the Mission — and the subsequent works of Poulin were published under the pseudonym of M. Gabrielovich.[118] There was something parallel on the Jerusalem side, at least as to the use of pseudonyms.[119]

The public announcement made to the journals and the appearance of the anonymous brochure *Panaghia-Capouli* seemed to be interpreted as a declaration of war, or so it would appear from the tenor of many of the writings which flourished after that time. Dr. Nirschl attacked Mary's home once again with a brochure of his own.[120] Leopold Fonck, S.J., the founder of the Biblical Institute of Rome, replied to Nirschl and wrote many articles after that, both in simple exposition and in defense of Mary's home. [121]

In the following years articles, brochures, and full-length books kept appearing on both sides of the controversy. Gabrielovich (Poulin) published a work called *Ephesus or Jerusalem* in 1897.[122] This was violently attacked by the work of Barnabé in 1903,[123] and Gabrielovich refuted him in 1905.[124]

De la Broise, S.J., wrote a brief article in 1897, in which he demonstrated his adherence to the Jerusalem tradition.[125] In that same year M. Jugie wrote a lengthy article, which also favored Jerusalem.[126]

Strangely enough, some of the most renowned authorities of that day contented themselves with expressing their views merely by way of reviews of articles or books. DeSmedt, for instance, in his appraisal of the work of Gabrielovich, said that the book did not change his opinion. He added:

> In truth I do not consider the tradition of Jerusalem as positively certain. But, at this point, I do not see any solid foundation for the tradition of Ephesus.[127]

And Lagrange declared his predilection for the Jerusalem tradition only through his review of the work of Zahn.[128] Lagrange and the *Revue Biblique* were accused by Euzet of having always attempted not to establish the Jerusalem tradition but to discredit the Ephesus tradition.[129]

In contrast to the generally negative approach, or nonconstructive efforts, toward confirmation of the Jerusalem tradition, the contributions from the proponents of Ephesus began to stand out like monuments, for example, masterful books by Gabrielovich (Poulin),[130] and excellent articles by Fonck[131] and Bardenhewer.[132] During the first years after the announcement of *Panaya* to the public, therefore, the literature assumed a general pattern, which it apparently never lost. The writers who were convinced of the merits of Ephesus had something to say about Ephesus, and then in their zeal, but not always, they compared the tradition with that of Jerusalem. Those who favored Jerusalem usually attacked Ephesus first, and only then mentioned what meager arguments they could scavenge in corroboration of Jerusalem.

It seems neither expedient nor desirable to review all the works that appeared subsequently, but certain ones must be included here; those chosen are representative of them all.

In 1898 Abbé Gouyet, the man who had visited Ephesus fifteen years earlier, lauded the Ephesus tradition in his admirable book about the discovery on Mary's Mountain.[133] In the following year Theodore Zahn, the learned Protestant professor of exegesis, berated Ephesus in a small booklet,[134] as did Le Camus in a work which dealt with many other subjects.[135] Le Camus will be remembered for the following statement:

> The most appreciable thing about the recent discovery (on the Mountain of Nightingales) is the good fortune of the Turk who through the intervention of a Christian has sold a loyal and enthusiastic religious [Sr. de Grancey] a ruin without any value for 35,000 francs.[136]

In 1906 Dr. Johannes Niessen of Cologne produced a well-documented and positive study on the authenticity of *Panaya*.[137] In a subsequent work he included a chapter on Ephesus,[138] and still later produced a second but smaller book on *Panaya*.[139] His death in 1938 thwarted his plans to revise and supplement the work of 1906. In the year prior to his death, however, Niessen made the following statement, which is like a legacy from this great intellectual:

> The further I advance in the literature on the subject, the more I prove that there is no serious objection to the contrary, and the more I am strengthened in the conviction that the site of the Dormition of the Virgin and of her Assumption is found at Ephesus.[140]

In the earliest years of *Panaya*, after the announcement of its discovery, many scholars actually visited Mary's home and drew their own conclusions. For example, the Baron Carra de Vaux from the Catholic Institute of Paris went to *Panaya* in 1896 in order to

Relevant Documents, Facts, and Studies

verify the descriptions of Catherine Emmerich. He returned home convinced of the authenticity of Mary's home.

> Also in 1896 Admiral Antoine, together with eight of his officers, was there with books, maps and pictures. His astonishment was such that he could not refrain from saying: "Indeed, one would be almost prone to think that the landscape and the house were designed and built on the very plans of Catherine Emmerich."[141]

Again, Paul Joüon, S.J., of the University of Beirut, wrote the following brief acknowledgment:

> Prior to climbing up to Panaya Kapulu on September 27, 1899, I was convinced, by the study of the Jerusalem tradition relative to the tomb of the Holy Virgin at Gethsemani and above all by the study of St. Epiphanius, that it was necessary to search for Mary's tomb other than in the environs of Jerusalem. This opinion was in no way motivated by the authority of Catherine Emmerich. Then, on the 27th of September I established between the description of C. Emmerich and the things of Panaya Kapulu a concordance such that I deem capable of only one explanation. C. Emmerich had contemplated in vision the site and the house actually called Panaya Kapulu.[142]

Another such acknowledgment was made by Jean Parrang, who resided at Smyrna from 1904 to 1913. It read as follows:

> There is no serious evidence in favor of Jerusalem, but more than enough against it. The possibilities in favor of Ephesus are very great. Can one ever arrive at the absolute certainty which history would like on this question?[143]

The following quotation contains still another acknowledgment:

> Among others who were able to go to Panaya we have yet to mention Prince George of Saxony, duly renowned for his profound knowledge and his piety. He was accompanied on his trip by Mr. Bendorf, director of the excavations at Ephesus (1908). When he returned from his pilgrimage, he exclaimed: "Veni, vidi, credo."[144]

Many of the men who published works for or against Ephesus never had the opportunity to visit Mary's home. They drew their conclusions from other sources, which included the treatises on Panaya that had already appeared. The following quotation mentions two such scholars whose names have not as yet been included in this section:

Many of those who could not take the trip became partisans of Panaya after careful study. Among those we will only mention Farges, Director of the Catholic University of Paris, and the very learned Vigouroux, member of the Biblical Institute of Jerusalem.[145]

In 1910 there were two interesting works, which would be worthy of mention because of their titles, if for no other reason. Marta, a canon of the Holy Sepulcher in Jerusalem, published *Neither Ephesus, nor Panaya Kapulu, but Jerusalem*, and Gabrielovich (Poulin), the Lazarist superior in Smyrna, produced *Neither Zion, nor Gethsemani, Farewell! Jerusalem*.[146]

The two world wars did not arrest the studies on Mary's home, but they did considerably decrease them. The first outstanding article during this period was that of Adhemar d'Ales,[147] and the second was one of Jean Brierre-Narbonne, who terminated his book on Mary Magdalen with a treatise on the sojourn of the Blessed Virgin in Ephesus.[148] Then the famous book of Martin Jugie concerning the death and Assumption of Mary appeared in 1944;[149] it contained certain material on Ephesus to which serious exception could be taken. Joseph Euzet did just that in an article of 1949, and answered satisfactorily every argument of Jugie.[150]

In 1950, when the dogma of the Assumption was defined, there began to appear a volume of literature on *Panaya*. B. Koetting denied the antiquity of the Ephesus tradition, but in his disavowal he conveniently ignored the council letter and the Marian basilica in Ephesus.[151] R. North, S.J., favored Jerusalem, but was scholarly and honest enough to admit the following truths among his conclusions:

> Any site which has a solidly probable claim to have been the last home of the mother of Jesus merits as such true veneration. . . .
> To rule out the claim of Ephesus altogether would be equivalent to suppression of relevant evidence.
> The Ephesus setting furnishes some few details to the imagination which fit the figure of Mary living in solitude better than what we see in Jerusalem.[152]

Then, in 1951, another article of Senior (Descuffi *et al.*) appeared, which summarized the arguments in favor of Ephesus, and which noted that the most uncompromising critic of modern times, Dom

Leclerq, favored Ephesus.[153] There also appeared in that year an article for Ephesus written by Eugene Borrel, who for many decades had labored over texts in the *Bibliotheque Nationale* in order to supply the Lazarists in Smyrna with information from the sources unavailable to them.[154] In 1952 Maurice Gordillo, S.J., published an article wherein he first belittled the arguments for Ephesus, and then attempted to refute them all.[155] He did not accomplish his designs by any means.

Canon Karl Gschwind, who was trapped in Turkey at the outbreak of World War II, took advantage of his years there and studied the antiquities of Asia Minor, and Mary's home in particular. After he returned to his diocese of Basel, Switzerland, he published a most knowledgeable work in favor of Ephesus.[156]

The most recent controversy was between Clemens Kopp and Joseph Euzet.[157] The former tried to destroy or at least minimize the manifold testimony for Ephesus; the latter did not hesitate masterfully to correct him and to reconfirm the arguments for Ephesus. The summary of Euzet reads as follows:

> In this matter, although *scientific* certitude, as they call it, is altogether impossible, the Ephesus tradition nonetheless appears by far the more probable, actually extremely probable, and morally certain. We are able to believe not only piously, but prudently, that *Panaya* is the place from which the Blessed Virgin Mary was assumed into heaven.[158]

In the interval between Kopp's book (1955) and Euzet's reply (1957) an article appeared by Maurice Tallon, S.J., which is worthy of note.[159] Tallon's study concerned the veneration of Mary in Asia Minor from the first to the fifteenth century. The following judgment and conclusion was as honest and fair as anything that had been written since the discovery of *Panaya*, sixty years earlier:

> If one will examine the facts with serenity and with absolute objectivity, one must acknowledge that they form a framework which limits the hypotheses. And we do not find a single major difficulty which contradicts the possibility of a sojourn of Mary at Ephesus, which sojourn, moreover, the ancient monuments and a very ancient oral tradition indisputably postulate.[160]

Finally, and before the introduction of some studies of a slightly different nature in the next section, the useful recent booklet of George Quatman, *House of Our Lady*, deserves an honorable mention.[161] Special praise is due to Joseph Euzet for his superb compilation, *History of the House of the Holy Virgin*, which covered the period of seventy years from the discovery of Mary's home in 1891 to the stage of its development in 1961.[162]

§ 5. *Archaeological Testimony*

This section relates to the preceding one almost as species does to genus; its subject matter, however, warrants distinct treatment. The two sections are similar, moreover, in that each is rife with disagreement. Archaeologists, architects, and other experts of this nature, are no more in agreement on *Panaya* than historians, Scripture scholars, and the like. The specific question for the archaeologist is whether the house, or more precisely its foundations, can truly be authenticated as construction of the first century. If *Panaya Kapulu* is in fact Mary's home, then even after slight architectural transformations through the centuries, and all else, there should still be substantial evidence that *Panaya* was built in the first century.

Before Mary's home had been discovered, a renowned French archaeologist and orientalist, Charles Lenormant (1802–1859), drew the conclusion, based on historical elements, that the Ephesus tradition was in perfect harmony with the conclusions to which the inductions of history led.[163] The archaeologist must use historical knowledge as one of the indispensable tools of his science, which is in many respects conjectural. When a date or equivalent evidence appears on a coin, medallion, plaque, or monument, the task of the archaeologist is simple. But in the many cases where he does not meet such good fortune, he has to gather all knowledge possible from related arts and sciences, so as to make his judgment at least conceivable, if not credible.

Some of the earliest experts to view *Panaya* were members of the Archaeological Institute of Vienna, whose research in Ephesus was headed then by Professor Otto Bendorff. Their consensus was that *Panaya* was a little chapel of the Middle Ages, which could be traced back as far as the fourth century.[164]

Mary's home in Ephesus before restoration.

The Shrine of Our Lady of Ephesus.

Our Lady of Ephesus.

The chapel in Mary's home.

The Shrine of Our Lady of Ephesus as viewed from the southeast.

The famous ruins in Ephesus.

The basilica of St. John in the process of restoration.

The pool below the esplanade of Panaya filled from the old spring.

The Plain of Ephesus as viewed from atop Mary's Mountain.

The summit of Mary's mountain.

The grounds of Panaya.

Lagrange, of the Biblical Institute in Jerusalem, visited Panaya twice, first in 1892 and again in 1905. On his first visit his colleague, Vincent, was with him. Vincent judged the house as a relic of the sixth century; Lagrange, of the seventh.[165] Fonck, of the Biblical Institute in Rome, also visited Mary's home twice, once in 1897 and again in 1907. His conclusion was that at least a part of the house could be verified as first-century construction.[166]

Abbé Wogh, professor of archaeology at Freiburg, studied Panaya in 1905. His pronouncement follows:

> The house may as easily be of the seventh century as of the first, and of the first as easily as of the seventh. I challenge anyone to prove the one rather than the other.[167]

As for the foundations, however, he established them to be of the first century.[168]

Then George Lambakis, a member of many academies and professor of sacred archaeology in Athens, came to Panaya in 1907. Later that same year he gave a lecture in which he placed Mary's home in the fourteenth century. He was famous for his mathematical categorization of religious architecture: first century to 312, 312 to 527, 527 to 842, and 842 to 1453. According to his judgment Panaya barely managed to fit in toward the end of the last division.[169] The opinion of Lambakis was manifestly a case of the archaeologist playing a good joke on the historian. In the fourteenth century there simply were no Christians in Ephesus or vicinity, except at Kirkindje, who could have built such a house. In answer to an inquiry from Lambakis, which concerned the inane attempt to remove Panaya two more centuries from its origin, Doctor Schuze, the eminent German archaeologist, replied as follows:

> As you claim it, the chapel of Panaya cannot date from the sixteenth century. It is definitely Byzantine in architecture, the architecture which was prevalent in the sixth century. But let us not forget that we can trace the Ephesus theory as far back as the fourth century.[170]

A representative number of archaeologists, and other scholars with archaeological ability, visited Mary's home. Several are mentioned in the following passage:

Mr. Ramsay, who is an authority on the archaeology of the Near East, favours the tradition of Ephesus. The well-documented book of Dr. Niessen of Cologne on Panaya, published in 1907, is conclusive.

The Rev. Fr. Adhemar d'Ales, S.J., was always favourably inclined toward Ephesus. . . .

The Rev. Fr. Joüon, S.J., Professor at the Beyrut University, visited Panaya (Sept. 27, 1899) and was immediately convinced. He says: "All this is a revelation of God."[171]

The following excerpt would indicate, moreover, that there was a kind of consensus in confirmation of the Ephesus tradition:

A number of archaeologists and architects agreed that part of the walls of the house could well have existed in the first century, but they thought that the rest was built in the seventh. It was the opinion of Father Wogh, professor of Archaeology and Byzantine Art at the University of Fribourg (1905), and Mr. Rosetti, official architect of the Italian government. It was also the opinion of Mr. Challier and Carre from Paris, and Mr. Hogarth from Oxford.[172]

None of the followers of the Ephesus tradition would deny that much of the walls and the entire front vestibule of the ruins of Panaya were of the seventh century. Catherine Emmerich said that the Apostles themselves had made Mary's home into a church after her death.[173] That subsequent generations of Christians would do likewise cannot be doubted. That there was even a Christian community on Mary's Mountain, practically at her threshold, seems certain.[174]

But what is most significant is that there were at least as many, if not more, archaeological experts who judged that the foundations of the house dated back to the first century, as there were who formed divergent opinions. The archaeologists were in truth divided on that question and cannot give us the final word. Apparently archaeology alone can neither prove nor disprove *Panaya's* authenticity.

The most notable recent archaeological report on the ruins of *Panaya* was addressed to the Tenth International Congress of Byzantine Studies held in Istanbul in 1955. It summarized the archaeological data, and reviewed the various discoveries made through the years. The paper was lengthy and detailed, especially in the section which presented the technical data on the various types of con-

Relevant Documents, Facts, and Studies 83

struction found, and the diverse architectures due to the superconstructions through the centuries. Its author concluded that part of the construction of the house itself belonged to the first century, or at the very least the foundations did.[175]

The most understandable and persuasive argument of all those contained in that report seems to be the simple combination of the following uncomplicated facts. In the ruins of Ephesus were found certain buildings which, together with their foundations, were unanimously judged as constructions of the first century. The foundations of Mary's home on the mountain were found to be identical with those first-century foundations down in Ephesus — they had the same identity of material construction, style, and art.[176]

CHAPTER V

Development of the Shrine

The actual discovery of Mary's home and the acquisition of the property have already been presented. There remain several very brief, but interesting, stories mostly about material aspects of *Panaya*. One concerns the commission for the ecclesiastical inquiry and the discoveries which followed this; another involves the efforts to reconstruct the shrine; still another reveals an American organization which has Mary's home as one of its subordinate beneficiaries. All this will introduce the societies which care for the shrine today, as well as recount the early discoveries and the years of struggle which preceded the development realized at present.

§ 1. *Examination and Excavation*

From the moment that Mary's home was discovered in July, 1891, André Timoni, the local ordinary, was kept informed of everything which took place at *Panaya*. After he had sufficient information and cause to take action, he formed a commission of five laymen and seven ecclesiastics, including himself. The purpose of the commission was to go to Ephesus and investigate *Panaya* in order to determine what official attitude the diocese of Smyrna should take toward the discovery.[1]

On December 1, 1892, only fifteen days after the property had been acquired, the commission arrived at Mary's home. The twelve members of the delegation scrupulously investigated the house and surroundings; every detail was considered minutely and at length. At the close of that examination the members unanimously agreed that a most striking correspondence of everything with the description of Catherine Emmerich was evident.[2]

The minutes of the official visit were recorded and submitted to

Development of the Shrine

the members of the commission, who signed in ratification of the content.[3] Part of the preliminary and general section of that official report may be advantageously included here.

> Minutes of the Official Visit made to Panaya Kapulu by the Most Rev. André Timoni, Archbishop of Smyrna and Vicar Apostolic of Asia Minor.
>
> We, André-Polycarp Timoni . . . as well as the subsigned, attest and certify the following:
>
> Some recent researches made according to the indications of Sister Catherine Emmerich have seriously attracted the attention of the country to a place situated near Ephesus and called Panaya Kapulu . . . we wished to ascertain for ourselves the exactitude of the reports which have come to us.
>
> For this end, on Thursday, December 1, 1892, we travelled to the said place of Panaya Kapulu. There we found the very well preserved ruins of an ancient house or chapel, the construction of which, according to competent archaeologists, may trace its origin to the first century of our era and which, both as to location and as to interior design, corresponds fully and entirely to those things which Catherine Emmerich said in her Revelations concerning the house of the Blessed Virgin at Ephesus.[4]

An enumeration of the individual points of that report, however, would seem at this stage neither necessary nor expedient. The first part concerned the position or location of the house. Archbishop Timoni reported: "All these details [those of Catherine] are rigorously exact," and he listed them one by one.[5] The second and final part concerned the house itself. A presentation of the particulars would be merely a repetition of Catherine Emmerich's own description.[6]

That report, of course, had some archaeological value by reason of the competent members on the commission, and thus could have been included in the preceding section. But its presentation was delayed until now, because it had greater import than that of mere expert testimony in favor of Mary's home. This was the official evaluation of a duly constituted ecclesiastical commission; by reason of the favorable judgment one could for the first time speak of a *shrine* of Our Lady of Ephesus. As a consequence of the inquiry *Panaya Kapulu* received local ecclesiastical approbation, which many years later was officially confirmed by the Pope himself.[7]

If any appreciable amount of work was to be accomplished at Mary's home, it would be necessary to have tools and some shelter which could serve as protection for the workers while they were there. A cottage was suggested by the Sisters of Charity in Smyrna so that, when it was unoccupied, it might shelter occasional pilgrims. In order to build the first such cottage near Mary's home, it was necessary to dig and smooth out the terrain. The pick first broke ground in July, 1894, and that marked the beginning of a series of discoveries. What began as ground breaking for the cottage continued as deliberate excavation by reason of the unexpected findings.[8]

Three vaults or arches, which were built as tombs, were among the first items uncovered. In one, a complete skeleton was found with its head facing the chapel and its hand clutching a medal of Emperor Constantius (337–350). In another, an almost entire skeleton, again with head facing the chapel, held a medal of Justinian (527–565).[9]

The excavations continued and other remains and more medals came to light; one medal was of Constantine the Great (324–337), another was of Anastasius (491–518). Many funeral lamps, vases, and similar objects appeared, which included a terra-cotta mold for making hosts, marked with corn and grapes. Everything indicated the presence of a Christian colony.[10]

But the greatest discovery of 1894 concerned Mary's home itself and occurred on August 23. In the process of excavating to investigate the foundations even more thoroughly, it was decided to dig behind the house in back of Mary's chapel. When the depth of five feet was reached, an octangular bend in this part of the foundation was disclosed.[11] This was the actual base of the angular construction which Catherine Emmerich had indicated for Mary's chapel.[12]

Items within the debris exposed in 1898 and 1899 included water jars, as well as water pipes used for drainage. More tombs hewn from rock, many bones, lacrimatory vials, urns, and mosaics in black and white, were among the numerous other discoveries.[13]

And in August, 1898, another momentous find concerning the

Development of the Shrine

house itself was made. After the thought came to one of the workers that there just might be some sort of pavement below the dirt floor of Mary's home, the ground inside the house was broken. Soon a few pieces of marble appeared, blackened on one side only — it looked as though there was a pavement after all. The digging was continued for about two more feet, where similar pieces were found. But they were all in one spot, as if disposed of in a hole. Then ashes, which were coagulated with soot and dirt, were also discovered in the same hole. Altogether, more than two cubic yards of such stones were removed.[14]

It was at about that point that the workers were shocked by their own mental processes. They had found pieces of marble blackened on one side only and coagulated ashes, and there they had just happened to dig in the middle of the house, between the two principal rooms, where according to Catherine, the hearth was supposed to be. These pieces of stone must have been part of the fireplace, demolished by the Apostles, or by Christians of a later era, when they transformed Mary's home into a chapel. These fragments must have been saved and buried in the hole, on the very spot of the former hearth, out of sentiment and respect. By reason of the subsequent miracles worked through the ashes, there would be difficulty in finding any other explanation.[15]

The final observation on the excavations concerns the tomb. The explorers of *Panaya* searched for it in vain from 1892 to 1914. You can be sure that Mary's home was enough of a discovery for them — they were supremely joyous and grateful for having found it. But they thought that the tomb might give still more proof of authenticity to *Panaya*, and with this attitude they persistently searched for it. Catherine had said that the tomb was underground and would one day be discovered.[16]

There was, however, one oddity about that remark of Catherine. Normally, as she related her visions, she introduced them with "I saw." But in the case of the tomb, she said: "I *believe* that this grave must still exist under the earth and will one day come to light."[17] Rather than a prophecy regarding the tomb, she perhaps elicited a pious wish.[18] At any rate, no tomb has yet been found.

Most of the futile search centered in the area of the little hill of Karatchali, where one of Mary's Stations of the Cross, presumed to be that of Calvary, was found.[19]

It is thought that several of these ancient stations have been found all along the mountain, toward the north, behind the house, on a line parallel to the Ephesus road and terminating on a hillock between the Ephesus and Arvalia (Eroglu) roads.[20]

But even if the tomb came to light tomorrow, it seems very doubtful that it would increase the number of believers in *Panaya*, or decrease the number of disbelievers. The discovery of the tomb would in reality add little to the present evidence of genuineness of either the Ephesus tradition or Mary's home itself. As mentioned previously, the question of a tomb, and even Mary's death for that matter, can readily be severed from the matter of authenticity of Mary's home.[21]

One benefit, and perhaps the greatest, that would attend the discovery of the tomb is the propagation of knowledge of Mary's home. Notices and new treatises would surely appear. There would undoubtedly be new controversies between the disciples of Ephesus and Jerusalem. But even the majority of such disputes are good — they seek the truth — and they serve the end of making *Panaya Kapulu* ever more known to the world.

For those who retain the Ephesus tradition in all its fullness, and recognize the perfect agreement of the house on the mountain with Catherine's descriptions, the tomb is surely there, at the side of a small hill at some distance from the house. But it does not really seem to matter in which direction. Mary's body is not there. In truth it was the whole site, together with the ancient home, that was Mary's dwelling place. And you might say, in view of the doctrine of the Assumption, that the entire area was Mary's tomb. For this reason it is quite fitting that today the mountain is called *Meryem Dagh* — Mary's Mountain.[22]

§ 2. *Restoration and Preservation*

After the site of Mary's home was purchased on November 15, 1892,[23] the new owner and collaborators were anxious to preserve and restore *Panaya*. They found themselves, however, buried in the

Development of the Shrine 89

minute details of bureaucracy in their attempts to obtain the necessary authorizations. That was the reason why nothing was done prior to July, 1894.[24]

Construction of any kind was a Herculean task as compared with excavation. All the building materials had to be carried up the mountain by means of pack animals and manpower. A visit to the site makes one appreciate the problems involved. The part-time excavations had occupied most of the efforts of the laborers on their occasional expeditions to Mary's home. And thus it was not until 1903 that a modest chalet, intended primarily for the use of the Sisters of Charity, was completed. Later it made excellent firewood for the soldiers during the war.[25]

For some intervening years, however, that little cottage, and Mary's home itself, offered shelter to a number of pilgrims who spent the night there. The object of primary concern in the matter of further construction was, of course, some structure to protect what remained of Mary's home. With that in view, a roof of timber frames and panes of glass, completely independent of the walls, was constructed over the remains of *Panaya*.[26]

Other work at this time included the improvement of the path which led to Mary's home; it was graded in part and planted with olive trees. Numerous evergreens also were planted here and there to adorn the landscape. And on a stone, which formed a sort of natural pedestal in the common or esplanade in front of *Panaya*, was placed a half-life-size brass statue of Mary with arms extended, as she appeared on the miraculous medal. An altar within Mary's home was then planned. What a labor it must have been to zigzag two camels carrying marble slabs up the mountain! But the project was completed, and a lovely altar was installed in Mary's own chapel.[27]

After World War I a brief talk with the captain who had charge of the artillery installed at the mountaintop revealed that his soldiers had found the brass statue in a ravine, and that he had ordered them to put it in the chapel. In 1926 it was missing again. After the full recovery of the property in 1931,[28] a caretaker named Aziz was hired for *Panaya*; he found the statue and restored it to its place of honor, shortly after he had been installed. When you first see that dark statue, you might well wonder why it was the object of so much attention and concern. The hands are missing, the nose is broken — it is not very attractive — but the arms still retain that tender gesture of a maternal welcome.[29]

Of all the war damage, the least regrettable perhaps was the destruction of that provisional glass roof. While it certainly protected the ruins from the elements, it also gave the ancient and venerable home an overall aspect of a temporary barracks. But the beautiful marble altar had been shattered too. In 1920 it was found in pieces, which were scattered all over the place.[30]

But there was still a happy thought. In 1914 plans were drawn and the money was raised for a building nearby which could house more pilgrims. Raymond Péré, the architect, had just barely begun the actual breaking of ground when the war broke out. Thus the building, which otherwise would have been built, was saved from its inevitable mutilation or destruction.[31]

The two world wars, together with Turkey's internal difficulties, prevented the long-desired restoration of Mary's home. They hindered also the fulfillment of the dreams of facilities for pilgrims and resident clergy, and other construction. There were in all over thirty years of forced neglect. And it was merely in the past decade or so that any of those projects were completed.

The most memorable event or date was the great pilgrimage, August 19, 1951,[32] which opened a new era in the history of Mary's home. Earlier in the same year Archbishop Descuffi had founded at Izmir the *Panaya Kapulu Derneği* — Mary's Home Association. It was recognized by the government and authorized to collect funds and make all necessary arrangements to put the Christian sanctuary to good use.[33]

The name was later changed to *Meryem Ana Derneği* — Society of Mother Mary — in order to avoid certain inconveniences arising from the original name.[34] Suffice it to say that the former name, with its hybrid expression *Panaya Kapulu* from Greek and Turkish, must have been offensive to many loyal Turks who, as you know, would be immediately inclined to despise anything Greek.

Development of the Shrine

Several years before the society was formed, the possibility of a modern road leading up the mountain was discussed. As early as 1948 the Turkish government was well disposed to the idea, and the Council of Ministers made the road practically a national cause. Once the Department of Tourism, in particular, became interested in the project, its director, Halim Alyot, naturally came to Archbishop Descuffi to discuss matters.[35] The bishop's knowledge of Turkish permitted him to confer directly with all the government officials. His intelligent and indefatigable activity on behalf of Mary's home gained for him the title of *Animator of Panaya*; he thereby joined the ranks of Jung, the *Discoverer of Panaya*, Sister de Grancey, the *Mother of Panaya*, and Poulin, the *Soldier of Panaya*.

In the negotiations which followed, the road was planned as nine kilometers in length and nine meters in width. Although the Turkish government merits a great deal of praise for consenting to and undertaking the project, it does not deserve all the credit. Over half the cost, for instance, was paid by Canon Gschwind with funds he had raised for this purpose.[36]

Work on the road was finally begun in April, 1951, and it was completed in only three months — a fine tribute to the builders, who were soldiers in the Turkish Army.[37] The road made possible the huge pilgrimage of August, 1951, mentioned earlier. In any event, the road may be viewed as a monument to the benevolent attitude and generous understanding of the government toward Panaya, which feelings continued through the following years to the present.[38]

It was while the road was being built that the Panaya society of Izmir was officially recognized and constituted on May 6, 1951. A description of both its purposes and accomplishments is surely in order. Its primary object was the restoration and then upkeep of Mary's home; a secondary end was the clearance and development of the area, which would allow larger pilgrimages. Work on the house was begun in earnest from the moment that the society was formed, and it was completed rapidly and satisfactorily through the generosity of the faithful of Izmir and of many foreign donors.

The work of restoration was reviewed and approved by a commission composed of the directors of the Izmir and Ephesus Museums, the chief architect of the municipality, the director of tourism, and other state officials. Some details of the reconstruction follow:

> The access paths were retraced in a straight line, the esplanade was considerably enlarged, and a semi-circular path now surrounds Our Lady's House. The more recent walls and arches of lighter color are easily distinguished from the darker ancient walls, which were respected, and are visible several feet above the ground, and are marked with a red paint line so one can readily distinguish the old, original structure, from the repaired portion. For the new parts, 7th century building materials, provided by the Museum's Administration, were used as far as possible. As much interiorly as exteriorly, the walls have been shed of their parget to give the building the ancient and rustic appearance demanded by public opinion.[39]

The work on the house was sufficiently completed by mid-August to allow its solemn dedication on August 19, 1951. From that day forward the shrine has remained open, in accordance with the wishes of Pope Pius XII, to all good men regardless of race, or creed, or any other differentiation.[40] Of the reconstruction in general, this may be said:

> In short, a special point was made of preserving as much as possible the lines and general appearance of the building. If, after so many centuries of ravages and alterations, some unimportant detail has disappeared, one can still find not only all the important features pointed out by Anne Catherine Emmerich, but also a number of complementary details which confirm the exactitude of her descriptions.[41]

And to that might also be added the following:

> Below the great modern arch which marks the junction between the Byzantine chapel and the oratory, dark flagstones show the spot where the "hearth," or chimney used to be. . . .[42]

The early years of the society were a bit trying and somewhat fumbling, because there was so much to do. Animated by its zealous president, Pol Clark, the society after having adequately restored Mary's home, and having effected some of the desired landscaping, erected a modest shelter for pilgrims and built a house destined for resident clergy.[43]

Development of the Shrine 93

Before October 26, 1955, there was no resident priest at the shrine, but on that day Archbishop Descuffi canonically installed Father Joseph Bouis of the *Petits Frères de Jésus* — Little Brothers of Jesus. In the following year Bouis received a confrere as companion in the person of Father Louis Couillard. With two resident priests at *Panaya* it became quite feasible to keep a journal which would record the events and some of the visitors at Mary's home. The daily report was summarized, and the more notable items were inserted in the chronicle of the *Revue of Our Lady of Ephesus*.[44]

Couillard stayed only a year and was replaced by Father François Saulais who, together with Bouis, remained until 1963.[45] In 1963 the transfer of the administration of the shrine to the Montfort Fathers was completed. One of them, Father Francis Allen, had already arrived on August 8, 1962, and his superior, Father François LeRoux, came exactly one month later. This overlap of time allowed the veterans to indoctrinate the neophytes, and also gave the latter an opportunity to learn some Turkish before being left alone in charge.[46] In November, 1962, even before the Little Brothers had left, the Turkish government gave permission for residence of four priests at the shrine in view of the increasing number of pilgrims and their need for adequate guidance, instruction, and general accommodation.

It is amazing that there are any priests at all at Mary's home, because such a situation is contrary to Turkish law. The government had made an exception to the law in the case of the first two resident priests, and then it granted a further dispensation and allowed two more. As a result of that permission Father Giuseppe Rum of Italy and Brother Benedictus of the Netherlands were added to the staff of LeRoux and Allen. Between those four gentlemen at that little international house, subject directly to the motherhouse in Rome, seven or more languages became available for the convenience and instruction of the foreign pilgrims.

The clerical garb is outlawed in Turkey, as is the fez for men and the veil for women, by reason of religious significance.[47] As a result, the priests at the shrine have no distinctive dress. Father Allen wrote the following on that point:

In summer I wear light pants and an open-collar sport shirt. In winter I wear a black or grey suit with shirt and tie. At the monthly clergy conferences at the Archbishop's residence, in winter it looks like a businessmen's conference, in summer it is a motley assortment of dress that enters the room.[48]

Although the *Panaya* society continues its maintenance of Mary's home, its resources are definitely limited. Foreign support is an absolute necessity, if the plans for future development of the shrine are to be realized. And in the life itself on the mountain there are very few of the comforts of home. While the priests there are forbidden to proselytize, they are missionaries in every other sense.[49]

The story of the resident Sisters at the shrine is a brief but pleasant one, and may be included here. The Sisters of Charity of St. Vincent de Paul had a vital interest in Mary's home from the beginning. You may recall that it was one of them, Sister Marie de Mandat-Grancey, who purchased a generous portion of Mary's Mountain in 1892.[50] Through the years those nuns made innumerable pilgrimages to Mary's home. And while their original little cottage there was only a brief reality,[51] they finally came to live at Panaya in 1962.

There were, however, other Sisters before them in brief residence at the shrine. With the new priests' house and the resident priests on the grounds, there was no longer need for a caretaker.[52] The little dwelling of the caretaker was remodeled sufficiently to house two Sisters. Official permission for the residence of two nuns was granted by the government, just as it had been for the priests. Thus, a pair of Little Sisters of Jesus arrived at the shrine in 1956, but they stayed only a few years.

Several years passed with no nuns permanently at Mary's home. Finally on May 24, 1962, two Daughters of Charity were assigned residence at the shrine: they were Sister Marie Emille and Sister Marguerite. In May, 1963, Sister Vincent was appointed to replace Sister Marguerite, who had previously spent over forty years as a schoolteacher in Izmir. Residence of Sisters at Mary's home is intended to be permanent, for the purpose of caring for the shrine itself — priests are notoriously poor housekeepers — and also of mind-

Development of the Shrine

ing the small religious article shop. The two Sisters of Charity, Emille and Vincent, who are currently assigned to Panaya, are both nurses from the French Hospital in Izmir.[53]

§ 3. American Society of Ephesus

The connection between Mary's home and the American Society of Ephesus (ASE·) is of minor import. Yet the very existence of an American organization dedicated to Ephesus comes as a surprise to most people.

The American society was conceived in 1955 by George B. Quatman, Sr., as a consequence of an apparition with which he was favored in Ephesus.[54] And while he was surely the driving force behind the society, he modestly described its formation as follows:

> Some American businessmen, realizing the need for financial assistance for the restoration of the sacred historical places of Ephesus, and to further spread the knowledge to the Christian world of the existence of these treasured relics of the second Holy Family — The Blessed Virgin, Christ's beloved Apostle St. John and St. Mary Magdalene — formed at the foot of the Cross, created The American Society of Ephesus.[55]

There is actually no intrinsic relation between the ASE, the scope of which is unlimited, and the Meryem Ana Society, which has ends delineated precisely and exclusively in relation to Mary's home. What confusion arises is principally explained by reason of the connection of certain persons with both organizations or, in other words, by the fact that the ASE has a Turkish subsidiary, some members of which are members also of the Meryem Ana Society. The following examples should elucidate this: Archbishop Descuffi of Izmir moderates the Meryem Ana or Panaya Society, and at the same time is protector and spiritual director of the ASE; P. A. Clarke and Suad Yurdkoru are members of the Turkish society and also members of the technical committee of the ASE.

Ever since Mary's home received the benefit of resident priests in 1955, the ASE has furnished funds for their personal support. This is the one and only connection between the American society and Mary's home. The ASE pays the modest salaries of the resident priests, while it is primarily engaged in other work, which will be mentioned momentarily. The Meryem Ana Society has as its exclusive purpose the maintenance of Mary's home and grounds, the expansion program, and everything else immediately connected with Panaya Kapulu. Very few of its members, however, are in a position to contribute much more than their prayers and labors, and thus financial support for the projects at Panaya must come from other sources. On that point Father Allen wrote the following:

> By far the major portion of our funds for construction comes from Canon Gschwind. He and his secretary have literally dedicated the last sixteen years of their lives to raising funds for Meryem Ana. The House [Mary's home] maintains itself through the offering box (very little comes in here), the candles (about 25 percent of the needed support) and the small kiosque.[56]

If any doubts remain as to the nature and purpose of the two societies, the American and the Turkish, a study of the preceding section along with the following brief treatment of the American society should resolve them.

The constitution and bylaws of the ASE were ratified and approved on December 16, 1955. The aims of the society and the means employed to accomplish them may be summarized as follows:

> TO PROMOTE the fundamental teachings of Christian doctrine which the rapid advancement of the material world has failed either through inadvertence, preoccupation or design to keep pace with in our governmental policy and international problems. No civilization can long endure unless its peoples accept and incorporate into their daily lives the teachings of Christ as disseminated by His Apostles — TO RESTORE AND PRESERVE the sacred sanctuaries of early Christian leaders in Ephesus where Mary, the Immaculate Mother of Christ, and St. Mary Magdalene spent their last days on earth and where St. John wrote his gospels and solidified Christianity through the establishment of Seven Bishoprics — TO DISTRIBUTE literature to promote such aims — TO ASSIST in caring for and restoring places of general worship — TO GRANT help to schools, universities or scholars in order to encourage and promote religious and spiritual studies — TO PROMOTE pilgrimages and other means of devotion.[57]

At present the ASE is engaged in restoring the tomb, basilica, and citadel of St. John at Ephesus. Its next aim is the restoration of the

Development of the Shrine

basilica of Mary, the council church, in the ancient city itself. After those projects are completed, it will most likely do something of a substantial nature in further development of the Shrine of Our Lady of Ephesus, Mary's home, if there be need for such by that time. The basilica of the Seven Sleepers and the tomb of Mary Magdalen are similarly included in the schedule of restoration of shrines at Ephesus.

While very much remains to be done on the first major undertaking of the ASE, much has been accomplished gradually over the past few years toward the restoration of St. John's tomb and basilica. The attitude of the Turkish government toward this restoration may be seen in the following quotation:

> This [restoration] is being done with the great and generous understanding, the moral support and encouragement of the Turkish Government, the Governor of Izmir (Smyrna), as well as all of the authorities concerned in Ephesus (Selçuk).[58]

The technical committee for the current restoration work includes Hakki Gultekin, director of the Smyrna Museum, Cevat Sezer, diplomatic architect of the same museum, Musa Baran, director of Ephesus Museum, and the previously mentioned P. A. Clarke and Suad Yudkoru.[59] Dr. Marko Žužić, executive director of the ASE, assists Archbishop Descuffi in the direct supervision of the work, as do Dr. Halim Tevfik Alyot for the Turkish government at Ankara, Canon Karl Gschwind of Basel, and Father Engelbert Kirschbaum, professor of archaeology at the Gregorian University in Rome. Dr. Žužić prepared for the ASE the small but engaging book, *A Short History of St. John in Ephesus*.[60]

A presentation of the numerous details of the work of excavation and restoration of St. John's basilica, which continues today, is beyond our scope.[61]

CHAPTER VI

Shrine of Our Lady of Ephesus

§ 1. *Pilgrimages*

Even before Mary's home was discovered, there were pilgrimages to Ephesus; it was believed that Mary and John had lived there and to this their basilicas bore witness. There were, as previously noted, pilgrimages to Ephesus during the Middle Ages[1] and even organized devotional visits were in vogue just prior to the discovery of *Panaya*. For example, Bishop Spaccapietra (d. 1878) led a group of Catholics from Smyrna to Ephesus in 1872. Timoni, his successor, continued the practice, first in 1884 and again in 1889, when it was decided to hold the pilgrimages to the ruins of the ancient city every five years. The pilgrims provided a colorful demonstration for the numerous, amazed orthodox and Moslem spectators — banners waved in the wind, processions moved to and fro, solemn Mass was sung — but most of this was localized at the mosque of Isabey, which was believed to be the site of St. John's tomb before the ruins of his basilica were unearthed.[2]

Once Mary's home on the mountain was discovered, pilgrimages were naturally directed there. In 1896, when it took two trains to transport the more than 1300 pilgrims from Smyrna to Ephesus, it was decided to form two groups. One would remain at Ephesus and have Mass as usual; the other, which comprised all those who had not only the desire but also the strength to climb the mountain, would go to *Panaya*. The majority elected *Panaya*. The train left Smyrna at 5:00 a.m., and the ride to Ephesus required less than two hours. It was 9:30 a.m., however, or more than two hours and a half after arrival at Ephesus, when the first of the long line of pilgrims reached Mary's home.[3]

The chapel had been decorated beautifully in advance. With such a crowd the little chapel was packed; it overflowed many times its capacity out into the esplanade. Archbishop Timoni, vested and with miter on head and crozier in hand, announced the plenary indulgence granted by Leo XIII, which had been authorized viva voce during an audience with the Holy Father. And the Mass began. After careful consideration of the old laws of the Eucharistic fast, the train ride, the grueling hike up the mountain, during which water had been offered to all who desired it — in view of all these things — the estimate was made and agreed upon that only from twenty to thirty persons would receive Holy Communion, and accordingly twenty-five hosts were consecrated. At Communion time the Hosts were broken, and rebroken, and broken again until one hundred and forty-four pilgrims had received.[4]

In 1898 and each year following until the war, similar pilgrimages took place, each with equal or greater enthusiasm than the preceding. By 1914 the pilgrims had totaled about twenty thousand. The war precluded the continuation of those joyous and pious demonstrations of allegiance and dedication to Mary.[5]

There were, of course, hundreds of other, but smaller, pilgrimages before the war. It would be impossible, however, to mention them all. In general it may be said that priests and religious of all orders and congregations came to see Mary's home — Assumptionists, Benedictines, Capuchins, Dominicans, and so on down the alphabet. And laymen of every walk of life also visited Panaya.

> Not only scholars came to see and study, but also a large number of pilgrims, famous people from France, Belgium, Holland, Austria, Poland and even from Chile. Artists from the School of Fine Arts in Paris, an imposing number of officials of all ranks from the French Navy, Dr. Spahn, Vice-President of the Reichstag (1909), the Baron Deterghem and Mlle. Lanoy from the Royal Court of Belgium. Even the Prime Minister of the Republic of Chile, Carlos Martinez. All of them went to Panaya and returned to their country convinced and in wonderment.[6]

In respect to the religious, both men and women, the following may be added:

> There was a constant flow of all the important religious orders who ascended the holy mountain of Panaya. At the head of the list

were the Fathers of the Assumption from Eskişehir and Konya. Fr. Logry, provincial of the Lazarists, Fr. Coubé, O.P., and the Rev. Father Bruno, O.F.M.C., spoke most eloquently of Panaya.

Rev. Fr. André, superior of the Jesuits, was there especially to meditate. The Brothers of the Christian Churches, the Sisters D'Ivrea, the Sisters of Charity were constantly bringing their pupils. And various fraternities and associations were endlessly coming. Also long processions of parish priests, Franciscans, Capuchins, and Dominicans were flocking there on holidays.

Mgr. Bonetti from Istanbul . . . Mgr. Macriniti, bishop of Syra, Mgr. Camilleri de Santorin, Mgr. Brindisi, archbishop of Corfu, all of them led pilgrimages and exalted the faithful by their heart stirring devotion.[7]

Most of the other notable pre-World War I visitors have been previously mentioned.[8] As a partial list here, however, the following names may be offered: Lagrange, Vincent, Vigouroux, Coubé, Fonck, Joüon, Grivet, Cardinal de Lai, Archbishop Netzhammer, Wogh, Hetzenauer, Prince George of Saxony, Baron Carra de Vaux, Blackler, Hogarth, Admiral Antoine, Baron Antoine de Mandat-Grancey.[9] From that list may be singled out R. Netzhammer, O.S.B., Archbishop of Bucharest, who led a pilgrimage to Mary's home in 1910 and declared: "I wish that Panaya would become known more and more, and become a place of world pilgrimage!"[10] His wish came true; Mary's home becomes known more and more each day and, as will be seen momentarily, has already beckoned pilgrims from all over the world.

World War I halted all pilgrimages. And the embryonic stages of Turkey as a national state forestalled their resumption. Once the cloud of the great war lifted, the problems of Turkey were clearly visible. The Treaty of Sèvres, August 10, 1920, which deprived Turkey of the Arab-speaking provinces and gave Ionia to Greece, was accepted by Sultan Mehmet VI. National elements led by Mustafa Kemal, however, defied the sultan's authority. Kemal made a treaty with Russia, routed the attacking Greeks, captured Smyrna, and finally, on November 1, 1922, deposed the sultan. In 1923 the Conference of Lausanne established essentially Turkey's present boundaries, and Turkey was proclaimed a republic on October 23 of that year. Kemal was chosen its first president, and religion and

Shrine of Our Lady of Ephesus 101

matters connected therewith began to suffer. Kemal took the name *Attaturk* — Father of the Turks — and his goal was complete cultural transformation and Occidentalization of his country. The democratic government, elected in May, 1950, manifested a more liberal spirit than that of the people's party; it thoroughly tolerated religion, and in some cases encouraged it. This is, of course, an oversimplification of Turkish history, but perhaps it may help you to appreciate some of the obstacles to pilgrimages to *Panaya* after World War I had ended.[11]

The first Mass offered at *Panaya*, after the year 1914, was celebrated rather stealthily in 1926.[12] Other than that visit and another fast trip in 1929 by Euzet and the Dominican, Grasso, there were no pilgrimages to Mary's home until 1932. In 1931 there were, however, several hasty excursions to Ephesus itself on the occasion of the fiftieth centenary of the Council of Ephesus. One of them was rather special by reason of the prelates in attendance. That particular visit to the council church included Archbishop Tonna of Izmir, Archbishop Filipucci of Athens, Bishop Margotti, apostolic delegate of Turkey, and Bishop Roncalli, then apostolic delegate of Bulgaria and later Pope John XXIII.[13]

On April 17, 1932, an excursion train became available for a trip to Ephesus and a group of sixty persons, which numbered nuns, priests, and laymen, visited Mary's home. This was the first postwar pilgrimage of any significant size. It was, indeed, a humble beginning, but nonetheless it did mark the desired reinstatement of organized pilgrimages to *Panaya*.[14]

Shortly after that the autorail came to Ephesus. It was presumably something like a self-propelled coach car, which could pick up its flanged steel wheels, after it had let down a set of pneumatic ones, and travel by road. But its most important feature was that it could be hired for the day. The autorail carried about fifty people to Ephesus on April 17, 1933. And again on May 21, 1934, it took about the same number. With the exception of that May pilgrimage and the one of 1896 (May 20), all others prior to 1951 took place in April, usually during the Easter holidays.[15]

Two notable pilgrims in that period were Father Hoffman, S.J., professor at the Oriental Institute in Rome, who came in 1934, and Father Benno Gut, O.S.B., of the Abbey of Einsiedeln, who came in 1935. Both were deeply impressed with *Panaya*, and Benno Gut wrote:

> Truly, the beloved apostle could not have chosen for himself and the Virgin a place more favourable by reason of the distance, the solitude, and the beauty of the landscape.[16]

On April 23, 1936, a group of sixty-five people climbed the mountain to Mary's home. After that there were no pilgrimages until 1949. There were several reasons for this moratorium. The earlier pilgrimages were composed of many of the same people each time. Some of them may have no longer welcomed the trip for any number of reasons, and others no doubt worried about returning under such difficult circumstances. Near-war conditions and World War II itself explained a sizable interval of that period. Then in 1949 a pilgrimage which required two motor coaches brought one hundred people to Mary's home. Archbishop Descuffi of Smyrna celebrated Mass.[17]

Dr. Karl Gschwind, a canon of Basel, who was caught in Istanbul by the beginning of the war (1939), took advantage of his forced sojourn and studied the Christian antiquities of Asia Minor. He loved Mary's home dearly.[18] In October, 1950, Gschwind conceived the idea of promoting a pilgrimage to *Panaya* that would coincide with the solemn definition of the Assumption on November 1 of that year.[19]

The actual pilgrimage took place on October 30 and could boast of few more than thirty participants. But one of its effects was immense. The announcement of the pilgrimage was carried by the Turkish press, and the Government Bureau of Tourism took cognizance of *Panaya* and became earnestly interested in the project of the road to Mary's home.[20] The road was perfectly timed with the revived discussion of Mary's death and tomb, which inevitably accompanied the definition of the Assumption, and the concurrent publicity accorded to *Panaya*. When the road was completed, people could for the first time drive by car, taxi, or autobus, to an altitude on the mountain identical with that of Mary's home; it was a

Shrine of Our Lady of Ephesus 103

matter of only a very short walk to the shrine from the parking area.

In April, 1951, the road was begun and by August it was finished. The road, even while in the process of construction, was a great help to the restoration of the shrine.[21] And it made possible, of course, the first truly large pilgrimage to Panaya. With the road completed by mid-August, and the house reconstructed sufficiently for dedication by that time, the first big pilgrimage was held on Sunday, August 19, 1951.

The local journals carried advance notices of that special event. Literally hundreds of true pilgrims, and thousands of curiosity seekers from the surrounding area, came to Mary's home that Sunday. There were no doubt more people gathered then at Panaya than at any previous time. If you could see Mary's home and the adjoining esplanade, you would agree that it was fortunate that no one was injured — the immediate open and passable area is relatively small. At any rate, Mass was celebrated, numerous pilgrims communicated, a sermon was delivered, and the mountain echoed with the enthusiastic chant of the joyous *Ave Maria* of Lourdes.[22]

The current diocesan days of official pilgrimage are still in August, on the fifteenth and the Sunday following the feast of the Assumption. They will probably remain unchanged. However, there are pilgrimages to Mary's home all through the year from various segments of the world, especially Europe and the Near East. Many pilgrimages originate at military bases.[23] A group of people, civilian or military, simply forms, usually with a chaplain, and departs for Panaya. In connection with the American military these words of Father Allen may be noted:

> With Americans coming and going all the time, the news about Mary's House is being spread through the whole of the United States. All of them visit here at least once, and many come time and time again. I have given days of recollection to large groups of them both here and in Izmir. The USO has a trip here about every two weeks all year round. One of my most frequent visitors was the Protestant chaplain's assistant [at Izmir] . . . he loved Mary's House and always brought up any visiting Protestant chaplains, some of whom, I noticed, were antagonistic. But it takes all sorts to make up the world and God works in roundabout ways — but He knows what He

is doing. Mary's House is having and will continue to have a profound influence on the world of the future. Of that I am convinced.[24]

One day soon Mary's home will surely be included in every Near East and Holy Land tour.[25]

Perhaps you may think our account of the road to Mary's home somewhat overdrawn or exaggerated; it really is not. The road was vitally important — it was the lifeblood of *Panaya* and radically affected the flow of people. After 1951 visitors and organized pilgrimages became so numerous that it would be cumbersome to deal with them here in any but the most general fashion. But why was Ephesus so neglected prior to 1951, while thousands were streaming to Lourdes and the other Marian shrines? If Mary was inviting her children to all those other places, then she surely should have been calling them to her home! But she was not. The following explanation may be postulated: Mary, ever maternal, did not beckon earlier by reason of the virtual inaccessibility of her home. The statistics of the last decade, or of any year after the road was completed, argue extremely well for such a hypothesis.

The number of visitors to *Panaya* has multiplied astoundingly in recent years. In 1956 there were 20,000.[26] The year 1957 saw 37,000 people come to Mary's home. In 1960 the visitors numbered 50,000,[27] in 1961 they increased to 71,000, and in 1962 they practically doubled from the preceding year to the amazing number of 133,000. All of those figures are quite conservative. If you were to think of the visitors of 1962 in more concrete terms, the average number to come each single day throughout that year would be about 365. Thus, for those 365 days there were 365 visitors each day. In 1963 there was another significant increase — the official count was 200,000. And the number of pilgrims continues to grow.

Of the American visitors to Mary's home the greater part at present is composed of military personnel. By reason of assignments in Europe, Africa, and especially the Near East, servicemen and their dependents have taken advantage of the opportunity to visit Mary's home. And it is similarly through the military that a great share of what little knowledge of *Panaya* there is in America has been propagated.

Shrine of Our Lady of Ephesus 105

It may come as a shock to learn that today the greatest percentage of pilgrims to Mary's home is not Christian. There are more Moslem visitors than Catholic, Jew, and Protestant combined. But it is by reason of the concurrent visits of all of them that this shrine is unique. Not all are pilgrims in the strict sense, of course, but many of them are. Regardless of the visitors' motives, however, the simple fact that they have such a common meeting place in Mary's home is indeed a most striking phenomenon, and one not duplicated elsewhere on earth.

> The people who come here are able to be placed into several categories. There are the purely curious, the interested but non-praying type, the Jews, and those who really come to pray. The curious are found mostly among those who come with groups from boats which reach port. They come and take pictures. For them this is just another stop on their trip. The interested are those who come either from the tourist boats, or who are foreigners living in Turkey. They would like to believe and ask Our Lady for what they need, but they just don't know how good such a procedure would be. The Jews are a particular group. They come to Mary's House from everywhere under the sun, including New York. If they have any religious education at all, they will argue about Mary and Jesus. There are others, however, who surprisingly come to pray. They will light candles and even ask that you say a prayer over them. I don't know what this attitude on their part indicates, but I like to think that Our Lady is working here in many mysterious ways among all sorts. The last group, the praying type, really have faith in Our Lady and come to her House to ask for the things they need, both material and spiritual. Many Turks fall into this category. I have met people from all over the world and of every religious persuasion under God's sun. Mary's House on Mary's Mountain, even though it is a Catholic Shrine, owned by the Catholic Church, is in reality a center of prayer for everyone. I don't know that there is another such spot on the face of the earth.[28]

There is one phrase in the above summary which may appear a bit equivocal. I thought I understood correctly the clause *they just don't know how good such a procedure would be*, but to make sure I requested the precise interpretation from the source. Although the ensuing response could be easily condensed, the entire answer is worthy of note:

> About that ambiguous sentence in my letter of April 8: what I

really mean is, they are people who are looking for something to hold on to. They are not too sure how to go about praying and, even though they would like to believe that prayer would be of help, they don't know exactly how to go about it. I think they are representative of many people today, who are looking for God. They know down deep that He is their only hope, but they are almost afraid to consciously admit this. When I explain the chapel to this type I usually leave the chapel before they do and let them stay there by themselves for a short time. I sincerely believe Our Lady has a very special mission and a very important one for her House. The tremendous increase in visitors and pilgrims, the exceptional cooperation and interest of Turkish government officials, and the selfless dedication of the members of the *Dernek* [Panaya society] is in startling contrast to the past. The Age of Mary is here and she seems to be pushing hard. As the song goes, "the future is not for us to see," but we can at least get an idea of what is going to happen.[29]

Inasmuch as the largest group of the visitors to Mary's home is Moslem, a word should be offered in explanation. According to Islam there is one God, Allah, and Mohammed (ca. 570–632) is his great prophet, and factual founder of the religion. But before Mohammed there lived other holy prophets, such as Abraham and Jesus. And just as Jesus is holy and merits veneration, so also his mother Mary. Mary is especially holy, moreover, because of the virgin birth of Jesus. All those concepts are tenets of Islam.

Mohammed's visions were collected and recorded in the *Koran*, the holy book of Islam, which is divided into one hundred and forty-four *surahs* or chapters. It is generally agreed that the *Koran* is substantially the work of Mohammed himself. Some of its chapters are very short, while others are quite long; the entire book, however, is smaller than the New Testament. In *Surah II*, Jesus is mentioned twice, each time as the son of Mary. In *Surah III*, the following is contained:

> And when the angels said: O Mary! Allah hath chosen thee and made thee pure, and hath preferred thee above (all) the women of creation. . . .
> (And remember) when the angels said: O Mary! Lo! Allah giveth thee glad tidings of a word from Him, whose name is Messiah, Jesus, son of Mary, illustrious in the world and the Hereafter. . . . He will speak unto mankind in his cradle and in his manhood, and he is of the righteous.

Shrine of Our Lady of Ephesus 107

> She said: My Lord! How can I have a child when no mortal hath touched me? He said: So (it will be). Allah createth what He will. If He decreeth a thing, He saith unto it only: Be! and it is.[30]

There are many other references to Mary in the *Koran*, but the passages above should be more than adequate to indicate the veneration that she receives from the Mohammedans. It seems no more than a logical conclusion that many of them would make pilgrimages to Mary's home. In connection with this notion of devotion to Mary, the following may be noted:

> Suad Yurdkoru, a Moslem, prominent merchant of Izmir and a student of the historical places in Ephesus of the Christian era wrote several articles entitled, "The Moslem Religion and Virgin Mary" and "Islam and Ephesus," in the Yeni Asir paper during the months of April and September of 1951, and later compiled a small book entitled *Mother (Virgin) Mary*.
> He points out that the Virgin Mary has a great spiritual value for both the Christians and the Moslem people and refers to the Koran to understand her Blessed existence. . . .[31]

Mary is one of the few links between Moslems and Christians, and thus she provides one of the areas of more or less common ground. That some Moslems visit Mary's home out of pure curiosity is probable, because many of them know little of their religion and of Mary's place in it. But that most of them are true pilgrims and altogether sincere is certain. They come to honor Mary, to pray, to offer a candle, to drink the water from the spring, and to take some home.[32]

The more fervent among the Moslem pilgrims leave scarves, or perhaps other strips of their own clothing, and tie them end to end starting at the top of a pole, which resembles a clothes tree or hat tree without any arms.[33] The short strips of varied cloths tied together form streamers and, when hung as they are from a common point of origin, they appear to be tall bouquets of flowers, or colorful Christmas trees. And Mary's altar is adorned with such sentinels standing guard on either side.

With the thought of the conglomeration of nationalities, races, and religions at Mary's home, you might well recall the phrase of the *Magnificat*, "Beatam me dicent omnes generationes" — "All generations shall call me blessed." There is no place in the world where those words are more sincerely and dramatically demonstrated than at the Shrine of Our Lady of Ephesus.

§ 2. Apparitions and Cures

Strange things happen on Mary's Mountain. Some of them are recorded here for your edification. In the early days of *Panaya* it was not too difficult to investigate the various apparitions and cures. But in recent years the cures especially have become so numerous that most of them are heard of only indirectly or not at all. Apparitions, of course, differ from cures in that there usually remains nothing tangible, after they have occurred, that could be used to substantiate them, other than the word of their beneficiaries. But several will nevertheless be presented before this chapter closes, two from the early days of *Panaya* and two from recent years.[34] Similarly, many wonderful cures from both those periods will be offered for your consideration. While all of them seem miraculous, several have even been declared such by ecclesiastical authorities after thorough investigation.[35] And thus you have every right to think in terms of the supernatural and miraculous being manifested at Mary's home.[36]

The first apparition that was investigated adequately and documented as far as possible occurred on August 13, 1902, between five and six o'clock in the afternoon, while the sun was still high.[37] After having gathered the wash that was spread on the bushes to dry, Helen, the daughter of the early caretaker Andréa, sat down to rest a while. She had worked all day and was a little tired.

Suddenly a lady dressed in black appeared, with her arms crossed on her breast. Her head was bowed in an attitude of profound sadness and was covered with a long veil, which hid part of her figure and fell to her feet on both the left and right. The lady remained still, with her eyes turned toward the chapel. The little girl, Helen, knew that it was the *Panaya*, the all holy Virgin, whom she saw.

The apparition lasted about thirty minutes. When Helen was asked what she thought of and did during that time, she replied: "I did not think of anything. I just looked, and looked, and

Shrine of Our Lady of Ephesus   109

looked!"[38] While the lady was fully visible at first, a cloud of white smoke formed at her feet and gradually enveloped her up to the knees.

After a while, because the lady was so immobile, Helen thought of calling the priest who happened to be at Mary's home at the time, and in the chapel at that particular moment. She took a few steps without taking her eyes off the lady, and called to her brother to fetch the priest. At the instant she called, the lady and the little white cloud began to rise slowly to the top of Karatchali, a small hill nearby.[39] On arrival at the crest of the hill, the cloud enveloped the lady completely and disappeared.

When the vision was later related, one sarcastic hypercritic ridiculed it, just as he had mocked almost everything connected with Mary's home. He stated in his book that an interpreter had told him that the black virgin, which the good girl saw, was none other than Father, evidently Jung, enjoying the fresh air and smoking his pipe.[40]

A second apparition occurred on the evening of October 15, 1903, at about 8:00 p.m.[41] Sister Guerlin, the visitatrix of the Daughters of Charity from Istanbul, was at *Panaya*, alone in the garden by the little cottage of the nuns. Her companions were out strolling elsewhere. Suddenly, from the side of Karatchali, an odd light attracted her attention. The light was not too large, but was very brilliant. It was so extraordinary that she could not help but be somewhat awed. Presently it followed slowly along the crest of the hillock.

Sister was so concerned and impressed with that unique light that she called her companions, four in number, who also saw exactly what she had seen — a light unlike a torch, or lamp, or lantern, or anything known to them. The weird light lasted about ten minutes. When it reached the point at which the lady and the cloud of the previous year had disappeared, it turned toward the south and without changing size grew dimmer and dimmer until it could be seen no more.

The vision which will be considered next is one of the more recent. This apparition occurred one evening at 7:45 p.m. in 1955.

An introductory word of background will make it all the more intelligible to you.

In 1954, Mr. and Mrs. George B. Quatman made a trip for the Marian Year to Europe in honor of our Blessed Virgin, Mother of Jesus, and received several special favors through her intercession to her Divine Son.

Desiring to do something of substance in return for our Blessed Mother, something here on earth that might please and honor her, he heard of the ruins of St. John's tomb and other holy, historic places in Ephesus. They prayed for one year for inspiration and guidance.[42]

The Quatmans are of Lima, Ohio. Among the several family favors which our Lady bestowed on them were the recovery of a grandson from polio and improved health for Mr. Quatman himself, who was then close to seventy years of age.

Then in 1955, they went to Jerusalem and from there traveled — as Mary and Saint John must have done 19 centuries before — some 700 miles northwest to Ephesus. It was a momentous journey and, on arrival, a thoroughly disheartening one.

The ruins the Quatmans had heard about were ruins with a vengeance — not soaring reminders like those of Rome or Athens but "more like three square miles of marble garbage dump."[43]

What upset Mr. Quatman most of all was the fact that the basilica of St. John was completely leveled and in a disgraceful plight due to the rock hovels of the squatters, and similar disgraceful conditions.

Stunned and angry, the man who gave America its first workable telephone dial system between cities turned instinctively to his wife with the proposal that they get in touch with somebody in authority at once to do something — anything. But although George holds some 150 communication-system patents and is steadily adding more, he learned something that very evening — as he and his wife made ready to return to Izmir (Smyrna) for the night — about getting your message through direct. Around 7:45, just as dusk closed in, Our Lady appeared in the heavens over the valley of Ephesus and showed the Quatmans a vision first of the hilltop laid out in rows of lighted walks and gardens around St. John's Basilica, then of her own restored Cathedral, and finally of her home in the adjacent mountains.[44]

The vision was interpreted by its beneficiaries as an indication of the manner in which Mary desired the expression of gratitude,

Shrine of Our Lady of Ephesus 111

which had been planned, though only in general. This then was the specific mode in which Mary wished to be thanked for her previous favors — a tripartite directive: (1) restoration of St. John's basilica; (2) restoration of Mary's church, the scene of the Council of Ephesus; (3) further development of the newly restored shrine on the nearby mountain. For those ends among others, George B. Quatman founded the American Society of Ephesus.[45]

There remains an enigma subsequent and relevant to that vision, and in that connection the following fact is significant:

> Quatman, who is a great believer in keeping his own counsel, said nothing about the vision when he communicated to Archbishop Descuffi, of near-by Smyrna, his plans for restoring the Ephesian shrines.[46]

Thus, while Quatman formed his society and began to pursue its objectives, he did not advertise the apparition. In view of his reticence, the following incident is most interesting:

> ... Pope Pius XII, of glorious memory, spoke in 1956 to Judge Joseph B. Quatman, son of George B. Quatman, about the apparition, although he had never been told about it by anyone.[47]

Thus, you see that word on the apparition came to Pius XII. The mode of communication is the element which is puzzling.

The second of the two recent apparitions included in this chapter will be reviewed later. The date of its occurrence was April 4, 1959. It differed from the ones mentioned earlier in that it took place around noon and inside Mary's home. The reason for its deferred treatment will be obvious when the vision is encountered.[48]

Just as only God knows the types and numbers of apparitions which have occurred at Mary's home, so also He alone knows the variety and frequency of the miraculous cures effected through Panaya. The cures which have been studied, and which follow, were all attributed to veneration of the Virgin Mary at her home at Ephesus. The early ones were effected materially, that is, in consideration of a tangible cause concurrent with the intercession of Mary and expression of faith in God, through the application of the ashes from the fireplace found in Mary's home in 1898; the later ones, through the contact with water from the spring which has its source under Mary's bedroom.[49]

The curative spring is not the one which Catherine Emmerich saw, and which the explorers found in existence in 1891 — the old spring responsible for the destruction of Mary's storeroom, which has not been restored — but a new one which appeared shortly after 1896.[50] This more recent spring is called *Hazreti Meryem Ana Suya* — Spring of Her Excellency Mother Mary. It has been channeled from its source in Mary's bedroom, through a spigot, for convenience of the pilgrims, and empties into a large pond below the esplanade. The source is marked on the floor of Mary's bedroom with dark flagstones.[51]

Miraculous cures can happen anywhere. The fact that those treated here occurred at or in connection with Mary's home, and that others happen there almost every day, can in no sense be considered proof of the authenticity of *Panaya*. Those cures are favors bestowed on certain individuals in recompense of the faith of those who pray. And as you will see, they are in no way limited to Catholics, or even to Christians for that matter. But regardless of your view as to Mary's sojourn in Ephesus, you cannot deny that she is there today.

From 1898 to 1906 five cures were recorded.[52] Of those, two will be presented in detail, and two may be summarized as follows:

> The ashes from the fire-place of the House of the Virgin Mary, found in 1898, have been used to cure many medically hopeless patients. . . .
> A certain woman, living on the Kordon in Izmir, was struggling with death at a difficult birth, but was saved by the application of these ashes to her body, and she delivered a perfectly normal baby.
> A Greek girl by the name of Katina Denazes had a bad abscess in her arm, but was completely cured by the application of some of these ashes. The patient's doctor could not hide his amazement at this miraculous cure, effected by divine intervention.[53]

Mr. Blackler of Boudja, near Smyrna, although English and Protestant, was a good friend of the Lazarists and the Sisters of Charity.[54] This man suffered a serious hand injury and his case quickly reached frightening proportions, despite the fact that second,

Shrine of Our Lady of Ephesus 113

third, and fourth doctors were called successively. The hand swelled considerably, then the arm, until everything was black up to his shoulder. After the doctors had exhausted their resources, they decided that amputation was indicated.

It was then that Sister Eudoxia suggested to the desolate Mrs. Blackler the application of the ashes from *Panaya*. The ashes were mixed with a little water, and the resultant lotion was applied. It immediately arrested the malady and gradually effected a complete cure. Both the arm and the hand were restored from something like gangrene. All that occurred in 1903. Out of love and gratitude Mr. Blackler gave an illustrated lecture on *Panaya Kapulu* at Oxford, under the chairmanship of the Duke of Norfolk. When you consider the circumstances, you will surely agree that Our Lady of Ephesus could not have had a more devoted lecturer.[55]

Another case, perhaps even more interesting, was that of the poor Catholic woman from the Bulgarian village of Moutlova, who came to the Daughters of Charity of Koukouch at the end of December, 1904.[56] She carried on her back her ten-year-old son, who was in agony and looked like a skeleton. The child's jaw had been eaten away by cancer; the wound was repulsive to look at, and its odor unbearable. After a day of rest they were sent to Salonika to consult the physician at the hospital directed by the Daughters of Charity. Two other doctors happened to be available to examine the child, and all three concurred in the same diagnosis — incurable cancer: death within a short time.

The distressed mother hurried back to Koukouch and implored the nuns to save her dying son. The sisters knew that neither doctors nor medicine could save the boy, and they decided to apply some ashes from Mary's hearth, mixed with a little water. This was done several times daily, and after ten days the child appeared somewhat better. Since the boy's mother was needed also at home, she then went back to her village with some ashes in her pocket and her son on her back.

Each week news arrived through the merchants that the boy was improving. In February progress accelerated; by April the healing process was complete. When the boy had fully recovered, he was brought back to the hospital and presented to the doctor, who was absolutely dumfounded. And although the physician was a Jew, he did not hesitate for a moment to record the following statement:

> I have just examined Cotcho, the child with cancer of the lower jaw and of the upper and lower lips. I am astounded at his truly miraculous cure. My sincere compliments to Sister Pascaut who worked a veritable miracle with her ashes.
> (Signed) Doctor Sciaky
> Physician at the Hospital of Salonika
> 12 May 1905[57]

Even though the cases above were studied and partially documented, none of the early cures was subjected to what you might call a canonical process of authentication. The first of several cures so investigated occurred in connection with the great pilgrimage of 1951.[58]

Miss Jeanne Koury, age thirty-five, suffered since 1950 with Pott's disease, which is characterized by decalcification of two dorsal vertebrae and two ribs. Her sickness had resisted thorough medical treatment and a competent operation. After her parents made the pilgrimage to Mary's home on August 19, 1951, they returned home with Ephesus water.[59] They gave some to their daughter to drink, and sprinkled some over her in the form of a cross. She fell asleep for four hours, and awoke completely cured.[60]

The cures at Mary's home in the last decade became quite numerous, and the official publication of *Panaya* almost always reported several of them.[61] The following terse accounts are offered as examples:

> It is reported that a girl suffering from tuberculosis of the bone visited the shrine in 1955 and slept on the ground, after drinking of this water, but awakened the next morning to find herself completely cured of her ailment.[62]
> In July 1960 there was reported a miraculous cure of a lady from angina pectoris; she had been under physicians' care for fifteen years.[63]

Such favors were granted not only to Christians, but to Mohammedans and others as well. For example, Lt. Col. Ahmet Tevfik Unalp was cured of a gall-bladder condition in 1954; Galip Agya, a sixty-year-old electrician from Izmir, was cured of asthma and angina

Shrine of Our Lady of Ephesus   115

pectoris when he drank the water at Panaya on September 17, 1956; Nasiba Devrim, Col. Kenan Albin, and little Nadia Giudice were cured of their respective ailments in 1959.[64]

The reports go on and on, but further individual treatment seems unnecessary. As a finale, therefore, it might be fitting to consider instead a few general remarks. Father Allen, who was stationed at Mary's home, wrote the following observation concerning the summer of 1962:

> This summer, especially, there have been many extraordinary cures which have taken place. We usually hear about them a day or so after they happen, and usually by reading about them in the papers. We have no way of checking on them. The great number of Moslems who come here is, for the most part, a result of the cures. As they express it: Mr. So-and-so from our town was paralyzed. He came to Meryem Ana and returned home cured. We know he is cured and so we have come to ask this, or that, from Meryem Ana. They come from hundreds of kilometers away, even from the extreme eastern parts of Turkey.[65]

At a later date Allen confirmed the statement above, and added a few interesting details, as follows:

> As far as miracles are concerned, they take place here seemingly quite often. That is one of the reasons why so many Turks show up. The usual way things happen is that someone will come from a village near or far. He will have some ailment, such as paralysis, or he will be crippled in some fashion. He will pray in Mary's House, bathe with the water from the spring, and become whole again. Without telling anyone here, he will return home and his fellow villagers, knowing him, will hear what happened. Then we have the whole village here. Every day, especially in the summer, we hear some story or other like this. The country Turk does not visit a doctor very often, if ever, so the cures cannot be authenticated in any way.[66]

With reference in particular to the atmosphere of Panaya, and in general to the wondrous events which are apparent at Mary's home, Father Allen made the following observation:

> It is hard for me to write down all the little things that happen here every day, and to speak about the very interesting people I meet. One thing I must say: perhaps we cannot prove with absolute certitude that Our Lady really did live here, even though it is very, very probable to my mind; yet I am absolutely convinced that she is here today. And I originally came here not knowing what to believe.[67]

Mary is present in such a way that by practically every pilgrim her presence is actually intuited at the Shrine of Our Lady of Ephesus.

§ 3. Environs

On many occasions in the earlier chapters, you have encountered the designations *Meryem Dagh,* Mary's Mountain, and *Bulbul Dagh,* Nightingale Mountain. They are simply two Turkish names, and their translations, for one and the same place.[68] In order to leave you with no false impression of the mountain, a few words should be said about it. The hill deserves to be called a mountain because it does stand out conspicuously from its surroundings; it is not an Everest, however. When contrasted with the ruins of Ephesus, which are only slightly above sea level, *Meryem Dagh,* which rises from the ancient city toward the south and to a height of 1722 feet, appears as a veritable mountain.

The view from the mountain is magnificent. That simple phrase is reminiscent of one writer who described *Panaya* as a place unique in the world, as well as the inexpressibly holy site of the Dormition of Mary.[69] Just as Catherne Emmerich said, from the summit you can see the beautiful plain of Ephesus below, and the sea, and the islands.[70]

> The site is one of the most picturesque in the area with a view, on the right, toward old downtown of Ephesus, and a little more to the right, toward the Hill of St. John. In front, to the West, a wonderful view is opened far over the Aegean Sea with numerous islands. St. John could scarcely find a better place to keep and protect the greatest treasure he inherited after the Crucifixion.[71]

Mary's home is situated close to the summit, on the western slope and at an altitude of 1508 feet. Its orientation is perfect. The door faces west and the sea; the back of the house, the east and the mountain; the right side, the south; and the left side, the north.[72] If you were to come out the door, turn right, and begin to walk around the house, you would expect to see the left arm or wing — the linen room or general storeroom — of the cruciform house. But you do not. The house runs straight to the rear with no projection on the left side. That missing room is the only part of Mary's

Shrine of Our Lady of Ephesus   117

house which has not been reconstructed. Its junction with the rest of the house has been walled up. Any attempt at restoration would meet the same fate that befell the original room.

> "To the left of the Oratory [as you would view it on entering the house] was to be found another room in which the Holy Virgin put her linen and furniture." On the left under the ancient arcade, the wall which has been built marks the old entrance to the former Vestiary. This part collapsed long ago, without leaving any traces. The spring of water which feeds the large pond and which runs beneath the foundations of the Vestiary must have destroyed and carried away everything. It is interesting to note that in the revelations of Catherine Emmerich, she said this spring would be found there.[73]

The spring just mentioned as the cause of destruction of the storeroom should not be confused with the smaller spring, which appeared after 1896 on the other side of the house, under Mary's bedroom.[74] And likewise, the large pond fed by the larger spring should not be confused with the special pond fed by the spring from Mary's bedroom.

The two springs and two ponds may be easily distinguished and remembered by picturing Mary's home as it originally existed in the shape of a cross. From each arm of the cross flows a spring. The one from the left arm is the old spring, which destroyed the room under which it flowed. It empties into a lovely circular pond in front of Mary's home beyond the esplanade and at a slightly lower level. The spring from the right arm of the cross is the one which originated after 1896 below Mary's bedroom. It empties into a rectangular pond, which is farther from the house than the circular pond and at a still lower level.

The "miraculous" spring which furnishes the Ephesus water is the one of more recent origin. Before it empties into that lower pond, it is channeled through pipes with a spigot outlet in a niche just below the esplanade and practically next to the circular pond. This is the place where the pilgrims drink the Ephesus water from cups provided at the niche, and likewise fill their containers from the spigot to take water home with them. The latest news in this respect is that the work described as follows is completed:

The outlet of the spring (which originates in Our Lady's bedroom in Mary's House) will be redone with stone arches, and more outlets added. A woman from Izmir . . . has donated the funds for a Lourdes-like bath for the sick. We will build two baths, so that there will be one for women and one for men. Those are projects for this spring and summer [1963].[75]

There are three principal buildings close to Mary's home, and two of lesser importance and proximity. All deserve at least brief mention. Of the latter two, one houses a post office and police station. The police are on duty on the days of large pilgrimages in order to facilitate the movement of the pilgrims around the grounds, which at such times become extremely congested. The double-purpose structure is the first you would see on the walk from the parking area to Mary's home. The next building that you would encounter is the Tea House, built by the *Panaya* society as a convenience for the visitors, with outside patios, tables, and chairs. The pilgrims who utilize it do so for rest and refreshment normally after visiting Mary's home and the grounds. The menu is limited to Turkish tea and coffee, soft drinks, eggs, and *Kofte* — Turkish meatballs. The Tea House is separated from the sanctuary grounds proper by terraces and a gateway.

The three remaining structures provide housing for the resident religious. The little cottage for the Sisters is near the entrance to the sanctuary grounds.[76] The house built by the *Panaya* society for the resident priests who came in 1955 is the closest building to the shrine.[77] And finally, a new residence for the priests stands behind the original rectory, and stretches out along the side of the mountain and away from the shrine. It was almost completed by, and in accord with, the regulations of the *Petits Frères*, but had to be enlarged for the Montfort Fathers by reason of the addition of personnel, and also so that they could accommodate a few visiting priests or seminarians.[78] In that regard, and also for the note on the weather at *Panaya*, the following is offered:

> At this very moment we are in the process of putting an extension onto the priests' residence. The house, as it stands today [April 8, 1963], has a chapel (very small), a sacristy, two bedrooms, a bathroom, a kitchen and a dining room (which is used for everything else). There is also a half-basement, used for storage. The new part

will contain five additional bedrooms (three for visiting priests or seminarians), a library (which will be used as a recreation room in the winter), a visiting parlor, an additional bath and at least two showers. The chapel will be enlarged. Since the weather is excellent from April to the end of September (no rain) and very good up until the middle of December (it rains on occasion), we will build a patio between the house and the mountain for our recreation room. It will all be set up as a religious house.[79]

The first house for the priests was called the *Guest House* after the new "rectory" had been started, and it became for a while a tiny hotel where several pilgrims could spend the night. It is still reminiscently called the *Guest House*, although it now functions as such in an even more restricted manner. An extension was built onto it so that it could become the Sisters' new convent, and provide accommodations also for visiting Sisters. Of course, now that the addition has been completed, the priests have moved to their newly enlarged residence, and the Sisters' old cottage is empty and able to serve as lodging for a few pilgrims.

At present, therefore, there are few accommodations for overnight visits of pilgrims at the shrine itself. Some tourists with automobiles stay at Seldjuk, a town of over six thousand inhabitants, which is at the foot of Mary's Mountain next to Ephesus. There is a new motel there and, while it has only fourteen rooms, it is excellent. Others prefer Kuşadasi, on the sea and about seven miles from Seldjuk. There is a new hotel there, which can accommodate about one hundred guests. Father Allen wrote: "It is the closest thing I have seen to a first-class American hotel. And, by American standards, the prices are quite reasonable."[80]

Still others prefer the city life of Izmir with its ample and diversified facilities, which include various modes of transportation to Ephesus.[81] The road from Izmir to *Panaya* is superb and the trip, which is about fifty miles, takes a law-abiding driver little more than an hour, unless he stops to photograph camel caravans, storks sitting in their nests on chimney tops, or some such thing. The Montfort Fathers forecast a guest house on the mountain itself as follows:

> . . . it is safe to say that the guest house will be built at least by the end of 1965. It is really needed and we are planning to give

conferences in our respective countries next winter in order to publicize Mary's House and to recruit some of the needed funds.[82]

Before leaving *Panaya*, to consider its less immediate environs, it should be noted that there is a tiny religious article shop between the spring and the enlarged Sisters' convent, that is, the Guest House. This is one of the many delightful and reassuring features of Mary's home — not that it has a shop for religious goods, but that it has such a small and pleasingly inadequate one. In a word, Mary's home is not commercialized.

> This little shop is the same as when you saw it [1959]. We have added a few articles but they all have to do strictly with Mary's House. Actually we have for sale only those articles which people have continually asked for over the past few years. We have discussed this over and over again in the past few months and we intend to keep this kiosque in its present modest state. This is sufficient for our present needs, and also conforms with our desire to avoid all commercialization.[83]

It is understandable that pilgrims should really want some small souvenir of their visit, and that such be made available to them. But a medal, postcard, or brochure of *Panaya* can be bought for pennies, and the Ephesus water is naturally free. It is refreshing not to have to fend off peddlers with their peephole Virgins, Marian ashtrays, and Madonna ties that glow in the dark, as you do at or in the vicinity of many other shrines of Mary. Around Mary's home there are no such distasteful objects and no aggressive or otherwise obnoxious salesmen. If anything, you may be disappointed at the meager selection of mementos which the Sisters have to offer.

In one of her visions of Mary's home, Catherine Emmerich stated: "Near here is a castle. . . ."[84]

> At a certain distance along the Aziziye (Camlik) road following the ravine and on the right when travelling southeast, one can find this castle. Its debris form a hillock where important remains can be seen and about which, for about 40 meters, extend the remains of a wall 80 centimeters thick. The stone blocks remind one of those of the ancient wall of Lysimachus (3rd Cent., B.C.).[85]

She also spoke of a plateau, with a Christian colony, near the castle.[86] The plateau is there, as well as vestiges of the colony.

Shrine of Our Lady of Ephesus 121

At a short distance from the castle, may be seen a platform or "terrace" (600 meters long, 300 meters wide) described by the seeress. The access she shows is along the ancient way coming from below in a southeasterly direction. This steep road is now abandoned.[87]

After the excursion to Mary's home, every visitor should take advantage also of the wealth of antiquities at Ephesus and review a bit of history in the ruins of the city itself.[88] Ephesus is located in the southern part of Asia Minor, on the west coast of Turkey, some two hundred miles south of Istanbul and about forty-two miles south of Izmir.

> Ephesus was once a mighty seaport whose fine anchorages the mud from the river Meander gradually rendered unusable. The town enjoyed, for centuries before its economic decline, identification with some of the most illustrious names of antiquity. From the picturesque countryside and offshore islands of this thriving metropolis, which on the eve of its Christianization had a population of some 600,000, had come such personages as Herodotus (the father of history), the epic poet Homer, Pythagoras (patriarch of mathematics), Hippocrates and Galen (progenitor and recreator of western medicine), the philosophers Heraclitus and Epicurus, and that paragon of austere virtue, Diogenes.[89]

Though the city passed through the Ionian, Hellenic, Roman, Byzantine, Seldjuk, Aydin, and Ottoman periods, most of the ruins on view today belong to the Roman period.[90] The ruins of the epochs which followed the Roman era are found mostly at Ayasoluk, the modern town of Seldjuk, just outside old Ephesus.[91]

The temple of Artemis (Diana), one of the ancient Seven Wonders of the World, was destroyed in the third century; the goddess cult was eventually replaced by the veneration of Mary. In the fourth century Ephesus became capitol of the vast Roman diocese of Asia Minor. The famed ecumenical council was convoked there in the fifth century. But such facts, and many more, can be found in any encyclopedia. It would better serve the immediate purpose to mention in summary fashion the ruins which may be visited in Ephesus today.

More than likely, the tour of the ancient city would begin in Seldjuk itself. There is a small museum there, which contains many of the relics of Ephesus, for example, a statue of Artemis, a sundial, mosaics, and the like. Very close by are the mosque of Isabey and outlines of the basilica of St. John in the process of reconstruction.[92] Along with that basilica, the monuments of special interest to Christians, which are found among the ruins of Ephesus, are Mary's basilica, which was the cathedral of Ephesus and the church where the council was held, St. Mary Magdalen's tomb, and the grotto of the Seven Sleepers. Then there remain the *gymnasium of Vedius*, the *stadium*, the gorgeous *Arcadian way*, the *market*, the enormous great theater, the *library of Celsus*, the *tombs of the heroes*, gates, fountains, baths, and other monuments in abundance.

A visit to Mary's home and some of the ruins of Ephesus could be accomplished in a single day with departure from and return to Izmir. But once that had been accomplished, the natural desire would be to return to Mary's home and view also the other ruins of Ephesus. It is highly recommended, therefore, that two or more days be scheduled for any visit to the Shrine of Our Lady of Ephesus.

§ 4. *Personal Visit*

My own visit to Mary's home was altogether delightful and absolutely unforgettable. It occurred in early April, 1959, and spanned a very brief two-day period. The cause of the trip may be traced to the U. S. Air Force, and more specifically to one of its finest Catholic chaplains, Father Robert F. Overman of the Archdiocese of St. Louis.

Major Overman was stationed in Athens in 1957, while I was living in Rome. Overman had more than enough duties to perform, and he accomplished them all extremely well. Among his charges were not only the Catholic military personnel and dependents in Athens, but also such souls in several other places where there was no Catholic chaplain. He faithfully visited his outposts beyond Athens, and was particularly concerned with the Iraklion Air Station on Crete by reason of the great number of Catholics stationed there. Through him and the dedicated Protestant chaplain, Rev. Bruno Caliandro, who was the only chaplain at Iraklion, arrangements were made to have the sole Greek Catholic priest

Shrine of Our Lady of Ephesus

on Crete, Father Roussos, say Mass on Sundays. But the Greek priest knew no English, and consequently could neither preach nor hear confessions. It was for those reasons, that on such great feasts as Christmas and Easter every effort was made to provide an English-speaking priest to minister to the American Catholics at the air station.

Thus it was that four times orders were cut which permitted me to fly from Rome to Crete between the Christmas of 1957 and the Easter of 1959. Overman was no longer at Athens during the last two trips, which were made possible solely through the efforts of Chaplain Caliandro on Crete. But while Overman was still in Athens, he had spoken to me quite enthusiastically about Mary's home in Ephesus, and strongly urged a visit. That sincere recommendation was disregarded until the Easter visit to Greece in 1959. I was truthfully in no big rush to see a simple stationary house, where Mary was reputed to have spent her last years, when back home in Italy I had an extraordinary house of Mary which, though now immobile, could boast of a miraculous flight from Nazareth.

On that Easter visit of 1959, however, with Overman's enthusiasm still ringing in my ears, together with encouragement from certain Catholics in Greece who had already seen Mary's home, I finally succumbed and made the short trip from Athens to Izmir. The one-hour flight was delightful both because of the low altitude flown and the abundance of island scenery on the way. On landing at Izmir and undergoing the usual formalities, I formed the presumption that all Turkish customs officers are thorough, courteous, and slow. The procedure left the personal impression, which is probably completely false, that the next foreign flight was not due to arrive for at least two hours and that, if the officials could not make the business of the current disembarkment last that long, they would not be remunerated for the intervening period of idleness.

Friends of friends were patiently waiting beyond the inner sanctum of customs. After the officials finally, and seemingly reluctantly, cleared and released the passengers from Athens, I was swept into the protective custody of knowing residents so rapidly that I scarcely had a chance to smile at the little men who just happened to be offering a special that day on Turkish pounds for American dollars. In Izmir arrangements had been made in advance, through the courtesy and generosity of friends and the local chaplain, which provided me the use of both an automobile and an apartment.

The residents of Izmir, with one unmentionable exception, were found to be genuinely kind and hospitable throughout the visit, and this was particularly evident during the evening strolls through the streets and various shops. The situation was completely different, for instance, from walking around Peiraeus, the seaport of Athens. Some Americans would never walk around that port at night without their cameras — not that they wanted to take pictures, but that a reason or excuse was thereby furnished for carrying a telescoped tripod for protection.

The morning of the first full day in Turkey witnessed my departure for Mary's home in the chaplain's car and in the company of friends. The drive to Ephesus was pleasing and rewarding. The road from Izmir to *Panaya* was excellent, and the sights along the way intriguing. There were peasants working in the fields, camel caravans traveling the ancient routes, buses driving on the wrong side of the road, and storks resting in nests atop most of the chimneys of the quaint houses enroute. Besides such exotic scenes along the highway, the landscape itself was perfectly exquisite and charming.

The drive up Mary's Mountain was exceptionally enchanting by reason of the rapidly changing view of the plain or valley of Ephesus. After a very short but lovely walk from the parking area near the mountaintop, Mary's home appeared among the trees — modest, unpretentious, and mystifying. At that moment I did not know what to think of the little stone structure. I had never heard of Catherine Emmerich; I enjoyed merely a passing acquaintance with St. John's activity in Asia Minor; I knew that there was a tomb of Mary in Jerusalem, because I had been there four years previously. In a word, I was rather incredulous internally, quite reserved externally, but not cynical in any way. It was only through subsequent study, all of which has appeared in this book, and the application

Shrine of Our Lady of Ephesus

of simple cold logic to known facts, that I became convinced of the authenticity of Mary's home on the mountain near Ephesus.

Father Bouis, one of the resident priests, appeared and offered to prepare the altar in the shrine after he was informed that I wished to celebrate Mass. Father Bouis was politely dismissed with the assurance that I had brought with me all the requisites and was willing to wait on myself, with his permission, of course. Preparations for Mass in Mary's bedroom were made, and the Holy Sacrifice was celebrated. After Mass I expected to see the priest at the door of Mary's home, just as I had found so many mendicants in other countries blocking with openmouthed burses the exits of places of religious interest. But Father Bouis was not there. This simply made him, and the knowledge of *Panaya* which he could impart, all the more desirable.

A brief walk about the grounds was enjoyed. Rev. Bouis or Father Joseph as he asked to be called, was found busy at construction of a new little rectory. His confrere, Father Saulais, was with him. After pleasant introductions, and just as a little information on *Panaya* was about to be requested, a little boy who had taken the ride from Izmir with my friends became indisposed. This practically necessitated an immediate return to Izmir, and all returned to the car for the drive back. I showed little frustration at all of this, and advised Father Joseph that I would return the following day both to celebrate Mass again at Mary's home and to visit the ruins in the city of Ephesus. The return trip to Izmir seemed rather uneventful, and the little boy was quite normal after his arrival at home.

The ride to *Panaya* the following morning was much the same as the first, except that the small boy was left behind. Mass was celebrated this time on the altar of Mary's oratory, the principal of the two altars in the shrine. The old statue of Our Lady of Ephesus presides in a niche over that altar. The statue is mentioned because it played an important part in the strange occurrence which transpired on that occasion.

After Mass, while I was busy at the altar placing all in order, the sole communicant attending the Mass ventured to the altar to see the window off on the Gospel side, which had been responsible for allowing the radiant but intermittent beams of light to play in the chapel. The unusual thing is that any rays were seen. I saw none, and in fact thought I had done a praiseworthy job of reading the missal in the dimly lighted chapel. And the communicant, who saw the light, became faint on arriving at the altar and looking toward the left of it for a window which was not there. There was nothing to be seen but a solid rock wall. And even if there had been a window to permit the passage of those rays of light, it still would have been a remarkable feat for the sun to produce almost horizontal beams at high noon.

The communicant was assisted to a chair in the chapel after the futile search for the source of the unexplainable light. The search had lasted only a moment. The sincere but confused inquiry uttered on the first glance at the solid wall, which seals the old access to the unrestored storeroom, is not easily forgotten. The words, inflected almost as a plea, were: "But where is the window?"

Nothing was said about that incident during the subsequent visit with Father Joseph. He took his visitors on a tour of the grounds, and explained as much about *Panaya* as time allowed. He also invited them for a cup of tea in the *Guest House*, which was in fact his own home. Throughout the visit he never stopped supplying valuable information, answering questions, condensing and evaluating facts and legends, and speaking in a commonplace tone of the daily cures effected through Mary's intercession and contact with the Ephesus water. It was also learned from Father Joseph that a single tea bag can with loving care be used more than twenty times and made to yield effectively as many cups. He treated his visitors, however, to fresh unused bags, thus sacrificing doubtlessly many cups of his favorite beverage.

When the visitors were ready to leave, Father Joseph was asked to accompany them to the religious article stand, so that they might obtain some literature and a few medals and postcards. He graciously fulfilled their request and also made sure that his visitors had taken some Ephesus water along. Father Joseph then accompanied them to the parking area. For all his kindness, which included even the often distasteful posing for pictures, he shall always be remembered.

The ruins of old Ephesus were visited that same afternoon, and it was not until the drive back to Izmir that evening that I learned some of the details of the enigmatic incident in the chapel. I am in a position to offer for your likely interest the personal and frank account prepared by the subject of the vision, apparition, or whatever you may wish to call it. The immediately following paragraphs comprise in the beneficiary's own words the report primarily of the occurrence in the chapel; they include also a few thoughts on the day in general.

> It was a fresh spring day and so quiet and peaceful up there on the mountain. I stood outside Mary's house and looked all over to enjoy the same scenery that she must have enjoyed, especially at that time of year with daisies scattered over the mountainside, a little olive grove beside the house, the view of the blue sea below and the mountain top not far above. There were many clouds in the sky and they kept passing in front of the sun, creating problems for taking pictures.
>
> Before long it was time to enter Mary's house for Mass. Right away I wanted to be sure I prayed for everyone who couldn't have the privilege of visiting there. I think I mentioned everyone by name or group, and especially those who suffer. As I stood for the Gospel, I thought "How beautiful it is here with the sun shining in and Mass being celebrated!"
>
> Now there were thoughts coming to me as though Mary herself was speaking to me: "We love them, dear. Why, the reward for suffering is so great that even if you were told you wouldn't know. Your minds aren't meant to know. . . . This life is no more than a short wave of the hand . . . with no more than a veil between." These and other ideas were like wonderful news to me, although I knew I had always believed them. I felt I could hardly wait to go to my sister and tell her. How happy she would be to know how truly blessed are children who are handicapped.
>
> Then I thought I should say the rosary — surely a rosary in Mary's house, of all places. As I recited the Apostles' Creed, each truth was so real to me, and the following prayers so meaningful! After a few Hail Marys of the first decade, with the realization that Mass was proceeding, I tried to make myself more conscious of the precise part and moment of the Mass. Despite my attempt to do this I could not, because the rays of the sun, shining in on the Gospel side of the altar, were too distracting. The fact that they were not constant, but kept going off and on as though little clouds were quickly passing before the sun, was the main source of distraction.

I looked at the light and mentally answered as in reply to a wish of the Blessed Mother: "All right, Mary! How *do* you look in your little house?" Then, without knowing why and with a strong impression of "statue" in the back of my mind, I looked to the other side of the altar. At first she wasn't there — then she was.

There was no surprise in all of this except that the Blessed Mother didn't look as I had always pictured her. Her hair was black instead of light. And because of this I said to her in my mind: "Of course you look like this; you were Jewish." Then I looked at her eyes. Because of having heard that Mary's smile was the most beautiful thing about her appearance, I continued: "They're wrong. It's your eyes that are most beautiful! So this is how love and happiness look — it's all in your eyes!" Then, looking at her cheek: "No, it's your cheek that is most beautiful!" I looked at her mouth. Her lips were parted as if she were about to speak. "No," I said, "it's your mouth that is most beautiful." Mary then smiled broadly. "Oh yes, they are right! It is your smile that is most beautiful." Mary looked toward the altar, and I said to her: "Oh, you are so pleased that we came to visit and that Mass is being said in your little house." I was so happy that she was pleased. I wish that more could be said about this moment, but there just aren't words.

Mary's hair was loose around her forehead. She wore a sheer veil, pale in color, which seemed to be folded back on her head and to fall longer than her shoulders. And I remember so well thinking of those beautiful amber eyes, so very round and full that all creation could be seen in them. I simply couldn't take my eyes from her face and, therefore, am unable to describe anything else Mary wore — I really don't know.

While I was admiring her beauty, there were still thoughts coming from Mary such as these: "Don't worry so, dear. You aren't meant to understand. We know! And we know that you don't know, that is why God is so merciful. Everything is as it should be according to God's plan. . . . We are with them."

I was looking at Mary, her cheek especially because I could see all her face that way, when the *Sanctus* announced the beginning of the Consecration. I looked away from Mary and thought no more about her until I went up to Communion.

I thought I'd look at the beautiful statue now that I was at the altar, and when I did I was looking at the old statue up in back of the altar. It was black metal; the nose was broken off, and the arms were broken at the wrists. The statue looked so ugly to me after expecting to see such beauty that I couldn't look away and put it out of my mind fast enough.

It wasn't until the Last Gospel that I looked back at the same statue above the altar. The sun was shining in once more, and in place of the ugly black statue I saw Mary once again. At the time

Shrine of Our Lady of Ephesus

I wondered how the statue could be so ugly from up close and so beautiful from the kneeling bench.

After Mass I picked up my belongings and walked up to the altar. I was ready to remark how pretty it was with the sun shining in, and at the same instant I looked up to see the window through which the sunshine should have been coming. There was no window — just a blank wall!

I asked the priest, who had just finished Mass, where the light had been shining from, and he answered that the only places where any light could enter were the miniature skylight of the chapel itself or a window of an adjoining room, all of which were too far removed from the spot whence the light should have come. I realized that none of those sources could have possibly produced the direct rays that I saw!

There were many things I wanted to know about Mary's house, and the priests who lived on the grounds were most informative. Father Joseph was so hospitable! He showed and explained everything he thought would be of interest, and answered my questions about Mary's sojourn in Ephesus.

The whole day continued to be just wonderful. After the visit at Mary's house I walked through the ruins of the old city of Ephesus. At one point beyond the edge of the ruins there was a shepherd with his flock standing under a flowering tree on a hillside. He was singing and it carried over Ephesus. I couldn't help but say aloud: "I am so happy!"

It wasn't until I knelt to say my night prayers and thought of my day at Ephesus that the full realization of it all came to me — everything that happened, just as I've told you. It will always be my wish that everyone might have the opportunity to visit Mary's house at Ephesus. One cannot help but feel at home there with the gracious welcome which I'm certain Mary extends to everyone who comes to her house.

Surely the account above speaks clearly for itself. It was written specifically and solely for inclusion in this work, and any commentary on it seems superfluous. It would in itself provide a fitting close to this narrative. But one of the results of that experience in the chapel furnishes perhaps an even more appropriate conclusion. After the details were related to an elderly and venerable lady, she was so inspired that she wrote a poem about Mary's home. She had been told only a few facts about *Panaya*, and been given the account as you have received it, whereupon she composed forthwith these previously unpublished verses:

MARY'S HOUSE

By M. Laura Leddy

Little House of Our Lady
Restored and standing anew
From centuries' devastation
On a mountainside she knew.
She came to you for haven
From a land beset with strife
Far from the stress and tumult
That threatened her holy life.

You sheltered her in her sorrows
Quietly soothing her fears
Filling the lonely hours
Throughout her declining years.
Warmth from your hearthstone fire
Its light on the walls aglow
Brought to her peace and comfort
That only she could know.

Little house she still remembers
Your gracious and loving care
And comes on light rays from heaven
To the dim lit chapel there.
Eyes have beheld her beauty
Minds have been freed from all fear
Hearts rejoice in the message
Of Our Lady standing near.

Our Lady of Ephesus.

Appendix

[A] Early law (ca. 400) on erection, etc., of shrines [cf. Chapter IV, note 42]:

Codex Canonum Ecclesiae Africae. Canon 83: *De falsis memoriis martyrum*. Item placuit, ut altaria quae passim per agros et per vias tamquam memoriae martyrum constituuntur, in quibus nullum corpus aut reliquiae martyrum conditae probantur, ab episcopis qui locis eisdem praesunt, si fieri potest, evertantur. Si autem hoc per tumultus popularis non sinitur, plebes tamen admoneantur, ne illa loca frequentent, ut qui recte sapiunt, nulla ibi superstitione devincti teneantur. Et omnino nulla memoria martyrum probabiliter acceptetur, nisi ubi corpus aut aliquae reliquiae sunt, aut origo alicuius habitationis vel possessionis vel passionis fidelissima origine traditur. Nam quae per somnia et per inanes quasi revelationes quorumlibet hominum ubicumque constituuntur altaria, omni modo improbentur. [Mansi, III, 782]

[B] Portion of brief of Pope Leo XIII, 18 April 1896 [cf. Chapter IV, note 81]:

Tandem, de apostolicae similiter potestatis Nostrae plenitudine, praesentium vi, itemque in perpetuum, in Sanctuarium quod ante memoravimus, Hierosolymae erectum, Nostrae Dominae Galliarum, indulgentiam plenariam transferimus Virginis Sepulcro adnexam, quod a Schismaticis detinetur et gravi absque discrimine a piis peregrinantibus visitari nequit. [ASS, 28 (1896), 685]

[C] Message from Pope St. Pius X, 6 April 1906, signed by Cardinal Merry del Val [cf. Chapter IV, note 86]:

Ce n'a pas été sans un particulier plaisir que le Saint-Père a reçu les trois opuscules publiés par Votre Seigneurie illustrissime, dans le but d'apporter autant que possible une nouvelle lumière sur le difficile problème du lieu de la mort et de l'Assomption de la très Sainte Vierge. Sa Sainteté a relevé avec une vive satisfaction toute l'importance des recherches faites sur ce grave sujet par Votre Seigneurie et par vos confrères. Aussi, en adressant à Votre Seigneurie un merci très spécial pour son bel hommage, Sa Sainteté se déclare reconnaissante aussi envers les autres prêtres de la Mission de Smyrne, et en vous accordant, ainsi qu'à ces Messieurs, la bénédiction apostolique, Elle prie de bon coeur et son auguste Mère de dispenser de plus en plus abondantes les lumières célestes à tous ceux qui, avec une affection de fils, consacrent leurs études à rechercher le lieu où s'élève la tombe de Marie. [*Historique*, pp. 40, 41]

[D] **Message from Pope Pius XI, 13 August 1922, signed by Cardinal Gasparri** [cf. Chapter IV, note 93]:

Je suis heureux de vous faire savoir que Sa Sainteté a fait le plus bienveillant accueil à la brochure dans laquelle vous exposez votre opinion au sujet de la dernière demeure de la Sainte Vierge. Agréant votre hommage et vous félicitant d'avoir ainsi ajouté votre contribution dans une question si disputée, le Souverain Pontife vous remercie paternellement et daigne vous envoyer, comme gage des faveurs divines, la bénédiction apostolique. Je saisis volontiers l'occasion qui m'est offerte, pour vous assurer, Monsieur, de mes sentiments dévoués en Notre-Seigneur. [*Historique*, p. 42]

[E] **Broadcast of Radio Vatican, 3 June 1951** [cf. Chapter IV, note 97]:

La Maison de la Sainte Vierge à Panaya Kapulu.

La tradition d'Éphèse et l'existence de la Maison de la T. Ste. Vierge à Panaya Kapulu ne sont pas des légendes issues des rêves d'une visionnaire, victime de son imagination.

Catherine Emmerich n'a pas créé la tradition; elle l'a simplement éclairée et confirmée, en fournissant des indications précises et des descriptions topographiques qui ont été rigoureusement contrôlées et vérifiées sur place par des hommes compétents et peu enclins à croire aux visions. Cependant ils ont dû constater que la voyante voyait la réalité à distance, et comme de Dülmen à Éphèse, la distance est grande, ce phénomène dépasse les forces de la nature et ne peut s'expliquer sans le secours spécial de Dieu.

La tradition d'Éphèse est basée sur des arguments solides, tirés de l'Ecriture Sainte et de l'Histoire. Elle accepte que l'apôtre St. Jean est venu de bonne heure en Asie. Ceux qui pretendent qu'il n'y est arrivé que fort tard, soit après l'an 66, ne peuvent produire aucun document historique à l'appui. L'Historien Eusèbe, dans son Histoire Ecclésiastique, affirme, textuellement que depuis déjà l'an 37 et dans les années qui suivirent, jusqu'en 42, les apôtres avaient été expulsés de Jérusalem, après avoir été véxés de mille manières. Ils étaient allés prêcher l'Evangile, chacun dans la région qui lui avait été assignée. Tout la tradition est d'accord pour affirmer que St. Jean avait reçu en partage l'Asie Mineure, et Tertullien, qu'il y est venu de bonne heure.

Si donc St. Jean est venu en Asie, entre 37 et 42 et avant 48, il n'a pu laisser la T.S. Vierge Marie toute seule au beau milieu de la persécution sanglante. La Ste. Vierge a dû le suivre en Asie, dans les environs d'Éphèse.

Cette croyance si vraisemblable est encore confirmée par des documents historiques. Ce sont les suivants:

1. L'existence à Éphèse, au moins dès le 3ème Siècle, d'une grande

Appendix

Eglise dédiée à Ste. Marie. D'apres les lois Liturgiques alors en vigueur, on ne pouvait construire d'eglises que sur les endroits où les Saints avaient vécu ou étaient morts. C'est dans cette Eglise que s'est tenu le Concile en 431.

2. La lettre des Pères du Concile d'Eglise d'Éhpèse au Clergé de Constantinople, où il est clairement fait mention de St. Jean et de Ste. Marie, dans une phrase qui est elliptique, mais dont le sens d'échappe à personne: St. Jean et Ste. Marie ont été présents de quelque façon à Éphèse.

3. Les documents écrits en faveur d'Éphèse paraissent au 6e. Siècle en même temps que ceux que l'on fait valoir pour Jérusalème. L'Eglise Syrienne et l'Eglise Jacobite sont pour Éphèse. Cette tradition se maintient ainsi jusqu'au 14e. siècle; elle est reprise et présentée dans toute sa force au 17e. et 18e. siècles par des historiens remarquables, comme Tillemont, Baronius, Ruinart, et Don Calmet.

Il n'est donc pas contraire au bon sens et à la prudence humaine de croire que la Maison de Panaya Kapulu décrite si exactement par le Vénérable Catherine Emmerich est exactement la Maison de la Ste. Vierge, d'autant plus que la tradition locale très ancienne et sérieusement contrôlée, celle des anciens chrétiens Kirkingiotes, établis en ce lieu depuis avant le 18e. siècle attestait également ce fait.

Dès lors, si l'on vient à établir par une série d'inductions historiques légitimes, que l'Apôtre St. Jean (qu'on ne peut confondre avec le presbytre Jean) est venu en Asie et en Éphèse, entre 37 et 48, la conclusion s'impose: il a dû emmener avec lui la Ste. Vierge dont il avait reçu la garde et la Ste. Vierge a vécu auprès de lui les derniers jours de son existence sur terre.

L'existence de la Maison de la Ste. Vierge sort ainsi du domaine des légendes et la croyance de sa Dormition à Panaya Kapulu devient une de ces traditions que le célèbre professeur d'Histoire à la Sarbonne, Mr. Charles Lenormant, n'hesitait pas à ranger, dès l'apparition du livre de Catherine Emmerich, en 1850 "parmi celles qui sont en accord parfait avec les conclusions auxquelles conduissent les instructions légitimes de l'Histoire."

Nous pouvons donc l'accepter sans crainte. Humainement parlant, nous avons en sa faveur assez de garanties morales. Puisse un coup de pioche providentiel permettre de découvrir des preuves materielles décisives.

Nous invitons donc les fidèles à faire le voyage d'Éphèse pour aller vénérer la Maison de la Ste. Vierge à Panaya Kapulu. Le voyage sera agréable et facile, surtout depuis que le Gouvernement Turc a montré sa bienveillance et sa générosité, en faisant construire une belle route qui conduit jusqu'au sommet de la Sainte Colline. [Duyuran, pp. 103–105]

[F] Decree of Pope Pius XII, 19 June 1951, as made public by Archbishop Descuffi [cf. Chapter IV, note 99]:

Aujourd'hui j'ai la grande joie et l'insigne honneur de révèler la communication officielle faite a moi par Sa Sainteté le Pape Pie XII, par une lettre autographe de Son Eminence Monseigneur Montini [Paul VI], Cardinal Secrétaire d'État du Vatican. D'apres cette communication officielle:

1. Sa Sainteté le Pape a bien voulu accorder le privilège de la célèbration de la messe votive de l'Assomption en ce lieu par tous les prêtres, au cours des pèlerinages qui seront effectués a la maison de la Sainte Vierge a Panaya Kapulu a Éphèse.

2. Sa Sainteté le Pape a bien voulu accorder également le privilège de la célébration de la messe votive de la Maternite divine dans l'église du Concile, sise dans l'antique ville d'Éphèse, ainsi que le privilège de la célébration de la messe votive de Saint Jean a l'église historique de Saint Jean à Selçuk.

3. Sa Sainteté le Pape a bien voulu m'accorder l'autorisation nécessaire pour bénir en son nom, à l'issue des messes, les pèlerins qui participeront au pèlerinage qui aura lieu 19 août 1951 à l'occasion de la restauration de la maison de la Sainte Vierge a Panaya Kapulu et de l'aménagement des routes menant à cette maison.

4. Sa Sainteté le Pape, ayant considéré juste le pardon des pêchés des pèlerins qui visiteront la Maison de la Sainte Vierge a Panaya Kapulu, a chargé de la question la Sacrée Penitencerie, autorisée a décider en la matiere. J'ai également reçu la bonne nouvelle que cette importante décision sera sous peu communiquée a notre archevêché. [Duyuran, pp. 109, 110]

[G] Decree of Pope John XXIII, 18 August 1961 [cf. Chapter IV, note 101]:

Décret du Sainte-Siège, Pie XII,
No. 258.115 — 19 Juin 1951

Confirmé pour toujours par décret du 18 août 1961. Jean XXIII, No. 6320/61 — 18 août 1961.

Indulgence plenière pour les pèlerins qui après s'être confessés et avoir communié visitent le Sanctuaire et prient aux intentions du Souverain Pontife.

    Sacrée Penitencerie Apostolique
    (Seal of Archbishop Descuffi)
    [Archdiocesan Archives of Smyrna]

[H] General section of the Minutes of the Official Visit of *Panaya*, 1 December 1892 [Cf. Chapter V, note 4]:

Procès-Verbal de la Visite Officielle Faite a Panaya-Capouli par Mgr. André Timoni, Archevêque de Smyrne et vicaire apostolique de l'Asie Mineure.

Appendix

Nous André-Polycarpe Timoni, archvêque de Smyrne et vicaire apostolique de l'Asie Mineure, ainsi que les soussignés, attestons et certifions ce qui suit:

De recherches récentes faites d'après les indications de la soeur Catherine Emmerich attirant serieusement, depuis seize mois, l'attention du pays sur un lieu situé près d'Éphèse et nommè Panaya-Capouli . . . (Porte de la Vierge), nous avons voulu contrôler par nous-mêmes l'exactitude des rapports qui nous etaient faits.

A cette fin, le jeudi ler decembre mil huit cent quatre-vingt-douze, nous nous sommes transportés audit lieu de Panaya-Capouli. Là nous avons trouvé les ruines assez bien conservées d'une antique maison ou chapelle dont la construction, au dire d'archéologues compétents, pouvait remonter au ler siècle de notre ère, et qui, tant pour *la position* que pour le *plan intérieur*, répond pleinement et entièrement à ce que dit Catherine Emmerich, dans ses Révélations, de la maison de la sainte Vierge à Éphèse. [Barnabé, pp. 216, 217]

[I] **Official report of a miraculous cure, 10 March 1955 [cf. Chapter VI, notes 35, 60]:**

Since 1950 Miss Jeanne Koury, 35 years of age, suffered from Potts disease. The disorder was clearly marked by decalcification of two dorsal vertebrae and two ribs. The sickness had resisted the most energetic treatments and even Ablee's operation which had not been successful. The deformity was apparent, the fistula flowed abundantly, the sufferings were acute, the paralysis had affected the lower members, the sufferer was confined to her bed. It was in this desperate state that she was abandoned by the doctors a month and a half before her miraculous cure. During this time, the devout invalid did not cease to pray to the Blessed Virgin and to beg her to cure her.

On the evening of the 19th of August 1951, the day of the solemn inauguration of the restored Sanctuary of the most blessed Virgin, the parents of the sick girl, upon returning from their pilgrimage, toward eight o'clock, brought her some water from Panaya which she had asked for, and which they gave her to drink, likewise applying some lotions in the form of a cross upon the affected and paralysed parts. Shortly afterwards, the sick girl settled into a tranquil sleep for four hours. On awakening, at about 2:00 a.m. of August 20th, she felt suddenly cured. The pains had ceased, the fistula no longer flowed, the invalid could freely move all parts of her body so that in the presence of her parents, as astonished as she was at this prodigy, she turned over twice in her bed with the greatest ease. All her relatives cried out: "a miracle," and gave thanks to the Blessed Virgin.

Since this date of August 19–20, 1951, all the symptoms of the sickness have disappeared; the fistula has dried up; freedom of all the members has been complete, and later on X-rays showed the complete recalcification of the vertebrae and the ribs. At the end of a week, Miss Jeanne could resume her fatiguing occupations without any inconvenience and since then until this day, March 10, 1955, she has enjoyed perfect health.

The attending physician and four out of five of the members of the medical staff who examined the case and visited the sick girl, came to the conclusion that this sudden and perfect cure in the space of four hours can in no way be explained from the medical viewpoint by the laws of nature thus far known.

In consequence His Excellency, the Archbishop, invites the faithful to thank the most blessed Virgin with all their hearts for this miracle which shows the power of her intercession and the merciful kindness of her maternal Heart.

Izmir, March 10, 1955
Mgr. Joseph Descuffi,
Archbishop of Smyrna
(Seal and signature)
[*Fatima Findings*, 10 (June, 1955), 1]

[J] **Prayer recited at Panaya during pilgrimages:**

Très Sainte et Immaculée Vierge Marie, qui avez suivi en Asie le Disciple bien-aimé et qui, à Éphèse, avez été proclamée Mère de Dieu, protégez l'Eglise de Smyrne, seule survivante des sept Eglises de l'Apocalypse, héritière de leurs traditions et Mère des Eglises des Gaules, en particulier de Lyon, d'Autun, de Langres, de Dijon et de Besançon. Entendez aussi, nous vous en supplions, à l'Eglise tout entière, sur l'Occident comme sur l'Orient, berceau de notre foi, le salutaire bienfait de votre maternelle protection.

O Notre Dame d'Éphèse, O reine montée aux cieux, Vous qui êtes notre Mère à tous, veillez sur nous, préservez-nous de tous les périls de l'âme et du corps; intercédez auprès de votre divin Fils, pour nous, qui à l'example de nos Pères, mettons en Vous toute notre confiance et tout notre amour. Ainsi soit-il.

Invocations en Langue Turque
Ey Hazreti Meryem Ana,
  Aslen lekesiz Bakire!
Hazreti Isa'nin Annesi!
Goklerdeki daimi Annemiz!
  Bizim için dua et!
    Amin. [*Marie*, 5 (1951), 21]

Notes

Chapter I — Notes

1. This name is a hybrid from Greek and Turkish meaning the house (or gate) of the all holy one: *domus sanctissimae*. Cf. below, Chapter II, note 42. (References to notes will sometimes refer primarily to their attendant texts.)
2. Preface of Abbé de Cazales to Catherine Emmerich's group of visions titled *The Dolorous Passion of Our Lord Jesus Christ*, 22 ed. (London: Burns & Oates, 1955), pp. 18, 19 (hereafter cited *Passion*).
3. A description of this event, as told by Catherine, may be found in *Passion*, p. 20.
4. *Ibid.*, p. 21.
5. Those and other details of her life may be found in *Passion*, pp. 15–63; these pages represent the synopsis of Catherine's life. There are many lives of Catherine, e.g., T. Wegener, *Sister Anne Katherine Emmerich of the Order of St. Augustine*, tr. by F. X. McGowan (New York-Cincinnati, 1898); K. Schmöger, *Life of Anne Catherine Emmerich*, 2 rev. ed. (New York, 1903).
6. *Passion*, p. 27.
7. All Souls' Day, 1812, marked the last time she was able to venture outside; cf. *ibid.*, p. 29.
8. Cf. A. Farges, *Mystical Phenomena*, tr. by S. P. Jacques (London, 1926), p. 560.
9. More details on Brentano and the controversy which he generated appear subsequently; cf. below, Chapter I, § 2.
10. In that year she related the whole Passion of our Lord, which she had made the subject of her Lenten meditations; these comprise the book *The Dolorous Passion*.
11. *Passion*, p. 63.
12. Statement of Sebastian Bullough, O.P., in the observations on his own notes, which are supplementary to those of Brentano, in Catherine Emmerich's *The Life of the Blessed Virgin Mary*, tr. by Sir Michael Palairet (Springfield, Ill.: Templegate, 1954), p. x (hereafter cited *Life of BVM*). In *Life of BVM*, therefore, two sets of notes appear: one of Brentano and one of Bullough, sometimes annotating the text directly, sometimes elucidating Brentano's notes.
13. Cf. Preface to the German edition, *Life of BVM*, p. vii.
14. Cf. *The Catholic Encyclopedia* (New York, 1907–1912), V, 406, 407.
15. Preface of Abbé de Cazales, *Passion*, pp. viii, ix.
16. Cf. T. Wegener, O.E.S.A., *Anna Katherina Emmerich und Clemens Brentano* (Dülmen i. W., 1900); G. Dirheimer, *Anne Cathérine Emmerich et Clément Brentano* (Paris, 1923); W. Hümpfner, O.E.S.A., *Clemens Brentanos Glaubwürdigkeit in seinen Emmerick-Aufzeichnungen* (Würzburg, 1923), and "Übersicht über die Literatur über A. K. Emmerick," *Theologie und Glaube* (Paderborn, 1909–), 16 (1924) 455–482; A.

Stockmann, S.J., "Die heutige Stand der Anna Katharina Emmerick-Forschung," *Stimmen aus Maria-Laach* (Freiburg i. Br., 1871–), 119 (1930), 292–306; H. Thurston, S.J., "The Problem of Anne Catherine Emmerich," *The Month* (London, 1864–), 138 (1921), 237–248, 344–356, 429–439, 519–530, and "The Authenticity of the Emmerich Visions," *The Month*, 143 (1924), 42–52.
17. Cf. above, p. 4. "La Congregation des Rites a écarté du procès de beatification de la vénérable stigmatisée tous les écrits publiés sous son nom par Clément Brentano, 'parce que la part de cet écrivain a tellement pénétré toute la trame des récits, qu'il est impossible de rien pouvoir attribuer en propre à la Voyante elle-même.'" — *Dictionnaire de la Bible, Supplément*, Vol. I, ed. L. Pirot (Paris, 1928), 649 (hereafter cited *Dict. Bib. Sup.*).

Chapter II — NOTES

1. An explanation of this name appears later; cf. below, Chapter II, note 42.
2. *Life of BVM*, pp. 346, 347.
3. *Ibid.*, pp. 347, 348.
4. Cf. *ibid.*, p. 367.
5. *Ibid.*, p. 348. The statement that Mary's home was the only one of stone is relatively significant. In the preceding quotation it was pointed out that the other people about lived in wooden huts, caves, or tents. But Mary's house was stone and, while not elaborate by present standards, it made her indeed Queen of the Mountain.
6. Since this is a crucial part of the description, having further implications when the discovery of the house is treated, the G. Theiner-Haffner edition of Brentano's *Das Marienleben* (Innsbruck: Marianischer Verlag, 1952) was quoted above. The German text reads: "Einzig das Haus der Mutter Gottes war von Stein. Es war viereckig und rückwärts innen rund und auszen eckig. . . ." — *Ibid.*, p. 535. Translation mine.
7. *Life of BVM*, p. 348.
8. *Ibid.*, pp. 348, 349.
9. *Ibid.*, p. 349. Catherine referred to the apse on another occasion when she spoke of the little churches built by the Apostles: ". . . yet all those I saw had at the back the semicircular or three-sided apse, like Mary's house at Ephesus." — *Ibid.*, p. 363.
10. *Ibid.*, p. 350.
11. *Ibid.*, p. 356.
12. *Ibid.*, p. 370.
13. It is obvious also from various statements of Catherine, e.g., "The Blessed Virgin could not see the altar from her bed . . ." — *Life of BVM*, p. 369.
14. "Mary's maidservant . . . and the other women . . . slept in the room behind the hearth. . . . In the meantime the women had woken and got up, and . . . retired from Our Lady's room." — *Ibid.*, pp. 377–379.
15. *Ibid.*, p. 350.
16. *Ibid.*, pp. 351, 352.
17. "Prière de respecter un pauvre voyageur inoffensif et sans ressources." — J. Euzet, *Historique de la Maison de la Sainte Vierge près d'Éphèse (1891–1961)* (Istanbul: Notre-Dame d'Éphèse, 1961), p. 2 (hereafter cited *Historique*). Translations from this source throughout the text are mine.

18. *Ibid.* Later, on hearing of the discovery by the Lazarists, Gouyet returned to Ephesus in 1896 and visited the site. After he went home to Paris, he published a beautiful book on the discovery, *Découverte dans la montagne d'Éphèse de la Maison où la T. S. Vierge est morte* (Paris, 1898).
19. "Éphèse n'est pas si loin . . . Il vaudrait bien la peine d'y aller voir!" — *Historique,* p. 3.
20. Cf. *ibid.,* pp. 3, 4. The priests of the Congregation of the Mission are commonly called Lazarists throughout Europe and some neighboring areas. In America, however, they are better known as Vincentians.
21. Cf. *ibid.,* pp. 4–6; cf. below, Chapter III, § 2.
22. In the declining years of Ephesus, when many of its inhabitants disliked the unhealthy climate caused by the silting up of the harbor, they moved up to the hill outside the city, on which a church was built over the tomb of St. John. "Toward the end of the Eleventh Century, the name Ephesus began to be forgotten, and the city was often referred to as Hagios Theologos, a nickname for St. John. Medieval sources changed this into 'Alto Luogo,' and the Turks called it Ayasoluk." — C. Toksöz, *Ephesus, Legends and Facts,* tr. by Dr. A. E. Uysal (Istanbul: Yenilik Basimevi, 1956), p. 24 (hereafter cited *Toksöz*). Ayasoluk was thus simply a corruption of the town's earlier name *Hagios Theologos* — Holy Theologian. The name Ayasoluk was changed in 1914 to Seldjuk, the name of the earliest Turkish dynasty in that region. The small town of Seldjuk today, therefore, lies just beyond the ancient ruins of Ephesus and is, in a sense, its offspring. Cf. *Historique,* p. 166. R. Duyuran added this further and more detailed note: "En 1914, Ayasuluk prit le nom de Selçuk, nom qui, après la guerre de l'Indépendence, fut remplacé par celui d'Akincilar, mais on le connaît aujourd'hui encore sous le nom de Selçuk." — *Éphèse* (Ankara: Direction Générale de la Presse, 1951), p. 16 (hereafter cited *Duyuran*).
23. *Life of BVM,* p. 348.
24. Cf. *Historique,* pp. 6–8.
25. They found Mary's home, therefore, on the third day of their search, July 29, 1891, and spent two more days examining it. Cf. E. Borrel, "A-t-on découvert à Éphèse la Maison ou mourut la Vierge Marie?" *Ecclesia, Lectures chrétiennes* (Paris, 1949–), 3 (Aug., 1951), 73, 74.
26. Cf. *Historique,* pp. 8–11.
27. Cf. below, Chapter III, notes 111–125.
28. Cf. *Historique,* p. 13.
29. Cf. below, Chapter IV, § 5; Chapter V, § 1.
30. Cf. below, Chapter V, notes 1–6.
31. Toksöz, pp. 107, 108.
32. *Life of BVM,* p. 382.
33. Actually the sole significant change was effected not by man but through the forces of nature — the storeroom of Mary's home was totally destroyed by a spring of water under its foundations; cf. below, Chapter VI, note 73.
34. "La conformité merveilleuse entre l'edifice découvert et la description de la voyante de Dülmen prouve qu'elle l'a réellement vue en ses visions et révélations . . ." — M. Gabrielovich, *Éphèse ou Jérusalem, tombeau de la sainte Vierge* (Paris-Poitiers, 1897), p. 109. Translation mine. Poulin used Gabrielovich as a pseudonym for reasons given later; cf. below, Chapter IV, notes 116–118.

35. Cf. above, Chapter I, § 2.
36. Cf. below, Chapter V, notes 11, 15.
37. Catherine had never heard of Ephesus; nor could she very well have read about it because she was for the most part illiterate. And Brentano had never been to Ephesus, much less to the nearby deserted mountain. But even if none of this were true, our conclusion would still stand because the revelations contained certain details which could have been known at the time by God alone. Intimately connected with these thoughts is the following quotation: "Il faut ajouter que Catherine Emmerich . . . n'avait jamais entendu parler d'Éphèse. Elle était de plus illettrée, sachant à peine le patois allemand. On ne peut pas accuser aussi Clément von Brentano de supercherie, car lui-même n'a jamais visité Éphèse, ni surtout la maison décrite par lui, reproduisant les Déclarations de la Voyante. Il eut fallu qu'il fût là, sur place, pour mesurer les lieux, donner des détails d'architecture, impossibles sans voir. Difficile à imaginer." — F. Psalty, *Notre Dame d'Éphèse, Les Ruines de la Maison de la Vierge Marie à Panaya-Capouli* (Istanbul: Güler Basimevi, 1955), p. 7.
38. *Mystical Phenomena*, p. 387.
39. Cf. *Dict. Bib. Sup.*, I, 648.
40. Cf. A. d'Ales, "Le tombeau de la Sainte Vierge," *Revue de l'Orient chrétien* (Paris, 1896–), 28 (1931–1932), 387. D'Ales supported the Ephesus tradition and stated: "En l'absence de toute clarté supérieure venue de Jérusalem, beaucoup de croyants préféreront tenir Éphèse . . ." — *Ibid.*, 389.
41. Probably the most offensive writer was Barnabé of Alsace [Meistermann], O.F.M., in *Le Tombeau de la Sainte Vierge à Jérusalem* (Jérusalem, 1903) (hereafter cited *Barnabé*). He devoted two thirds of his book to an ineffectual refutation of the Ephesus tradition.
42. As noted earlier, *Panaya Kapulu* is a mixture of Greek and Turkish meaning the gate or house of the most holy one (feminine); cf. above, note 1. It was the name used for Mary's home at Ephesus by the orthodox Christians who visited it from time immemorial — more on them later; cf. below, Chapter III, § 3. *Panaya* (*Panagia*, transliterated in French as *Panaghia*) is the Greek element meaning "all holy," equivalent to the Latin *sanctissima*, a modifier of the Virgin Mary; *Kapulu* (*Kapoulu*, similarly transliterated as *Capoulu*, and sometimes appearing as *Capouli* or *Capuli*) is the Turkish element, derived from *Kapou* meaning "gate" or "house." The two-word name was a short form of *Panaya utch Kapoulu Monastiri*, and was itself shortened to simply *Panaya*. Cf. *Historique*, pp. 155, 156, for a more detailed explanation. M. Hetzenauer, O.M.C., offered this concise explanation: "Hoc nomen est graeco-turcicum. 'Panagia,' i.e., sanctissima, est titulus Mariae; 'capu' idem est ac porta, i.e., habitatio; 'li' demonstrativum est. Ergo 'Panaghia Capuli' = habitatio Sanctissimae." — "De peregrinatione B. Mariae V. in Panaghia Capuli prope Ephesum," *Verbum Domini* (Romae, 1921–), 2 (1922), 252. Cf. also M. Dierickx, S.J., "Panagia Kapulu of Meryem Ana," *Streven* (Amsterdam, 1945–), 15 (1962), 712.
43. The greater portion of this account has been gleaned from *Historique*, pp. 17–21, 121–127. Euzet included therein quotations from the *Registers of Historical Manuscripts of Panaya* kept at the French hospital in Izmir.
44. "J'y pensais déjà! Achetez!" — *Ibid.*, p. 19.

45. The following statement is incorrect: "Die Lazaristen kauften 1898 diese kleine Kirchenruine, die sie mit dem Wohnhaus Mariens identifizierten, und das umliegende Gelände." — J. Aufhauser, "Wo befindet sich das echte Mariengrab?" *Actes du X. Congres International d'Études Byzantines, Supplément* (Istanbul: Comite d'Organisation, 1957) [single page unbound summaries] (hereafter cited *Actes, Sup.*).
46. Cf. below, Chapter V, § 2; Chapter VI, § 1.
47. "Il est bien entendu, note E. Poulin, que Soeur de Grancey resta Seigneure et maîtresse de Panaghia, comme avant le transfert, le dit transfert n'ayant pour but que d'assurer la propriété après sa mort (1915) et non de la dépouiller elle-même." — *Historique,* p. 20.
48. Cf. below, Chapter VI, note 11.
49. Cf. *Historique,* pp. 122, 128.
50. "Comment puis je . . . inscrire au nom de J. Euzet une propriété qui n'appartient pas à E. Poulin?" — *Historique,* p. 123.
51. The finger of God is seen throughout the history of *Panaya,* and Euzet has written a little appendix about this in *Historique,* pp. 157-165. He presented it precisely under the title, "Le Doigt de Dieu dans l'Oeuvre de Panaya Kapoulu."
52. It is a striking coincidence that the decision favorable to returning Mary's home to Catholic possession was delivered on the feast of Our Lady of Ransom.
53. "A Panaghia on verra des Choses extraordinaires. Moi, je ne les verrai pas, mes enfants les verront. Ce sera comme un paradis." — *Historique,* p. 126.
54. Cf. *ibid.,* pp. 126, 164. For formation of the Society of Mother Mary, cf. below, Chapter V, notes 33-35.
55. "En 1896, un manifeste anonyme adressé 'au Monde chretien' par Mgr. Timoni, archevêque de Smyrne et vicaire apostolique de l'Asie Mineure, annonçait la découverte, sur les indications de la voyante westphalienne, Anne Catherine Emmerich, de la maison où était morte la sainte Vierge, au Bülbül Dagh, montagne voisine des ruines d'Éphèse." — *Dict. Bib. Sup.,* I, 647. Translation mine.

Chapter III — Notes

1. "Si autem Patres in quodam textu interpretando unanimes non sunt, liberi manent catholici exegetae quantum est ex parte Patrum, et unam prae alia interpretationem eis seligere licet." — J. Filogrossi, S.J., "Traditio Divino-Apostolica et Assumptio B.V.M.," *Gregorianum* (Roma, 1920-), 30 (1949), 456. Cf. H. Denzinger, *Enchiridion Symbolorum, Definitionum et Declarationum de Rebus Fidei et Morum* (30 ed., Friburgi Brisgoviae: Herder, 1955), n. 1788 (hereafter cited Denzinger).
2. Jn 19:27.
3. Cf. Hetzenauer, art. cit., 246.
4. Cornelius à Lapide, S.J. (1567-1637), *Comm. in Io.* 19:27, as in *The Great Commentary of Cornelius à Lapide,* tr. by T. Mossman (6 vols., London, 1887), VI, 243, 244. The role of the Council of Ephesus in this question is considered later; cf. below, Chapter IV, § 1.
5. Such a thesis based on Scripture appeared in Dierickx, art. cit., 705-709.
6. J. Descuffi, C.M., "De loco transitus B. Mariae Virginis," *Divus Thomas* (Piacenza, 1880-), 52 (1949), 213 (hereafter cited Descuffi, "De loco").

Translation mine. Another such chronological argument from Scripture is found in M. Tallon, S.J., "Le Culte de la Vierge Marie en Asie Mineure du Ier au XVe Siècle," *Maria, Études sur la Sainte Vierge*, Vol. IV, ed. H. du Manoir, S.J. (Paris: Beauchesne et ses Fils, 1956), 889, 890.

7. C. Clemen, "The Sojourn of the Apostle John at Ephesus," *The American Journal of Theology* (Chicago, 1897–1920), 9 (1905), 643.
8. *Ibid.*, 656. For arguments for John's residence in Ephesus, treated in detail, cf. *ibid.*, 660–676.
9. Toksöz, *op. cit.*, p. 34. The final sentence of the quotation refers to Mary and is taken from St. Epiphanius; cf. below, Chapter III, note 21.
10. *Adv. Marc.*, IV, 5: "Habemus et Ioannis alumnas ecclesias. Nam etsi Apocalypsim eius Marcion respuit, ordo tamen episcoporum ad originem recensus, in Ioannem stabit auctorem." — J. Migne, *Patrologiae Cursus Completus, Series Latina* (221 vols., Parisiis, 1844–1855), 2, 366 (hereafter cited *MPL*).
11. "Ioannes vero in Asia a Domitiano imperatore [81–96] in Patmos insulam relegatus, ubi etiam Evangelium conscripsit, ac apocalypsim vidit sub Traiano [98–117] obdormivit Ephesis. Eius reliquiae cum fuissent quaesitae, non sunt inventae." — J. Migne, *Patrologiae Cursus Completus, Series Graeca* (161 vols., Parisiis, 1857–1866), 10, 951 (hereafter cited *MPG*). That his relics were missing refers to the legend of John's assumption; cf. M. Žužić, *A Short History of St. John in Ephesus* (Lima, Ohio: The American Society of Ephesus, 1960), pp. 42, 43 (hereafter cited Žužić). "The Oriental Rites and Churches have a special liturgical feast of St. John's Assumption into Heaven, celebrated on September 26. Approximately 155 millions of faithful Christians, and among them approximately three million Americans of different Eastern Churches and Rites, glorify St. John also on that day, i.e., as *assumptus est in coelo*." — Žužić, p. 52.
12. "Sed et Ioannes, qui supra pectus Domini recubuit, fuitque sacerdos Dei laminam gestans, et martyr et doctor, hic, inquam, Ioannes in urbe Epheso conditus iacet." — *MPG*, 20, 279.
13. Cf. *MPL*, 22, 687.
14. *Adv. Haer.*, III, 1, 1: "Postea et Ioannes discipulus Domini, qui et supra pectus eius recumbebat, et ipse edidit Evangelium Ephesi Asiae commorans." — *MPG*, 7, 845. Cf. *MPG*, 7, 851, 852. This is found also in J. Quasten, *Patrology*, Vol. I, *The Beginnings of Patristic Literature* (Westminster, Md.: The Newman Press, 1951), 307.
15. *Hist. Eccl.*, III, 23: "Sed et Ephesina Ecclesia, quae a Paulo quidem fundata est, Ioannem vero usque ad Traiani tempora habuit praesidentem, testis locupletissima et apostolicae traditionis." — *MPG*, 20, 258.
16. "Cum post tyranni ex insula Patmo Ephesum rediisset Ioannes." — *Loc. cit.*
17. *Hist. Eccl.*, III, 1: "Ioanni Asia obvenit, qui plurimum temporis in ea commoratus, Ephesi tandem diem obiit." — *MPG*, 20, 215.
18. *Eccl. Hist.*, III, 1; *The Fathers of the Church*, Vol. XIX, *Eusebius Pamphili Ecclesiastical History* (New York: Fathers of the Church, Inc., 1953), 137, 138 (hereafter cited *Eusebius Pamphili*). Cf. *MPG*, 20, 215.
19. Cf. *Hist. Eccl.*, III, 5; *MPG*, 20, 222.
20. *Hist. Eccl.*, V, 24; *Eusebius Pamphili*, 335. Cf. *MPG*, 20, 494, 495.
21. *Panarion*, 78, 11: "Ac cum Ioannes interim in Asia profectus sit, nusquam tamen B. Virginem itineris comitem secum illum habuisse significat; sed de ea re penitus Scriptura conticescit . . . ne hominum animos maiorem

quemdam in stuporem coniicerit." — *MPG*, 42, 715. Translation mine. Cf. H. Daniel-Rops, *The Book of Mary*, tr. by A. Guinan (New York: Hawthorn Books, Inc., 1960), pp. 135, 136.
22. Cf. Descuffi, "De loco," 213, 214.
23. Cf. J. Descuffi, "La Maison de la Sainte Vierge à Éphèse," *Ecclesia, Lectures chrétiennes*, 14 (Aug., 1962), 34 (hereafter cited Descuffi, "La Maison").
24. *De vir. illustr.*, 9: ". . . redit Ephesum . . . totas Asiae fundavit rexitque Ecclesias . . . iuxta eamdem urbem sepultus est." — *MPL*, 23, 625.
25. ". . . Ephesum . . . in qua urbe et hospitiolum et amicos amantissimos sui habebat." — *MPL*, 27, 603. In connection with the house, cf. below, note 30.
26. Cf. A. d'Ales, *art. cit.*, 382. Of St. Jerome he said: "Et l'on a pu observer que l'idée d'un miracle tel que l'Assomption corporelle ne paraît pas avoir traversé la pensée de saint Jérôme." — *Loc. cit.*
27. "Gethsemani, locus ubi Salvator ante Passionem oravit. Est autem ad radices montis Oliveti nunc ecclesia desuper aedificata." — *MPL*, 23, 903.
28. *Lib. mirac.*, I, 4: "Posthaec dispersi sunt per regiones diversas ad praedicandum verbum Dei (An. 36). Denique impleto a beata Maria huius vitae cursu, cum iam vocaretur a saeculo, congregati sunt omnes apostoli de singulis regionibus ad domum eius (An. 48)." — *MPL*, 71, 708. Translation mine.
29. "Mortuam autem eam Ephesi fuisse doctorum virorum est sententia." — *Ibid.*, note e.
30. *Lib. mirac.*, I, 30: "In Epheso autem habetur locus in quo hic apostolus Evangelium quo ex eius nomine in Ecclesia legitur scripsit. Sunt autem in summitate montis illius proximi quatuor sine tecto parietes. In his enim orationi insistens, Dominum assidue pro delictis populi deprecans, morabatur; obtinuitque ne in loco illo imber ullus descenderet, donec ille Evangelium adimpleret. Sed et usque hodie ita praestatur a Domino, ut nulla ibi descendat pluvia, neque violentus adveniat." — *MPL*, 71, 730. In this connection the following may also be cited: "Saint Grégoire de Tours (570) et saint Willibrod (720) rapportaient que les pélerins se rendaient au sommet de la colline pour voir 'une maison avec quatre pans de mur, sans toit,' où saint Jean allait prier et offrir des sacrifices pour les péchés du monde." — Descuffi, "La Maison," 40.
31. E.g., Hippolytus of Thebes would have John preaching in Ephesus while Mary stayed at his home: "Sic igitur recepit Deiparam in domum suam, verbum veritatis Christi Ephesi in Asia praedicans . . ." — *MPG*, 117, 1039; yet, he appeared to imply that the home of John was in Jerusalem; cf. *ibid.*, 1030, 1031.
32. Cf., e.g., J. Euzet, "Remarques sur 'Jérusalem?-Éphèse?' de Clemens Kopp," *Divus Thomas*, 60 (1957), 47–72 (hereafter cited Euzet, "Remarques"); D'Ales, *art. cit.*, 376–389.
33. D'Ales, *art. cit.*, 378.
34. Tallon, *art. cit.*, 916.
35. *Dictionary of the Holy Bible* (ed. C. Taylor, rev. E. Robinson, Boston, 1832), p. 389.
36. Cf., e.g., M. Jugie, "La Mort et l'Assomption de la Sainte Vierge dans la tradition des cinq premiers siècles," *Échos d'Orient* (Paris, 1897–), 25 (1926), 5–20, 129–143, 281–307 (hereafter cited Jugie, "La Mort"); G.

Roschini, O.S.M., *Lo Pseudo-Dionigi l'Areopagita e la Morte di Maria SS.* (Roma: Edizioni "Marianum," 1958) (hereafter cited *Roschini*). For other studies, cf. Bibliography.

37. "Toute l'Eglise greque et latine celebre aujourd'hui la mort et la glorification de la Ste Vierge le 15 d'août. Les Grecs appellent cette feste *le sommeil* [dormitio], et quelquefois *le passage* [transitus] de la Ste Vierge. Les Latins se sont aussi servis du nom de *sommeil*: mais ordinairement ils luy donnent celui d'*Assomption* [assumptio]." — L. S. le Nain de Tillemont, *Memoires*, Vol. I, *Le Temps de N.-S., et les Apostres* (Paris, 1936), 500, 501 (hereafter cited *Memoires*). Translation mine.

38. "Transitus B. Mariae antonomastice Assumptio nominatur, quia prius est assumpta in anima et postmodum sicut pie creditur assumpta est in corpus." — Siccardus Cremonensis, *MPL*, 213, 420.

39. W. Burghardt, S.J., "The Testimony of the Patristic Age Concerning Mary's Death," *Marian Studies* (Washington, D. C., 1950–), 8 (1957), 76–79. A reasonably complete list of the writings on the Dormition in *MPG* is offered for convenience: Modestus Hier., 86, 3277–3312; Andreas Cretensis, 97, 1045–1110; Ioannes Damascenus, 96, 699–762; Germanus I, 98, 339–372; Theodorus Studita, 99, 719–730; Iosephus Hymnographus, 105, 999–1004; Leo Imperator, 107, 157–172; Ioannes Euchaita, 120, 1075–1114; Isidorus Thessalonicensis, 139, 117–164; Nicephorus Chumnus, 140, 1497–1526; Theophanes Ceromeus, 132, 1047–1060; Manuel Palcologus, 156, 91–108; Andronicus Senior, 161, 1095–1108. The writings of the Latin authors are too numerous to list here; they may be found in the Index of *MPL*, 220, 495–497.

40. Cf. Bull *Munificentissimus Deus*, 1 Nov. 1950 — *Acta Apostolicae Sedis, Commentarium Officiale* (Romae, 1909–1929, Civitate Vaticana, 1929–), 42 (1950), 753–771 (hereafter cited *AAS*); Denzinger, 3032, 3033.

41. Cf. *Dictionnaire d'Archéologie chrétienne et de Liturgie*, Vol. I, Pt. 2 (ed. F. Cabrol, H. Leclercq, Paris, 1924), 2995 (hereafter cited *DACL*).

42. Cf. U. Holzmeister, S.J., "De anno mortis Deiparae Virginis," *Marianum* (Romae, 1939–), 4 (1942), 179.

43. *Ibid.*, 182.

44. "La tradition, sans doute, n'est pas unanime sur la question de sa mort." — Jugie, "La Mort," 307. *DACL*, I, 2995, is in error on this point.

45. M. Jugie, *La Mort et L'Assomption de la Sainte Vierge* [Studi e Testi, 114] (Città del Vaticano: Biblioteca Apostolica Vaticana, 1944), p. 508 (hereafter cited simply *La Mort*, thus distinguishing Jugie's book from his article cited above, Chapter III, notes 36 and 44).

46. Cf. *loc. cit.* Cf. also above, Chapter III, note 39.

47. *The Teaching of the Catholic Church* (ed. G. Smith), Vol. II (New York: The Macmillan Co., 1949), 1015.

48. The description of Catherine Emmerich is at least as worthy of credence as the apocrypha.

49. Cf. A. Le Hir, "De l'Assomption de la sainte Vierge et les livres apocryphes qui s'y rapportent," *Études bibliques*, Vol. X (Paris, 1866), 514–555; C. Bonnet, "Bemerkungen über die älteste Schriften von der Himmelfahrt Maria," *Zeitschrift für wissenschaftliche Theologie* (Leipzig-Frankfurt, 1858–1914), 23 (1880), 222–247; C. Tischendorf, *Apocalypses apocryphae* (Leipzig, 1886), pp. 94–136.

50. Cf. A. Rush, C.SS.R., "Assumption Theology in the *Transitus Mariae*,"

The Ecclesiastical Review (New York-Philadelphia, 1889–), 123 (1950), 97.
51. Cf. M. James, The Apocryphal New Testament (Oxford, 1924), pp. 209–216.
52. W. Wright, "The Departure of My Lady Mary from this World," Journal of Sacred Literature (London, 1848–), 7 (Apr., 1865), 139.
53. Cf. La Mort, p. 106.
54. Cf. Roschini, pp. 20–24.
55. "Liber qui appelatur Transitus, id est Assumptio sanctae Mariae, Apocryphus." — MPL, 59, 162. Translation mine.
56. Hom. II in Dorm. B.M.V., 18 — MPG, 96, 747–751. Cf. Nicephorus Callistus who reported all this in MPG, 147, 44. Cf. also MPG, 145, 816. The story is summarized in DACL, I, 2996.
57. If he had, it would have been ridiculous and contradictory for St. Germain, Patriarch of Constantinople fifty years before John Damascene wrote the Euthymian story, to preach as he did that Mary ascended to heaven together with the loculus and winding sheets and that there was never anything at the Blachernae except a robe of Mary; cf. Senior [Descuffi, J., et al.], Ephesus or Jerusalem (Izmir: no pub., 1951), p. 7 (hereafter cited Senior).
58. Cf. below, Chapter IV, notes 65–68.
59. "Nous savons enfin que Juvénal de Jérusalem chercha, à l'aide de faux documents, à se soustraire à la juridiction d'Antioche et à obtenir une autorité patriarcale sur la Palestine, la Phénicie et l'Arabie." — Dictionnaire de Droit Canonique (ed. R. Naz, incomplete, Paris: Librairie Letouzey et Ané, 1953–), V, 363.
60. Cf. M. Abel, O.P., "Sanctuaires Marials en Palestine," Maria, Études sur la Sainte Vierge, IV, 864.
61. Cf. M. Gordillo, S.J., "La muerte de Maria madre de Dios en la tradicion de la Iglesia de Jerusalén," Estudios Marianos (Madrid, 1942–), 9 (1950), 52. He offered a brief history of that church; cf. ibid., 52, 53.
62. "D'après le Typicon géorgien de l'Anastasis, l'eglise du Tombeau de la Vierge à Gethsemani serait l'oeuvre de l'empereur Maurice (582–602) qui imposa par décret le 15 août à tout l'empire comme date de la mort de Marie. Il est probable qu'avant cette consécration officielle il y ait eu depuis Juvénal vers 450 un culte ayant pour objet un sépulcre ancien taillé à la base du mont des Oliviers dans le Cédron ou Valée de Josaphat." — Abel, art. cit., 864.
63. Cf. Life of BVM, pp. 353, 354.
64. G. Quatman, House of Our Lady (Lima, Ohio: The American Society of Ephesus, 1962), p. 28 (hereafter cited Quatman).
65. H. Clarke, Ephesus (Smyrna, 1863), p. 28. Cf. Quatman, p. 12.
66. "Cum Patribus illis divino afflatis (et nos ipsis adessemus) tempore obdormitionis sanctissimae dominae nostrae Deiparae . . ." — MPG, 3, 699. Cf. ibid., 681.
67. Cf. op. cit., p. 9; above, Chapter III, note 36.
68. Cf. ibid., pp. 19, 20.
69. Cf. ibid., p. 20.
70. Cf. ibid., pp. 20–24.
71. Cf. ibid., p. 24.
72. Cf. loc. cit.

73. Cf. loc. cit.
74. Cf. Roschini, p. 25.
75. Cf. ibid., p. 26.
76. Cf. ibid., pp. 30–37.
77. Cf. ibid., p. 34.
78. Cf. S.R.C., 27 Apr. 1951 — AAS, 43 (1951), 385–399; S.R.C., 23 Mar. 1955, effective 1 Jan. 1956, Tit. II ad 11 — AAS, 47 (1955), 220.
79. Cf. op. cit., p. 66.
80. "Ci auguriamo che tutti coloro i quali vorranno ancora parlare della 'morte' di Maria SS., si astengono, perlomeno, dall' appellarsi ad una inesistente 'Tradizione' sulla medesima." — Ibid., p. 69. Cf. Jugie, "La Mort," 307.
81. Cf. below, Chapter IV, §§ 1, 2.
82. A. Neufeld, O.M.C., "Where did the Blessed Virgin Die?" *The Ecclesiastical Review*, 90 (1934), 164. One author who criticized the Ephesus thesis admitted at least the possibility, which cannot even be imagined for Jerusalem, that the Ephesus tradition predated the Council of Ephesus (431). Of this possibility before 431 he said: "The evidence for Ephesus is meagre, vague, equivocal. It does not justify a confident affirmation, though it may permit a temporate conjecture, that before 431 a tradition existed which localized the grave of Our Lady in Ephesus." — Burghardt, art. cit., 99.
83. ". . . l'existence d'un tombeau de la Sainte Vierge à Jérusalem ou dans les environs est complètement ignorée de la tradition des cinq premiers siècles et jusque vers l'an 570." — La Mort, p. 681. Translation mine. Cf. Roschini, p. 24.
84. Cf. La Mort, p. 681. Cf. also MPL, 22, 483–492; 54, 1101. To those significant omissions may be added also many others, e.g., that of Eusebius, an expert on Church history, and that of St. Helena who erected so many monuments during her stay in Palestine (ca. 326), but built none over a tomb or a site marking the Assumption.
85. Cf. La Mort, pp. 684, 685.
86. Cf. ibid., pp. 686, 687.
87. "La cause . . . est facile à trouver. Ce sont les recits apocryphes du *Transitus Mariae* qui ont insensiblement influencé la tradition topografique de la Ville Sainte." — Ibid., p. 686.
88. ". . . la Sainte Vierge semble bien être morte à Jérusalem, et qu'il est peu probable qu'elle soit jamais venue en Asie Mineure." — R. de la Broise, S.J., "Les dernières années de la Sainte Vierge," *Études* (Paris, 1856–), 72 (1897), 301. Translation mine.
89. "La Iglesia 'ortodoxa,' a pesar de su tradición litúrgica y literaria, unánime en colocar el sepulcro de la Virgen en Jerusalén, empieza a inclinarse abiertamente en favor de Efeso." — M. Gordillo, "Panaghia-Kapulu," *Ephemerides Mariologicae* (Madrid, 1951–), 2 (1952), 366 (hereafter cited Gordillo, "Panaghia").
90. Cf. La Mort, p. 383. Jugie, however, is not strictly an adversary of the Jerusalem tradition; in fact, he favors it slightly over Ephesus.
91. E.g., H. Vincent et F. Abel, *Jérusalem*, Vol. II, *Jérusalem Nouvelle* (Paris, 1926), 808.
92. Cf. below, Chapter IV, § 4.
93. Cf. loc. cit.
94. Cf. above, Chapter II, note 41.

95. Cf. *Life of BVM*, p. 362.
96. The first time, and only time as far as I can tell, that such a distinction was made was in 1922 by M. Hetzenauer, who wrote: "Salvo meliore iudicio, ego quidem censeo, quaestionem utrum Maria Ephesi peregrinata sit necne, a quaestione ubi mortua et sepulta et in coelum assumpta sit, penitus secernendum esse." — *Art. cit.*, 254.
97. Quatman, p. 6.
98. Cf. Senior, p. 14.
99. Cf. *MPG.*, 5, 943, 944.
100. Cf. Quatman, p. 8. This letter may very well exist, but I was unable to verify its source; I could not find it in *MPG*, 5, and, even if I had located it, would still have reason to doubt its authenticity.
101. Cf. *loc. cit.*
102. Cf. below, Chapter IV, § 1.
103. Quatman, p. 8.
104. Cf. *loc. cit.*; Senior, p. 14; Dierickx, *art. cit.*, 709.
105. "Jean prêcha à Antioche; ensuite, il s'en alla à Éphèse et la Mère de Notre-Seigneur l'accompagna. Aussitôt, ils furent relégués dans l'île de Patmos. En revenant d'exil, il prêcha à Éphèse et y bâtit une église. Ignace et Polycarpe le servaient; il ensevelit la bienheureuse Marie. Il vécut 73 ans et mourut après tous les apôtres; il fut enseveli à Éphèse." — *La Mort*, p. 96, note 3. Translation mine.
106. Cf. Quatman, p. 8; Senior, p. 14; Dierickx, *art. cit.*, 709.
107. Cf. *La Mort*, *loc. cit.*; Dierickx, *loc. cit.* The text of Bar Hebraeus follows: "Ioannes . . . fundavit Ecclesiam Ephesi. Eidem ministrarunt Ignatius et Polycarpus. Idemque beatam Mariam sepelivit, nec quisquam novit ubi eam posuerit." — *La Mort*, p. 305, note 2.
108. Cf. *La Mort*, p. 305.
109. Cf. *ibid.*, pp. 303, 305.
110. Cf. *ibid.*, p. 96, note 3.
111. Cf. Quatman, p. 9.
112. "A trois lieues d'Éphèse, vers l'orient, existe un gros village du nom de Kirkindje, composé de quatre mille habitants, tous grecs schismatiques." — Barnabé, p. 265.
113. Cf. above, Chapter II, note 42.
114. This means the Mountain of Nightingales. In 1959 the name was changed by the Turkish Government to *Meryem Dagh* — Mountain of Mary. Cf. Dierickx, *art. cit.*, 712; below, Chapter V, note 22.
115. E. Poulin reported that for the feast of the Assumption, 1897, there were more than two hundred Kirkindjites who climbed the mountain to Panaya; cf. *Historique*, p. 26.
116. Cf. *loc. cit.*
117. "Huius pagi Christifideles, qui originem ab antiquis ephesinis deducere videntur, in sacello modo memorato, iuxta patrum suorum localem traditionem, quae tamen doctrinae totius Ecclesiae orthodoxae, Hierosolymis faventi, contradicit, quotannis cum magno populi clerique concursu festum B. Mariae V. dormitionis celebrant ibique, praeter suos liturgicos libros, sacra faciunt." — Descuffi, "De loco," 215.
118. Cf. *Historique*, p. 166.
119. "Après le crucifiement de N.-S. J.-C., notre sainte Vierge mère de Dieu était sous la garde de saint Jean; et ils vivaient à Éphèse . . . de là elle se

porta sur le mont Bulbul-Dagh . . . et c'est là dans sa demeure de Capouli qu'eut lieu sa 'Dormition' dont on fait la fête le 15 août." — *Dict. Bib. Sup.*, I, 651. Translation mine. This is but a brief excerpt from the lengthy document. For more details of this investigation, as well as for satisfactory answers to a group of objections raised by the opponents of Ephesus concerning this testimonial, cf. Euzet, "Remarques," 63–66.

120. Cf. *Historique*, p. 27. "Mais enfin, leur temoignage de parole et de fait, s'il n'est pas décisif, ne doit-il pas être considéré comme d'un grand poids?" — Euzet, "Remarques," 66.
121. Cf. above, Chapter II, note 42.
122. ". . . ils parlaient plutôt turc . . ." — *Historique*, p. 25.
123. "Quam domum sacelli ad instar super antiquissima fundamenta extructam, vicinioris pagi (Kirkinge dicti) incolae, religione graeci-schismatici, sermone autem Turcarum loquentes, idiomate ex graecis turcisque derivationibus mixto 'Panaghia Capuli' (id est Sanctissimae portam seu domum) appellant." — Descuffi, "De loco," 215.
124. This is obvious from what has been said of its transformation into a church; cf. above, Chapter II, notes 31–33. It is clear also from other archaeological indications, e.g., a small vestibule was added to the front of the house in the seventh century; cf. below, Chapter IV, notes 172, 173.
125. Cf. Quatman, p. 12.
126. Cf. below, Chapter V, § 2.
127. Cf. below, Chapter VI, notes 28–33.
128. Žužić, p. 81.
129. *Ibid.*, p. 76.
130. Quatman, p. vi.
131. *Lib. mirac.*, I, 30: "In Epheso autem habetur locus in quo hic apostolus Evangelium quod ex eius nomine in Ecclesia legitur scripsit. . . In ea urbe Maria Magdalena quiescit, nullum super se tegumen habens. . . In ea et septem Dormientes habentur. . ." — *MPL*, 71, 730, 731. Translation mine.
132. Cf. Descuffi, "La Maison," 34.
133. J. Richter, "The Monuments of Christian Art at Ephesus," *The Academy* (London, 1869–1920), 14 (1878), 98.
134. Cf. Descuffi, "La Maison," 34. The dates given for the transfer of the relics to Byzantium vary somewhat but fall within the reign of Leo VI, the Philosopher (866–911). After two centuries the relics were moved to Alsace, and from there to southern France.
135. ". . . Madeleine . . . est morte à Ephese: et il est assez naturel de croire qu'elle y avoit accompagne le Ste Vierge." — *Memoires*, I, 492.
136. E.g., Clarke, *Ephesus*, pp. 28, 29.
137. The archaeological expert is named in the following quotation: "We know today, quite positively, that Mary Magdalene, too — long before the Seven Sleepers, was buried there. Louis Massignon, professor at the Collège de France in Paris, an outstanding expert in Christian archaeology, recently identified the large sarcophagus (coffin) of St. Mary Magdalene at the very entrance of the cave of the Seven Sleepers. On the other hand, the Austrian Institute of Archaeology of the Vienna University had the fortune to discover the entire area of the Basilica and the necropolis around it (containing some 700 different caves, with many graves of martyrs)." — Žužić, p. 75. Cf. Descuffi, "La Maison," 34.

138. Ibid., p. 78.
139. Ibid., pp. 73–75.
140. Cf. ibid., p. 79.
141. Cf. Toksöz, pp. 102, 103.
142. Žužić, p. 79. "It is here [grotto of the Seven Sleepers] where according to the Koran — the first trumpets of the Last Judgment have to resound and where Jesus Christ will judge all men of all generations, of all nations, races and faiths." — Quatman, p. 2.
143. Cf. Clarke, Ephesus, p. 31.
144. Loc. cit.
145. Cf. Žužić, p. 81.
146. Ibid., pp. 80, 81.

Chapter IV — Notes

1. Cf., e.g., Z. Zitelli-Natali, *Epitome Historico-Canonica Conciliorum Generalium* (Romae, 1881), p. 68; J. Mansi, *Sacrorum Conciliorum Nova et Amplissima Collectio* (53 vols. in 60, Parisiis, 1901–1927), IV, passim (hereafter cited *Mansi*).
2. J. Quasten, *Patrology*, Vol. II, *The Ante-Nicene Literature after Irenaeus* (Westminster, Md.: The Newman Press, 1948), 81.
3. "Quare et Nestorius impiae haereseos instaurator, cum in Ephesiorum civitatem pervenisset, *in qua Ioannes Theologus, et deipara Virgo sancta Maria,* a sanctorum patrum et episcoporum coetu seipsum abalienans. . ." — Mansi, IV, 1242. Translation and italics are mine.
4. ". . . dans le pays des Éphésiens, à l'endroit où arrivèrent Jean le théologien et la Sainte Vierge Marie mère de Dieu. . ." — Euzet, "Remarques," 59, note 8. Translation and italics are mine. Euzet has reproduced the study of E. Delebecque, "Sur une lettre du concile d'Éphèse," which appeared originally in *Bull. de l'Ass. Guillaume Budé,* 1956, 74–78. Professor Edouard Delebecque of the Faculty of Aix held without reservation for the arrival and sojourn. Cf. Descuffi, "La Maison," 36.
5. Cf. above, Chapter III, § 1; below, Chapter IV, § 2.
6. "In talibus propositionibus ellipticis secundum optimos grammaticos Krüger et Kühner-Gerth communiter tertia persona indicativi *praesentis* intelligenda est; quod si contextus tempus praesens excludit, tertia persona indicativi *imperfecti* intelligatur." — Hetzenauer, art. cit., 248. Translation mine.
7. "Quae cum ita sint, in fine propositionis relativae non *sunt,* sed *erant* addere debemus, quo facto sensus propositionis: 'in qua civitate personae Ioannis Theologi et deiparae Virginis sanctae Mariae *erant,*' i.e. aliquando commorabantur." — *Ibid.,* 249. Translation mine.
8. Cf. Mansi, IV, 1233.
9. Cf. Mansi, IV, 1123, 1230, 1238, 1242, 1251, 1306, 1318, 1331, 1465, plus the one just mentioned, of course, 1233.
10. Cf. Hetzenauer, art. cit., 248.
11. Cf. below, Chapter IV, § 2.
12. Cf. *The Great Commentary of Cornelius à Lapide,* pp. 243, 244.
13. *Memoires,* I, 496.
14. Cf. *Memoires,* I, 496.
15. *Dictionary of the Holy Bible* (5 vols., London, 1829), II, 117.
16. Cf. above, Chapter III, note 35.
17. "Aliqui subintelligunt, aliquando habitarunt, alii aedes habent." — Mansi,

IV, 1242. Translation mine. Aedes may be understood as homes, churches, or any buildings, but by contrast with habitarunt probably meant churches.
18. Cf. "Kleine Kritiken," Literarische Rundschau für das katholische Deutschland (Aachen-Freiburg i. Br., 1875–1914), 22 (1896), 345, 346.
19. Cf. DACL, V, Pt. 2 (Paris, 1922), 135, 136; Dict. Bib. Sup., I, 646.
20. "Les mots: Jean le Théologien et la Vierge Théotocos Sainte Marie désignent par les noms de ses deux patrons et titulaires l'église principale d'Éphèse, où fut réuni le concile." — La Mort, p. 97.
21. Cf. loc. cit.
22. Cf. Mansi, IV, 1230.
23. Cf. MPG, 76, 472.
24. Cf. Mansi, IV, 1238.
25. Cf. La Mort, p. 98.
26. "Vos hortor, fratres beatissimi, respiciatur illa sola dilectio, in qua utique, secundum vocem Ioannis apostoli, cuius reliquias praeferentes veneramini, manere debemus." — Mansi, IV, 1286. Translation mine.
27. E.g.: "Ephesis ergo, quibus est nota fidei praedicatio. . ." — Loc. cit.
28. Cf. La mort, p. 98.
29. ". . . sacra templa, invictissimorumque martyrum aedes praeclusisse, ita ut ne orare quidem volentibus licuerit; e locis usque adeo remotis venientibus, sanctorumque ac triumphatorum martyrum, maxime vero beatissimi Ioannis theologi ac evangelistae (quem summam apud dominum nostrum fiduciam familiaritatemque obtinuisse constat) monumenta omnia complectendi desiderio flagrantibus." — Mansi, IV, 1275. Translation mine. This is part of the letter which also excommunicated Cyril and Memnon, who threw the council into disorder.
30. The preferential mention of the tomb of St. John is in perfect accord with the theory that in the early centuries of Christianity in Ephesus the cult of St. John overshadowed that of the Blessed Virgin Mary; cf. below, Chapter IV, notes 54, 55.
31. Various scholars proposed dates ranging from the first century to the time of the council. Cf. T. Wood, Discoveries at Ephesus (London, 1877), p. 99; Gordillo, "Panaghia," 374; Tallon, art. cit., 895; Hetzenauer, art. cit., 250; Žužić, p. 63.
32. Cf. Žužić, p. 65. The Museion was very likely destroyed in 263 by a Gothic invasion; cf. Gordillo, loc. cit.
33. The Kathisma, first church in Jerusalem dedicated to Mary, was built in 450 or later; cf. Toksöz, p. 35; above, note 72. The Chacepratene, first in Constantinople, was completed in 458; cf. Toksöz, p. 35. Santa Maria Maggiore in Rome was built in commemoration of the Council of Ephesus and its definitions: "Il ricordo del Concilio di Efeso è perpetuato a Roma dalla grande basilica di S. Maria Maggiore, che il papa Sisto III (432) fece costruire dopo il Concilio e dedicò alla Madre de Dio. . . ." — Enciclopedia Cattolica (11 vols., Città del Vaticano, 1948–1952), V, 118. Cf. also DACL, V, 136.
34. Toksöz, pp. 62, 63. Cf. DACL, V, 135–137; Hetzenauer, art. cit., 249.
35. Žužić, pp. 65–67.
36. E.g., DACL, V, 135–137; Dict. Bib. Sup., I, 646; Dictionnaire de la Bible (ed. F. Vigouroux, 5 vols., 2 ed., Paris, 1912), II, 1843.
37. "Etrange échappatoire heureusement fermée depuis qu'en 1930 fut découverte, dans le nartex de la basilique, la plaque où l'archevêque Hypatios,

Notes

du temps de Justinien, mentionne que c'est bien là l'église Sainte-Marie où eut lieu le concile." — Descuffi, "La Maison," 36.

38. "Felix Romanus, patre Constantio, Aureliano imperatore praefuit Ecclesiae. Constituit, ut Missa supra memorias et sepulcra Martyrum celebraretur." — Breviarium Romanum, 30 May.
39. J. Jungmann, S.J., *The Early Church* [*Liturgical Studies*, Vol. VI], tr. by F. Brunner, C.SS.R. (Notre Dame, Ind.: University of Notre Dame Press, 1959), p. 186. Cf. L. Duchesne, *Christian Worship, its Origin and Evolution* (New York & Toronto: The Macmillan Co., 1949), p. 402; S. Many, *Praelectiones de locis sacris* (Parisiis, 1904), p. 25.
40. "Fuit id prioribus Ecclesiae temporibus usu receptum, ut Ecclesiae seu Templa nonnisi in memoriam, ac sub nomine Sanctorum Martyrum, qui pro Christo fortiter certantes occubuerunt, conderentur. Martyrum vero nomine comprehenduntur Apostoli, qui et ipsi omnes Martyres sunt, nec excluditur Beatissima Virgo Deipara quae a S. Hieronymo plusquam martyr appellatur." — C. Guyet, S.J., *Heortologia* (Urbini, 1729), p. 36. Translation mine. Cf. M. Righetti, *Manuale di Storia Liturgica* (4 vols., Milano: Editrice Ancora, 1950), IV, 377.
41. ". . . et quidem plerumque iis ipsis locis, in quibus passi fuerant, aut ubi eorum corpora reposita iacerent, erigi consuevissent." — Guyet, *loc. cit.*
42. *Codex Canonum Ecclesiae Africae* (419) — Mansi, III, 782. Translation mine; the Latin text is found in the Appendix [A]. The *Codex* derived this text from canon 14, V Council of Carthage (398), and canon 50, African Council (399). Canon 14 is practically identical to the text cited. The word *property* used above is for *possessio* in the text. Whether *possessio* was used in its legally specific sense or in a vulgar sense as translated above is unimportant to the meaning, for in either case a physical place is connoted which was frequented by the saint, and which had some special connection with the saint by reason of either possession or actual ownership. It may also be noted here incidentally that Emperor Theodosius I had authorized on February 26, 386, the erection of a large monument over the tomb of a dead person regarded as a saint. *Cod. Theo.*, IX, 17, 7: "Habeant vero in potestate, si quolibet in loco sanctorum est aliquis conditus, pro eius veneratione quo martyrium vocandum sit addant quod voluerint fabricarum." — *Theodosiani Libri XVI* (ed. T. Mommsen, Vol. I, Pt. 2, 2 ed., Berolini: Apud Weidmannos, 1954), 466.
43. Cf. Hetzenauer, *art. cit.*, 250. He noted that even Theodore Zahn, the Protestant exegete, now admits that the only possible reason for Mary's basilica in Ephesus is that she lived there; cf. *loc. cit.*
44. Cf. above, Chapter III, § 1.
45. For details, cf. Žužić, p. 37.
46. *Ibid.*, p. 39.
47. ". . . cuius reliquias praeferentes veneramini. . ." — Mansi, IV, 1286.
48. The rescript is reconstructed in *DACL*, V, 139.
49. Cf. above, Chapter III, § 1.
50. Richter, *art. cit.*, 98. The Latin phrase in the quotation means: "They walked to St. John the Evangelist [Church] *in a lovely place near Ephesus*." The legend of the manna and assumption of John may be found in Žužić, pp. 42, 43.
51. Cf. *loc. cit.*
52. Cf. below, Chapter V, note 61.

53. Wood, *Discoveries at Ephesus*, p. 183. Cf. above, Chapter II, note 22.
54. Ephesus was the first Marian city of the Christian world. "Éphèse, avec la maison de la Sainte Vierge et la basilique du Concile, fut la première ville mariale du monde chrétien." — Descuffi, "La Maison," 42.
55. "Le culte marial, aux premiers siècles, déjà en bonne voie de développement, était bien loin d'avoir l'ampleur que nous le voyons acquérir dans la suite. Elles étaient bien rares les églises portant son nom à Jérusalem, à Constantinople, à Rome. Quel contraste, quand on pense à la floraison des cathédrales dédiées à Notre-Dame pendant le moyen-âge!" — Euzet, "Remarques," 53. Translation mine.
56. E.g., those of Tillemont, Serry, Dom Calmet, Natalis Alexander, C. Fleury, and others.
57. "De Feria Sexta in Parasceve," c. 7, 101 — *Omnia Opera* (12 vols., Romae, 1747–1751), X, 229, 230.
58. "De Festo Assumptionis Beatissimae Virginis ad diem 15 Augusti," c. 8 — *Ibid.*, 595–616.
59. "Ut autem praecipuum suum in Matrem amorem declaret, ei dixisse, ut Ioannem deinceps in filii loco diligeret; itidemque Ioanni, ut B. Mariam perinde ad Matrem coleret: Ioannem mandata Christi abunde implevisse, qui omni officio, et pietate B. Mariam semper coluit, domi secum habuit, donec mansit in Palestina, profectusque Ephesum eam secum adduxit, ubi tandem Beata Mater ex hac vita ad Coelum convolavit. Quod autem Christus Ioanni Matrem commendaverit, sacri inde Interpretes arguunt, D. Iosephum tum temporis in vivis non fuisse." — *Omnia Opera*, X, 229, 230. Translation mine.
60. Cf. above, Chapter III, notes 21–23.
61. "Huius nihilominus gravissimi Patris sensus, aliorum et, quod caput est, Ecclesiae universae sensui adversatur, qui mortuam eam censent: ita ut tota controversia sit, num in civitate Ephesina, an in civitate Hierosolymitana mortua fuerit, iuxta erudite collecta a Tillemont. . ." — *Omnia Opera*, I, 117.
62. In his treatise on the Assumption, Benedict showed that the common opinion of both Greeks and Latins was that Mary died: "Itaque concludendum, B. Virginem obiisse, eiusque animam corpore fuisse seclusam. . ." — *Ibid.*, X, 597.
63. "Sed nihil ea de re quidquam ut exploratum certumque definiri potest. . . ." — *Ibid.*, 598.
64. Cf. *loc. cit.*
65. "Huc accedit, Iuvenalem a Cyrillo Alexandrino, et Leone Magno seditionis multorumque scelerum, ac praesertim corruptarum tabularum reum eius existimari." — *Omnia Opera*, X, 600.
66. "Qui autem aliorum scripta falsare solitus erat, annon falsam Epistolam Marciano, et Pulcheriae scribere potuit? Falsam, inquam, non quae suum mentiretur Auctorem, sed quae falsum de Mariano Sepulchro Gethsemani iuxta Hierosolymam extante testimonium contineret." — *Loc. cit.*
67. "Nemo est qui non videat." — *Loc. cit.*
68. ". . . iuxta iurisperitos *falsus in uno praesumitur falsus in omnibus.*" — *Loc. cit.*
69. "Qui Iuvenalis auctoritatem respuunt, nec sibi persuadere possunt, B. Virginem Hierosolymis obiisse, putant mortuam esse Ephesi." — *Loc. cit.*

70. ". . . nulla alia huic loco tribui potest sententia quam quod Ioannis et B. Virginis sepulcra essent Ephesi." — *Omnia Opera*, X, 601.
71. "Hanc autem sententiam quidam minime probant." — *Ibid.*, 600. Translation and italics are mine.
72. ". . . putant [Mariam] mortuam esse Ephesi." — *Loc. cit.* Cf. above, Chapter IV, note 69.
73. ". . . concludamus . . . suspicemus. . ." — *Omnia Opera*, X, 600.
74. Cf. *ibid.*, 601.
75. Cf. Barnabé, p. 101.
76. "Ioannes . . . profectusque Ephesum eam secum adduxit, ubi tandem Beata Mater ex hac vita ad Coelum convolavit." — *Omnia Opera*, X, 230.
77. Senior, p. 15.
78. ". . . Beatissimam Virginem in ea cum Apostolis diu moratam fuisse." — *Pii IX pontificis maximi Acta* (9 vols., Romae, 1854–1878), I, 59.
79. Cf. *Historique*, pp. 34–37.
80. Cf. *ibid.*, p. 38.
81. *Acta Sanctae Sedis* (Romae, 1865–1908), 28 (1896), 685; *Analecta Ecclesiastica*, 4 (1896), 144. The strategic portion of the document appears in the Appendix [B]. Shortly after this Leo granted a plenary indulgence for the pilgrimage to Mary's home on May 20, 1896; cf. below, Chapter VI, note 4.
82. ". . . ita ut per haec indulgentiae visitationi illius sanctuarii adnexae perinde acquirantur, ac si Sanctuarium fuisset reapse visitatum." — *Loc. cit.*
83. Cf. Senior, p. 21.
84. "De his factis edoctus Leo PP. XIII anno 1903 hanc adnotationem, quondam ablatam, in diario romano die XV augusti restituit: 'Ephesi . . . ubi iuxta probabiliorem opinionem Maria mortua est.'" — Descuffi, "De loco," 215. Cf. Duyuran, p. 97.
85. Cf. Descuffi, *loc. cit.*; Duyuran, *loc. cit.*; *Historique*, p. 40.
86. Cf. Descuffi, *loc. cit.*; *Historique*, *loc. cit.* The complete text of the letter, as reproduced by Euzet, appears in the Appendix [C].
87. "Le Pape sainte Pie X, convaincu par le texte de saint Jean: *Accepit eam in sua*, se déclara en particulier pour Panaya." — Descuffi, "La Maison," 41.
88. Cf. *Historique*, p. 41. The short quotations above read: "A-t-on trouvé le Tombeau?" — "Pas encore Saint-Père . . . Très Saint Père, je sais que vous croyez comme votre illustre prédécesseur Benoît XIV que la Sainte Vierge est morte à Éphèse." — *Loc. cit.* The following quotations also indicate the preference of St. Pius for the Ephesus tradition: "Pie X . . . avoue n'avait jamais pu concevoir l'hypothèse que la Sainte Vierge fut morte à Jérusalem." — Duyuran, p. 16; "Quant à l'attitude du St.-Siège à part Benoît XIV, nous avons eu dans nos pours les Papes Léon XIII et Pie X, qui l'ont favorablement accueillie." — *Ibid.*, p. 97.
89. For the pilgrimages to Panaya, cf. below, Chapter VI, § 1.
90. Cf. Senior, pp. 21, 22.
91. Cf. Duyuran, p. 64. The substance of the lecture was printed in *Verbum Divinum*, 2 (1922), 246–254, under the title "De peregrinatione B. Mariae V. in Panaghia Capuli prope Ephesum."
92. It was called *Un dernier Mot sur le Lieu où est morte la Sainte Vierge* (Rome-Paris, 1921).
93. Cf. *Historique*, p. 42. The complete text of the letter, as reproduced by Euzet, appears in the Appendix [D].

94. Cf. above, Chapter III, note 40.
95. Cf. below, Chapter IV, § 4.
96. Cf. below, Chapter V, note 40; Chapter VI, note 22.
97. The broadcast was the *Emission Française: Dimanche, 3 Juin, 13 h. 1/4*. The text of the program, "La Maison de la Sainte Vierge à Panaya Kapulu," appears in the Appendix [E].
98. Cf. Quatman, p. 29.
99. Cf. Duyuran, pp. 109, 110. The substance of this document, No. 258.115 — 19 June, 1951, as reproduced by Archbishop Descuffi, appears in the Appendix [F].
100. Cf. *loc. cit.*
101. The document was No. 6320/61 — 18 Aug. 1961. The decree, as authentically reproduced and sealed by the Archbishop of Smyrna, appears in the Appendix [G].
102. Cf. *Historique*, pp. 130, 165.
103. The reason why Pope John did not visit Mary's home is not known to me or to Archbishop Descuffi himself. It surely could not have been a lack of volition. It may well have been, however, a lack of time, or any of innumerable possibilities, which do not exclude the adverse conditions in Turkey at the time, difficulty of ascent to the top of Mary's Mountain, and inadequate facilities for the unavoidable overnight stay.
104. Quatman, p. 29.
105. Quatman, p. 31. *Meryem Ana* means Mother Mary; cf. below, Chapter V, note 34; Chapter VI, note 65.
106. "Eccovi qui . . . il *Motu proprio* che fissa la data della solenne apertura del Concilio Ecumenico Vaticano II. Questa data è l'11 ottobre dell'anno 1962, ora incominciato: festa liturgica della Maternità divina di Maria SSma, richiamo quindi al Concilio di Efeso — terzo ecumenico — che questo dogma Mariano proclamò." — Allocutio . . . in festo Purificationis B.M.V. post oblatos Beatissimo Patri cereos, 2 Feb., 1962; *AAS*, 54 (1962), 103. Translation mine.
107. Cf., e.g., Appendix [F].
108. Cf. Tillemont, "Que la Vierge est aparemment morte à Ephese." — Memoires, I, 491–493; Benedict XIV, *Omnia Opera*, X, 595–616. Among other early scholars who favored Ephesus were Serry, Enger, Dom Calmet, Baronius, Baillet, N. Alexander, C. Fleury, C. Lenormant, E. Hello, Curtus, L. Bloy, and Farges.
109. For the announcement, cf. above, Chapter II, note 55.
110. Cf. below, Chapter V, notes 1–7.
111. "Les visions de C. Emmerick ne sont qu'une abominable imposture. Dans quelle mesure la prétendue voyante et son associé Cl. Brentano se partagent le mérite d'avoir compilé tant d'evangiles apocryphes et de légendes mensongères, ce n'est pas à moi de la définir et je crois que l'on peut employer plus utilement son temps. . . . Pardonnez-moi de vous parler ainsi, mais je suis breton et j'ai l'habitude d'appeler un chat un chat. D'autre part, ma conscience religieuse et morale me fait un devoir de protester contre l'establissement d'un sanctuaire dans de telles conditions. C'est ici que je voudrais avoir l'eloquence de saint Paul pour vous supplier de ne pas aller plus loin et de ne pas exposer votre société et même l'Eglise aux sarcasmes trop mérités qui ne manqueront pas d'accueillir votre découverte. Je crois voir que vous être plus entraîné que convaincu. Pour l'amour de Dieu,

Notes 155

résistez!" — *Historique*, p. 29. Translation mine. The original of this letter is in the archives of the Lazarist motherhouse in Paris, Rue de Sèvres, 95.
112. Cf. *ibid.*, pp. 29, 30. At a later date, October 1, 1897, the superior general congratulated Poulin for his accomplishments and confessed his belief in Mary's home; cf. *ibid.*, p. 107.
113. Cf. *ibid.*, pp. 32, 33.
114. "Das Mariengrab in Ephesus," *Der Katholik* (Mainz, 1821–1918), 74, 2 (Ser. 3, 10, 1894), 385–407.
115. *Wo ist das Grab der heiligen Jungfrau Maria?* (Würzburg, 1895).
116. "Quand même la chose serait vraie, ce ne serait pas à notre congrégation de faire de cette question son affaire propre." — *Historique*, pp. 38, 39. Translation mine.
117. Cf. *loc. cit.* The brochure appeared anonymously, with the approbation of Timoni, as *Panaghia-Capouli ou maison de la sainte Vierge près d'Éphèse* (Paris-Poitiers, 1896).
118. Cf. Bibliography.
119. E.g., M. J. Berger was the pseudonym adopted by Arsène du Châtel, Capuchin provincial of Istanbul, for his offensive articles in *Saint François et la Terre-Sainte, Échos de Terre-Sainte*, 1897–1899. Later, and for a somewhat different reason, Senior was adopted as a pseudonym by Archbishop Descuffi for the publication of works which had several collaborators.
120. *Das Grab der heiligen Jungfrau Maria* (Mainz, 1896). He attacked Ephesus for the third time in 1900 with *Das Haus und das Grab der heiligen Jungfrau Maria* (Mainz, 1900).
121. The article of reply was "Über Ephesus nach der 'Wohnung Marias' auf dem Nachtigallenberge," *Stimmen aus Maria-Laach*, 51 (1896), 471–493. For some of his other articles, cf. Bibliography.
122. *Ephèse ou Jérusalem, tombeau de la sainte Vierge* (Paris-Poitiers, 1897).
123. Cf. above, Chapter II, note 41.
124. The refutal was *Le Tombeau de la sainte Vierge à Éphèse* (Paris-Poitiers, 1905).
125. Cf. above, Chapter III, note 88.
126. Cf. above, Chapter III, note 36.
127. "A la vérité je ne regarde pas comme positivement certaine la tradition de Jérusalem. Mais, jusqu'ici, je ne vois pas de fondement solide pour la tradition d'Éphèse." — Euzet, "Remarques," 70. Translation mine. Cf. *Analecta Bollandiana* (Paris-Bruxelles, 1882–), 16 (1897), 189–191. DeSmedt's successor, Peeters, tried unsuccessfully to inspire doubts about the authenticity of the council text; cf. *ibid.*, 51 (1933), 133, 134.
128. "Que si nous ne pouvons avoir une certitude absolue sur les lieux précis, du moins nous devons admirer la pensée de l'Église de Jérusalem." — "La Dormition de la Sainte Vierge et la Maison de Jean-Marc," *Revue Biblique* (Paris, 1892–), 8 (1899), 599.
129. Cf. Euzet, "Remarques," 69. Cf. also *Revue Biblique*, 6 (1897), 136–138; 8 (1899), 142, 597. Euzet's remark is accurate, except for the earliest notice of *Panaya* in the *Revue Biblique*, which was quite a contrast to the attitude of later years; cf. *ibid.*, 1 (1892), 463.
130. Cf. Bibliography.
131. Cf. above, Chapter IV, note 121.
132. Cf. above, Chapter IV, note 18. Cf. also "Ist Maria zu Jerusalem oder zu

Ephesus gestorben?" *Theologische Revue* (Münster i. W., 1902–), 5 (1906), 569–577; this was an article-review combination.
133. Cf. above, Chapter II, note 18.
134. *Die Dormitio Sanctae Virginis und das Haus der Johannes-Markus* (Leipzig, 1899). This appeared also as an article in *Neue Kirchliche Zeitschrift* (Leipzig, 1890–1933), 10 (1899).
135. *Voyage aux sept Églises de l'Apocalypse* (Paris, 1899).
136. "Ce qu'il ya a de plus appréciable dans la découverte récente (au mont du Rossignol), c'est la bonne fortune du Turc qui par l'entremise d'un chrétien a vendu à une religieuse enthousiaste et loyale pour 35,000 francs une ruine sans valeur." — *Ibid.*, p. 135. Translation mine.
137. *Panaghia Kapuli: Das neuentdeckte Wohn-und Herbe-Haus der heil. Jungfrau Maria bei Ephesus* (Dülmen i. W., 1906).
138. *Mariologie des hl. Hieronymus* (Münster i. W., 1913).
139. *Ephesus. Die letzte Wohnstätte der hl. Jungfrau* (Münster i. W., 1931).
140. Portion of the letter of Niessen, 27 May 1937, to L. Dworschak: "Plus j'avance dans la littérature du sujet, plus je constate qu'il n'y a pas d'objection sérieuse contre, et plus s'affermit en moi la conviction que le lieu de la Dormition de la Vierge et de son Assomption se trouve à Éphèse." — *Historique*, pp. 100, 101. Translation mine.
141. Senior, p. 19. For details on Carra de Vaux, cf. *loc. cit.*
142. "Avant de monter à Panaghia-Capouli, le 27 Septembre 1899, j'étais convaincu, par l'étude de la tradition hiérosolymitaine relative au tombeau de la Sainte Vierge à Gethsémani et surtout par l'étude de saint Epiphane, qu'il fallait chercher le tombeau de la Vierge ailleurs que dans les environs de Jérusalem. Cette opinion n'était nullement motivée par l'autorité de C. Emmerick. Or, le 27 Septembre j'ai constaté entre la description de C. Emmerick et les choses de Panaghia-Capouli une concordance telle qu'elle ne me semble susceptible que d'une seule explication. C. Emmerick a contemplé en vision le site et la maison actuellement dénommée Capouli-Panaghia." — *Historique*, p. 32.
143. "Rien de serieux pour Jérusalem, mais beaucoup contre. Grandissimes probabilités pour Éphèse. Arrivera-t-on jusqu'à la certitude absolue que l'histoire voudrait sur cette question?" — *Ibid.*, p. 95. The statement appeared in the periodical *Annales de la Mission*, 1942, 140, a publication of the French Vincentians.
144. Senior, p. 20.
145. *Loc. cit.*
146. J. Marta, *Ni Éphèse, ni Panaghia-Capouli, mais Jérusalem* (Jérusalem, 1910); M. Gabrielovich, *Ni Sion, ni Gethsémani, Adieu! Jérusalem* (Constantinople, 1910).
147. Cf. above, Chapter III, note 40.
148. Cf. *Vie de Saint Marie-Madeleine* (Paris, 1933). One of his articles, "L'Habitation de la Vierge à Éphèse," later appeared in *Revue Notre Dame d'Éphèse* (Istanbul, 1957–), 4 (1960), 171–180.
149. Cf. above, Chapter II, note 45.
150. "Le Père Jugie et la question de lieu où est morte la Sainte Vierge," *Divus Thomas*, 52 (1949), 345–359.
151. Cf. *Peregrinatio Religiosa* (Regensburg, Münster, 1950), pp. 172, 173.
152. "Mary's Last Home," *The Ecclesiastical Review*, 123 (1950), 261.
153. "Et un critique des plus intransigeants de notre temps, Don Leclerq,

retient que 'la tradition universellement reçue marquait a Éphèse la mort de la Sainte Vierge Marie et qu'on y conservait un édifice regardé comme son tombeau. Le Concile lui-même consacra cette tradition.'" — "Éphèse ou Jérusalem," *Marie* (Nicolet, Quebec, 1947–), 5 (1951), 16.
154. Cf. above, Chapter II, note 25.
155. Cf. above, Chapter III, note 89. This author had published an article on Mary's death and tomb in Jerusalem in 1950 and, as an exception to the rule, it did not attack Ephesus; cf. above, Chapter III, note 61. He repeated the weak and tired arguments of the apocrypha, sepulcher, and writings that favored Jerusalem. Then great publicity was accorded Panaya throughout Europe in 1951, on and after its dedication. Gordillo's article of 1952 appeared almost as if in defense and justification of his article of 1950.
156. *Wiedererwachendes Ephesus* (Basel: Verlag-Stiftung "Für Ephesus," 1953).
157. Kopp, *Das Mariengrab. Jerusalem?-Ephesus?* (Paderborn: Ferd. Schöningh, 1955); Euzet, "Remarques"; cf. above, Chapter III, note 32. Euzet's reply was more than adequate.
158. "Quamvis hac de re *scientifica*, ut aiunt, certitudo sit omnino impossibilis, attamen ephesina traditio longe probabilior immo probabilissima apparet et moraliter certa. Panaya . . . ut hunc locum esse a quo Beata Virgo Maria in coelum assumpta est non solum pie, sed prudenter credere possumus." — Euzet, "Remarques," 47. Translation mine.
159. Cf. above, Chapter III, note 6.
160. "Si l'on veut examiner les faits avec sérénite et en toute objectivité, on doit reconnaître qu'ils forment un cadre qui limite les hypothèses. Mais nous ne trouvons aucune difficulté majeure qui contredise la possibilité d'un passage de Marie à Éphèse, que postulent par ailleurs de façon indéniable, des monuments anciens et une très ancienne tradition orale." — Tallon, *art. cit.*, 896. Translation mine.
161. Cf. above, Chapter III, note 64. While the booklet is by and large a summary of information from other sources, and practically a reprint of Senior, *Ephesus, Hazreti Meryem Ana Evi, House of Our Lady* (Izmir, Korsini Basimevi, 1959), it does contain some new information and, by reason of format, size, and readability, serves a definite need and purpose.
162. Cf. above, Chapter II, note 17. Euzet died in Izmir, June 20, 1961, several months after he had compiled and published his book at the age of 87. His sources included the *Registers of Historical Manuscripts of Panaya* and the *Journal du Superieur*, the diary of Poulin; they are at present kept at the French Hospital in Izmir.
163. Cf. Quatman, p. 1.
164. ". . . d'après l'Institut Archéologique de Vienne, la ruine de Panaghia Capouli peut remonter au IVe siècle." — *Historique*, p. 44. Cf. *Dict. Bib. Sup.*, I. 650.
165. Cf. *Historique*, p. 45.
166. "Une partie au moins de l'édifice remonte au Ier siècle." — *Loc. cit.*
167. "La Maison peut être aussi bien du VIIe siècle que du Ier et du Ier que du VIIe. Je mets en défi de prouver l'un plutôt que l'autre." — *Historique*, pp. 44, 45. Translation mine.
168. "Pour ce qui est des fondements, il les estime du Ier siècle." — *Ibid.*, p. 45.
169. Cf. *ibid.*, pp. 46, 47. Shortly after that lecture Lambakis published his *Hoi*

heptà Astéres tēs Apokalýpseos (Athenai, 1909) — Seven Stars of the Apocalypse.
170. Senior, p. 19.
171. Ibid., p. 18.
172. Ibid., p. 19.
173. Cf. Life of BVM, p. 382; above, Chapter II, note 32.
174. Cf. below, Chapter V, note 10.; Quatman, pp. 19, 25.
175. "La construction de la Maison de la Vierge Marie appartient-elle au Ier siècle, ou tout au moins ses fondations. . . ." — F. Psalty, "Les ruines de la maison de la Vierge Marie à Panayakapouli," Actes du X. Congres International d'Études Byzantines (Istanbul: Comite d'Organisation, 1957), 154.
176. Cf. Psalty, Actes, Sup. Psalty's report to the congress was enlarged and printed as a monograph: Notre Dame d'Éphèse, Les Ruines de la Maison de la Vierge Marie à Panaya-Capouli; cf. above, Chapter II, note 37. All further references to Psalty will be to the monograph (hereafter cited Psalty). The following may be quoted here in connection with the statement above: "Cette manière de construction rappelle exactement celles des premiers monuments d'Éphèse. Des archéologues de sont déjà prononcés à ce sujet." — Psalty, p. 10.

Chapter V — Notes

1. Cf. Historique, p. 21.
2. Cf. ibid., p. 23; above, Chapter II, note 45.
3. Cf. ibid., p. 24.
4. Barnabé, pp. 216, 217. Translation from this source mine; the French text appears in the Appendix [H]. The complete report appeared also in Poulin's work of 1896; cf. above, Chapter IV, note 117.
5. "Tous ces détails sont rigoureusement exacts . . ." — Barnabé, p. 217. Cf. ibid., pp. 217–219, for individual details.
6. Cf. ibid., pp. 236–239.
7. Cf. above, Chapter IV, note 98. The successors of Timoni were all protectors of Panaya: Marengo, O.P., Zucchetti, O.M.C., Tonna, Descuffi, C.M. And even before Timoni and the discovery of Mary's home, his predecessor, Spaccapietra, was convinced of the Ephesus tradition; cf. Descuffi, "De loco," 215.
8. Cf. Historique, p. 56.
9. Cf. Psalty, pp. 12, 13.
10. Cf. loc. cit.
11. Cf. Historique, p. 57.
12. Cf. above, Chapter II, note 6.
13. Cf. Psalty, p. 14.
14. Cf. Historique, p. 58; Psalty, p. 15.
15. Cf. Psalty, pp. 14, 15; Historique, p. 58. Cf. also below, Chapter VI, § 2, for the miraculous cures.
16. Cf. Historique, p. 116; Life of BVM, p. 362.
17. Life of BVM, p. 362.
18. Cf. Historique, p. 116.
19. Cf. ibid., pp. 116, 117.
20. Quatman, p. 27.
21. Cf. above, Chapter III, notes 95, 96.

Notes

22. Cf. *Historique,* p. 118; above, Chapter III, note 114.
23. Cf. above, Chapter II, note 45.
24. Cf. above, Chapter V, note 8.
25. Cf. *Historique,* pp. 52, 53.
26. Cf. *ibid.,* pp. 53, 54.
27. Cf. *ibid.,* pp. 54, 55.
28. Cf. above, Chapter II, note 52.
29. Cf. *Historique,* p. 55.
30. Cf. *loc. cit.*
31. Cf. *loc. cit.*
32. Cf. below, Chapter VI, note 22.
33. Cf. *Historique,* p. 150.
34. The change of name occurred in 1959; cf. Dierickx, *art. cit.*, 712. The offices of the *Meryem Ana Dernegi* are located at 210 Atatürk Bulvari, Izmir, Turkey.
35. Cf. Descuffi, "La Maison," 41. Interest was particularly aroused by the public announcement, carried by the press, of the pilgrimage of 1950; cf. below, Chapter VI, notes 19, 20.
36. Cf. above, Chapter IV, note 156; below, Chapter VI, notes 18, 19. The total cost of the road exceeded $600,000; cf. Žužić, p. 70.
37. Cf. Quatman, p. 15.
38. In 1952 a Carmelite Father, obstinately faithful to the Jerusalem tradition, remarked to Euzet, who accompanied him to Panaya, "I just don't know why they made such a big road for such a little ruin": "Je ne peux pas comprendre que, pour une si petite ruine, on ait fait une route si importante." — *Historique,* p. 163. Dr. Mukarem Sarol, Minister of State in charge of tourism in 1955, said on a visit to Panaya: "The cause of Panaya for us is not at all a simple matter of tourism; it has for us a high moral significance": "La Cause de Panaya n'est point pour nous une simple affaire de tourisme, elle a pour nous une haute portée morale." — Psalty, p. 3. The road was improved in later years, e.g., it was widened in 1954. By 1959 a new and improved road had been completed by the government. It is entirely paved and wholly acceptable even by critical American standards. Typical of many other kind gestures of the government was the issuance on December 8, 1962, of a lovely set of four stamps in full color depicting various views of Panaya.
39. Quatman, pp. 15–17.
40. "Comme le Souverain Pontife le désire, le sanctuaire de Panaya est ouvert à tous les fidèles de n'importe quelle race et de n'importe quelle religion." — Descuffi, "La Maison," 42.
41. Quatman, p. 17.
42. *Ibid.*, p. 19.
43. Cf. *Historique,* p. 151.
44. Cf. *loc. cit.* The bimonthly bulletin was initiated at Istanbul in 1957 as *Revue Notre Dame d'Éphèse*. Its publication was suspended with the November-December, 1962, issue due to circumstances beyond the control of Archbishop Descuffi and the Panaya society; there is no hope of resumption until sometime in 1965.
45. The names Couillard and Saulais have sometimes appeared as Coulland and Saulois. I am not absolutely certain, therefore, whether my choice for the text is correct. At any rate, Bouis left on January 2, and François S.

on February 22. They went to Ankara for a course in nursing which lasted until May; they then proceeded to El Azig in eastern Turkey to care for the lepers.
46. LeRoux is from France and Allen is from the United States. It is to Father Allen that credit must be given for unraveling certain important facts, which in several sources remain ambiguous, and for supplying information on developments at the shrine since my visit in 1959.
47. The fez and turban were banned by decree in 1925, while the veil disappeared through the initiative of certain groups. In 1935 the use of ecclesiastical costume in public, other than inside places of worship, was banned. Cf. *The Catholic Encyclopedia, Supplement II* (Vol. 18) (New York: The Gilmary Society, 1950), s.v. *Turkey*.
48. Personal letter of April 8, 1963. Allen left *Panaya* on September 11, 1964.
49. Any donation may be sent to Father Allen, Montfort Fathers, 101-18 104th St., Ozone Park, N. Y., or to his replacement at *Panaya*, Father Hubert Pocock, S.M.M., Meryem Ana, Selçuk, Izmir, Turkey. Pocock arrived November 27, 1964.
50. Cf. above, Chapter II, note 45.
51. Cf. above, Chapter V, note 25.
52. The old caretaker Aziz, who spent twenty years at *Panaya*, had died in 1950; cf. above, Chapter II, note 53. Between that time and the arrival of the priests, the presence of the workers of the *Panaya* society guaranteed adequate protection of the shrine.
53. Letter of May 22, 1963, from Father Allen, containing data related by Archbishop Descuffi and the Sisters of Charity. In 1853 the Sisters of Charity were installed at the French Hospital, built in 1757 for the French Navy. The Sisters were called the *Yedi Kizlar* — Seven Girls, the name given to the first seven Sisters of Charity to arrive in Smyrna in 1839. In 1922, when the hospital was turned over to the needs of the city, the French doctors were replaced by Turkish doctors, but the Sisters remained.
54. Cf. also below, Chapter VI, note 44. Mr. Quatman died on September 25, 1964, but the ASE continues as a nonprofit organization, with Mr. George Quatman, Jr., as president.
55. Quatman, p. vi.
56. Personal letter of June 10, 1963. The small kiosk is the tiny religious article shop; cf. below, Chapter VI, note 83.
57. *Pictorial Report of the Restoration Work at St. John's Tomb* (Lima, Ohio: The American Society of Ephesus, 1961), p. 1 (hereafter cited *Pictorial Report*). The ASE is a nonprofit organization and has been certified by the U. S. Treasury Department for religious tax exemption; donations are, therefore, deductible. Membership in the society is open to all, and members receive regular reports of the society's activities and accomplishments. For further information write ASE, 122 South Elizabeth Street, Lima, Ohio.
58. Žužić, p. viii.
59. Cf. *Pictorial Report*, p. 11. The Turkish Ministry of National Education must approve all work of restoration and assume responsibility for its genuineness; scientific and artistic evaluation is effected in cooperation with the study of the Austrian Institute of Archaeology; cf. Žužić, p. 86.

60. Cf. above, Chapter III, note 11. The other publications of the ASE are a pamphlet containing its constitution and bylaws, the periodical reports of the society's activities, and the booklet by Quatman, *House of Our Lady*; cf. above, Chapter III, note 64.
61. Some of the discoveries made during the work of excavation included the following: several crypts below the sanctuary floor; coins of the third century; fragments of lamps and vases; pieces of columns, many with their capitals; segments of marble altars, reliefs, railings, and floors; a chapel decorated with paintings of John and other saints; inscriptions on many of the objects just mentioned. For further information on discoveries and general progress of this laudable project, cf. *Pictorial Reports*, which are available from the ASE; cf. also J. Conniff, "Return to Ephesus," *Columbia*, (New York-New Haven, 1921-) 43 (April, 1963), 22, 23.

Chapter VI — Notes

1. Cf. above, Chapter IV, note 50.
2. Cf. *Historique*, pp. 59, 60.
3. Cf. *ibid.*, pp. 61, 62.
4. Cf. *ibid.*, pp. 62–64.
5. Cf. *ibid.*, p. 68.
6. Senior, pp. 19, 20.
7. *Ibid.*, pp. 20, 21.
8. Cf. above, Chapter IV, §§ 4, 5.
9. For a more complete list, cf. *Historique*, pp. 68–73.
10. "Je souhaite que Panaya soit de plus en plus connu et devienne un lieu de pèlerinage mondial!" — Duyuran, p. 63. Cf. *Historique*, p. 71.
11. Cf. *The Catholic Encyclopedia*, Supplement II, s.v. Turkey.
12. Cf. *Historique*, pp. 122, 128; above, Chapter II, note 49.
13. Cf. *Historique*, pp. 128–130.
14. Cf. *ibid.*, p. 131.
15. Cf. *ibid.*, pp. 132, 133.
16. "Vraiment, l'apôtre bien-aimé n'avait pas pu choisir pour lui et la Vierge un endroit plus favorable par l'éloignement, la solitude et la beauté du paysage." — *Historique*, p. 141. Benno Gut later became abbot primate of the Confederated Benedictines, San Anselmo, Rome.
17. Cf. *ibid.*, pp. 134–136.
18. Cf. above, Chapter IV, note 156; Chapter V, note 36.
19. Cf. *Historique*, p. 162.
20. Cf. above, Chapter V, notes 35–38.
21. Cf. above, Chapter V, note 40.
22. Cf. *Historique*, p. 163. The couplets of the canticle of Lourdes were adapted to *Éphèse-Panaghia*; cf. *ibid.*, p. 132.
23. The American military in Turkey make not only pilgrimages to, but even retreats at, Mary's home. Among military pilgrimages from nearby bases, for instance, there were many led from Athens in the late 1950's by Father Robert Overman and his replacement, Father Robert Flanagan. Again, there was the pilgrimage of May, 1960, which included approximately seventy-five members of the general staff of NATO.
24. Personal letter of April 8, 1963.
25. For details on current tours, consult a specialist in pilgrimages, e.g., Hodgson Travel Service, Inc., Dupont Circle Bldg., 1346 Connecticut Ave., N.W., Washington, D. C.

26. Cf. Dierickx, art. cit., 702.
27. Cf. *Historique*, p. 152. The diocesan pilgrimage of August 15, 1960, alone saw more than 2500 pilgrims at *Panaya*; cf. Quatman, p. 32.
28. Personal letter of April 8, 1962, from Father Allen.
29. Personal letter of June 10, 1963, from Father Allen.
30. Quatman, p. 7.
31. *Ibid.*, p. 6; cf. also p. 34.
32. Cf. below, Chapter VI, notes 49–51.
33. Cf. Descuffi, "La Maison," 42.
34. One of those recent apparitions appears in a subsequent section; cf. below, Chapter VI, § 4.
35. The complete official report of one such cure appears in the Appendix [I].
36. In conformity with the decree of Pope Urban VIII (1623–1644) it is hereby stated that all reports of seemingly miraculous events contained herein are sustained solely by human authority and are submitted without reserve to the judgment of the Holy See.
37. The details of this apparition were gathered from *Historique*, pp. 74–78.
38. "Je ne pensais à rien. Je regardais! je regardais! je regardais!" — *Historique*, p. 76.
39. Karatchali was the place where Mary's Station of Calvary was found; cf. above, Chapter V, note 19.
40. Cf. Barnabé, p. 78.
41. The details were gathered from *Historique*, pp. 78, 79.
42. Žužić, p. 57.
43. Conniff, art. cit., 22.
44. Conniff, loc. cit.
45. Cf. above, Chapter V, § 3.
46. Conniff, loc. cit.
47. Žužić, p. 57.
48. Cf. below, Chapter VI, § 4.
49. "This water is authenticated to be miraculous. . . ." — Žužić, p. 70.
50. Cf. below, notes 73–75. The date is given vaguely inasmuch as no one was present when the spring first appeared. It was not in evidence during the pilgrimage of 1896. But it was there after that; cf. Quatman, p. 22.
51. Cf. Quatman, pp. 22, 23.
52. Cf. Senior, p. 18.
53. Toksöz, pp. 108, 109.
54. Details of his cure were gathered from *Historique*, pp. 82, 83.
55. Cf. Senior, pp. 18, 19.
56. Details were gathered from *Historique*, pp. 80–82.
57. "Je viens d'examiner Cotcho, l'enfant au cancer du maxillaire inférieur et des lèvres supérieure et inférieure. Je suis surpris de sa guérison vraiment miraculeuse. Mes sincères compliments à la Soeur Pascaut qui a opéré avec sa poudre un vrai miracle." — *Historique*, pp. 81, 82. The original document is in the archives of the Archbishop of Smyrna.
58. "Canonical inquiries of the Archdiocese [Smyrna] admitted several miracles and cures." — Žužić, p. 70.
59. Cf. below, Chapter VI, note 75.
60. Cf. J. Descuffi, "The Official Report of the Cure," *Fatima Findings* (Baltimore, 1946–), 10 (June, 1955), 1. The complete official report of that

Notes

cure appears in the Appendix [I]. Cf. also R. Larson, "Panaya Kapulu," Extension (Chicago, 1906–), 50 (May, 1956), 27.
61. Cf. *Historique*, p. 152.
62. Toksöz, p. 109.
63. Quatman, p. 32.
64. Cf. Dierickx, art. cit., 712, 713.
65. Letter of November 26, 1962.
66. Letter, April 8, 1963.
67. Loc. cit.
68. Cf. above, Chapter III, note 114; Chapter V, note 22.
69. Léon Bloy (1846–1917) in *La Vieux de la montagne*, p. 334; cf. *Historique*, p. 88.
70. Cf. *Life of BVM*, p. 348.
71. Žužić, p. 71. The island of Samos itself, with its numerous summits, gives the illusion of several islands.
72. "L'orientation est parfaite. . . La porte regarde l'ouest et la mer, le fond de la maison, l'est et la montagne de Bulbuldagh, le côté droit, le sud, et le côté gauche, le nord." — Psalty, p. 6.
73. Quatman, pp. 21, 22. The sentence in quotation marks indicates a statement of Catherine Emmerich; cf. *Life of BVM*, p. 350; above, Chapter II, note 10.
74. Cf. above, Chapter VI, notes 49–51.
75. Personal letter of April 8, 1963, from Father Allen.
76. Cf. above, Chapter V, note 52.
77. Cf. above, Chapter V, note 43. There is a tiny shop with religious articles between the house mentioned and the spring, but as a building it is insignificant; cf. below, Chapter VI, note 83.
78. Cf. above, Chapter V, notes 45, 46.
79. Allen's letter of April 8, 1963. The priests need some sort of a chapel in their house for celebration of Mass, when visiting priests are occupying the two altars of Mary's home, as well as for community prayers and other exercises, which would often be difficult or impossible in Mary's home itself by reason of the visitors.
80. Letter of November 26, 1962.
81. Izmir is served by a railroad which comes from Istanbul and continues south through Ephesus, but the service would not meet the requirements of the average traveler. There are many fine tourist agencies in Izmir, such as *Ege Turizm* and Henry Van Der Zee & Co., which will aid in making the most desirable arrangements (bus, taxi, and so on) according to individual tastes. Izmir itself is served by *Turk Hava Yolari*, the Turkish airlines, with flights from Athens, Istanbul, and Ankara. It is the largest seaport on the west coast of Turkey, the capitol of the province of Smyrna, and quite a metropolis.
82. Letter of May 22, 1963, from Father Allen.
83. Letter of June 10, 1963 from Father Allen.
84. *Life of BVM*, p. 348.
85. Quatman, p. 25.
86. Cf. *Life of BVM*, pp. 347, 348.
87. Quatman, p. 25.
88. Most guidebooks on Ephesus are more than adequate. For one who seeks the ultimate, however, the publication of the Austrian Archaeological In-

stitute is recommended: Josef Keil, *Ephesos, Ein Führer durch die Ruinenstätte und ihre Geschichte* (Wien, 1957). It should be noted with respect to the Austrian maps, however, that they mistakenly apply the name *Bulbul Dagh* to the Coressus; cf. Quatman, p. 25.
89. Conniff, art. cit., 40. Cf. Žužić, pp. 6, 7.
90. Cf. Toksöz, p. 37. The booklet by Toksöz, incidentally, is a very handy guide to the individual monuments of the ruins; he devoted about a page to each.
91. Cf. loc. cit.
92. Cf. above, Chapter V, note 58.

Bibliography

AUTHORS AND REFERENCE WORKS

(N.B. Where authors have definitely favored either the Ephesus or the Jerusalem tradition, the letter [E] or [J] respectively follows their works.)

Acta Apostolicae Sedis, Commentarium Officiale, Romae, 1909–1929, Civitate Vaticana, 1929 —.
Acta Sanctae Sedis, Romae, 1865–1908.
Alexander, N., Historia Ecclesiastica, Venetiis, 1758. [E]
Barnabé (d'Alsace) [Meistermann], O.F.M., Le Tombeau de la Sainte Vierge à Jérusalem, Jérusalem, 1903. [J]
Baunard, Mgr., L' Apôtre Saint Jean, 4 ed., Paris, 1883. [J]
Benedict XIV, Omnia Opera, 12 vols., Romae, 1747–1751. [E]
Brentano, C., Das Marienleben, ed. G. Theiner-Haffner, Innsbruck: Marianischer Verlag, 1952.
Brierre-Narbonne, J., Vie de Saint Marie-Madeleine, Paris, 1933. [E]
Calmet, A., Dictionary of the Holy Bible, 5 vols., London, 1829. [E]
——— Dictionary of the Holy Bible, ed. C. Taylor, rev. E. Robinson, Boston, 1832. [E]
Catholic Encyclopedia, The, 15 vols., New York, 1907–1912.
——— Supplement II (Vol. 18), New York: The Gilmary Society, 1950.
Clarke, H., Ephesus, Smyrna, 1863. [E]
Daniel-Rops, H., The Book of Mary, tr. by A. Guinan, New York: Hawthorn Books, Inc., 1960.
Denzinger, H., Enchiridion Symbolorum, Definitionum et Declarationum de Rebus Fidei et Morum, 30 ed., Friburgi Brisgoviae: Herder, 1955.
Dictionnaire d'Archéologie chrétienne et de Liturgie, ed. F. Cabrol, H. Leclercq, Vol. I, Pt. 2, Paris, 1924, Vol. V, Pt. 2, Paris, 1922.
Dictionnaire de Droit Canonique, ed. R. Naz, incomplete, Paris: Librarie Letouzey et Ané, 1924 —.
Dictionnaire de la Bible, ed. F. Vigouroux, 5 vols., 2 ed., Paris, 1912.
——— Supplément, Vol. I, ed. L. Pirot, Paris, 1928.
Dirheimer, G., Anne Cathérine Emmerich et Clément Brentano, Paris, 1923.
Duchesne, L., Christian Worship, its Origin and Evolution, New York & Toronto: The Macmillan Co., 1949.
Duyuran, R., Éphèse, Ankara: Direction Générale de la Presse, 1951. [E]
Emmerich, A. C., The Dolorous Passion of Our Lord Jesus Christ, 22 ed., London: Burns & Oates, 1955.

―――― *The Life of the Blessed Virgin Mary*, tr. by Sir Michael Palairet, Springfield, Ill.: Templegate, 1954. [E]
Enciclopedia Cattolica, 11 vols., Città del Vaticano, 1948–1952.
Euzet, J., *Historique de la Maison de la Sainte Vierge près d'Éphèse (1891–1961)*, Istanbul: Notre-Dame d'Éphèse, 1961. [E]
Farges, A., *Mystical Phenomena*, tr. by S. P. Jacques, London, 1926. [E]
Fathers of the Church, The, Vol. XIX, Eusebius Pamphili Ecclesiastical History, New York: Fathers of the Church, Inc., 1953.
Fleury, C., *Ecclesiastical History*, Oxford, 1844. [E]
Gabrielovich, M. [Poulin, E., C.M.], *Éphèse ou Jérusalem, tombeau de la sainte Vierge*, Paris- Poitiers, 1897. [E]
―――― *Le Tombeau de la sainte Vierge á Éphèse*, Paris-Poitiers, 1905. [E]
―――― *Ni Sion, ni Gethsémani, Adieu! Jérusalem*, Constantinople, 1910. [E]
―――― *Panaghia-Capouli ou maison de la sainte Vierge près d'Éphèse*, Paris-Poitiers, 1896. [E]
―――― *Un dernier Mot sur le Lieu où est morte la Sainte Vierge*, Rome-Paris, 1921. [E]
Golden Legend of Jacobus de Voragine, The, tr. and adapted by G. Ryan and H. Ripperger, 2 vols., New York: Longmans, Green & Co., 1941.
Gouyet, M., *Découverte dans la montagne d'Éphèse de la Maison où la T. S. Vierge est morte*, Paris, 1898. [E]
Great Commentary of Cornelius à Lapide, The, tr. by T. Mossman, 6 vols., London, 1887. [E]
Gschwind, K., *Wiedererwachendes Ephesus*, Basel: Verlag-Stiftung "Für Ephesus," 1953. [E]
Guyet, C., S.J., *Heortologia*, Urbini, 1728.
Hello, E., *Regards et lumieres*, Paris, 1929. [E]
Henze, C., C.SS.R., *Anna Katharina Emmerich schaut Maria*, Wiesbaden: Credo-Verlag, 1954.
―――― *Meryem Ana (Panaya Kapulu)*, Würzburg, 1961. [E]
Hümpfner, W., O.E.S.A., *Akten der kirchlichen Untersuchung über die stigmatisierte Augustinerin A. K. Emmerick nebst zeitgenössischen Stimmen*, Würzburg, 1929.
―――― *Clemens Brentanos Glaubwürdigheit in seinen Emmerick-Aufzeichnungen*, Würzburg, 1923.
James, M., *The Apocryphal New Testament*, Oxford, 1924.
Jugie, M., *La Mort et L'Assomption de la Sainte Vierge* [Studi e Testi, 114], Città del Vaticano: Biblioteca Apostolica Vaticana, 1944. [J]
Jungmann, J., S.J., *The Early Church* [Liturgical Studies, Vol. VI], tr. by F. Brunner, C.SS.R., Notre Dame, Ind.: University of Notre Dame Press, 1959.
Keil, J., *Ephesos, Ein Führer durch die Ruinenstätte und ihre Geschichte*, Wien, 1957.

Bibliography

Koetting, B., *Peregrinatio Religiosa*, Regensberg, Münster, 1950. [J]
Kopp, C., *Das Mariengrab. Jerusalem?-Ephesus?*, Paderborn: Ferd. Schöningh, 1955. [J]
Lambakis, G., *Hoi heptà Astéres tēs Apokalýpseos*, Athenai, 1909.
Le Camus, Mgr., *Voyage aux sept Églises de l'Apocalypse*, Paris, 1899. [J]
Le Nain de Tillemont, L. S., *Memoires*, Vol. I, *Le Temps de N.-S., et les Apostres*, Paris, 1693. [E]
Lupus, C., *Synodorum Decreta et Canones*, Vol. II, Venetiis, 1724.
Mansi, J., *Sacrorum Conciliorum Nova et Amplissima Collectio*, 53 vols. in 60, Parisiis, 1901–1927.
Many, S., *Praelectiones de locis sacris*, Parisiis, 1904.
Marta, J., *Ni Éphèse, ni Panaghia-Capouli, mais Jérusalem*, Jérusalem, 1910. [J]
Migne, J., *Patrologiae Cursus Completus, Series Graeca*, 161 vols., Parisiis, 1857–1866.
────── *Patrologiae Cursus Completus, Series Latina*, 221 vols., Parisiis, 1844–1855.
Mommert, C., *Die Dormitio und das deutsche Grundstück auf dem traditionellen Zion*, Leipzig, 1899. [J]
Niessen, J., *A. K. Emmerichs Charismen und Gesichte*, Trier, 1918. [E]
────── *Ephesus. Die letzte Wohnstätte der hl. Jungfrau*, Münster i. W., 1931. [E]
────── *Mariologie des hl. Hieronymus*, Münster i. W., 1913. [E]
────── *Panaghia Kapuli: Das neuentdeckte Wohn-und Herbe-Haus der heil. Jungfrau Maria bei Ephesus*, Dülmen i. W., 1906. [E]
Nirschl, Dr., *Das Grab der heiligen Jungfrau Maria*, Mainz, 1896. [J]
────── *Das Haus und das Grab der heiligen Jungfrau Maria*, Mainz, 1900. [J]
Nissen, B., O.P., *Der Rembrandtdeutsche*, Freiburg i. Br., 1926. [J]
Pictorial Report of the Restoration Work at St. John's Tomb, Lima, Ohio: The American Society of Ephesus, 1961.
Pictorial Report . . . No. 2, Lima, Ohio: The American Society of Ephesus, 1962.
Pii IX pontificis maximi Acta, 9 vols., Romae, 1854–1878.
Psalty, F., *Notre Dame d'Éphèse, Les Ruines de la Maison de la Vierge Marie à Panaya-Capouli*, Istanbul: Güler Basimevi, 1955. [E]
Quasten, J., *Patrology*, Vol. I, *The Beginnings of Patristic Literature*, Westminster, Md.: The Newman Press, 1951.
────── *Patrology*, Vol. II, *The Ante-Nicene Literature after Irenaeus*, Westminster, Md.: The Newman Press, 1948.
Quatman, G., *House of Our Lady*, Lima, Ohio: The American Society of Ephesus, 1960. [E]
Reineccius, C., *De Septem Dormientibus*, Lipsiae, 1702.
Righetti, M., *Manuale di Storia Liturgica*, 4 vols., Milano: Editrice Ancora, 1950.

Roschini, G., O.S.M., *Lo Pseudo-Dionigi l'Areopagita e la Morte di Maria SS.*, Roma: Edizioni "Marianum," 1958.
Schmöger, K., *Life of Anne Catherine Emmerich*, 2 rev. ed., New York, 1903.
Senior [Descuffi, J., et al.], *Ephesus, Hazreti Meryem Ana Evi, House of Our Lady*, Izmir: Korsini Basimevi, 1959. [E]
────── *Ephesus or Jerusalem*, Izmir: no pub., 1951. [E]
Serry, J., *Exercitationes de Christo*, Venetiis, 1719. [E]
Teaching of the Catholic Church, The, ed. G. Smith. Vol. II, New York: The Macmillan Co., 1949.
Theodosiani Libri XVI, ed. T. Mommsen, Vol. I, Pt. 2, 2 ed., Berolini: Apud Weidmannos, 1954.
Tischendorf, C., *Apocalypses apocryphae*, Leipzig, 1866.
Toksöz, C., *Ephesus, Legends and Facts*, tr. by Dr. A. E. Uysal, Istanbul: Yenilik Basimevi, 1956. [E]
Vincent, H., et Abel, F., *Jérusalem*, Vol. II, *Jérusalem Nouvelle*, Paris 1926.
Wegener, T., O.E.S.A., *Anna Katharina Emmerich und Clemens Brentano*, Dülmen i. W., 1900.
────── *Sister Anne Katherine Emmerich of the Order of St. Augustine*, tr. by F. X. McGowan, New York-Cincinnati, 1898.
────── *Wo ist das Grab der heiligen Jungfrau Maria?*, Würzburg, 1895. [E]
Wood, T., *Discoveries at Ephesus*, London, 1877.
Zahn, T., *Die Dormitio Sanctae Virginis und das Haus der Johannes-Markus*, Leipzig, 1899. [J]
Zitelli-Natali, Z., *Epitome Historico-Canonica Conciliorum Generalium*, Romae, 1881.
Žužić, M., *A Short History of St. John in Ephesus*, Lima, Ohio: The American Society of Ephesus, 1960. [E]

ARTICLES

Abel, M., O.P., "Sanctuaires Marials en Palestine," *Maria, Études sur la Sainte Vierge*, Vol. IV, ed. H. du Manoir, S.J., Beauchesne et ses Fils, 1956, 855–866.
Aufhauser, J., "Wo befindet sich das echte Mariengrab?" *Actes du X. Congres International d'Études Byzantines, Supplément*, Istanbul: Comite d'Organisation, 1957 [single page unbound summaries].
Bardenhewer, O., "Ist Maria zu Jerusalem oder zu Ephesus gestorben?" *Theologische Revue*, 5 (1906), 569–577. [E]
────── "Kleine Kritiken," *Literarische Rundschau für das katholische Deutschland*, 22 (1896), 345, 346. [E]
Bonnet, C., "Bemerkungen über die älteste Schriften von der Himmelfahrt Maria," *Zeitschrift für wissenschaftliche Theologie*, 23 (1880), 222–247.
Borrel, E., "A-t-on découvert à Éphèse la Maison où mourut la Vierge Marie?" *Ecclesia, Lectures chrétiennes*, 3 (Aug., 1951), 71–75. [E]

Bibliography

Brierre-Narbonne, J., "L'Habitation de la Vierge à Éphèse," *Revue Notre Dame d'Éphèse*, 4 (1960), 171–180. [E]

Burghardt, W., S.J., "The Testimony of the Patristic Age Concerning Mary's Death," *Marian Studies*, 8 (1957), 58–99.

Clemen, C., "The Sojourn of the Apostle John at Ephesus," *The American Journal of Theology*, 9 (1905), 643–676.

Conniff, J., "Return to Ephesus," *Columbia*, 43 (Apr., 1963), 21–23, 38–40. [E]

D'Ales, A., "Le tombeau de la Sainte Vierge," *Revue de l'Orient chrétien*, 28 (1931–1932), 376–389. [E]

De la Broise, R., S.J., "Les dernières années de la Sainte Vierge," *Études*, 72 (1897), 289–303. [J]

Descuffi, J., C.M., "De loco transitus B. Mariae Virginis," *Divus Thomas*, 52 (1949), 213–216. [E]

——— "La Maison de la Sainte Vierge à Éphèse," *Ecclesia, Lectures chrétiennes*, 14 (Aug., 1962), 33–42. [E]

——— "The Official Report of the Cure," *Fatima Findings*, 10 (June, 1955), 1. [E]

Dierickx, M., S.J., "Panagia Kapulu of Meryem Ana," *Streven*, 15 (1962), 702–713. [E]

Euzet, J., "Le Père Jugie et la question de lieu où est morte le Sainte Vierge," *Divus Thomas*, 52 (1949), 345–359. [E]

——— "Remarques sur 'Jérusalem?-Éphèse?' de Clemens Kopp," *Divus Thomas*, 60 (1957), 47–72. [E]

Filogrossi, J., S.J., "Traditio Divino-Apostolica et Assumptio B.V.M.," *Gregorianum*, 30 (1949), 443–489.

Fonck, L., S.J., "Bemerkungen zu den ältesten Nachrichten über das Mariengrab," *Zeitschrift für katholische Theologie*, 22 (1898), 481–507. [E]

——— "Das Grab der Gottesmutter," *Stimmen aus Maria-Laach*, 52 (1897), 143–156. [E]

——— "Über Ephesus nach der 'Wohnung Marias' auf dem Nachtigallenberge," *Stimmen aus Maria-Laach*, 51 (1896), 471–493. [E]

Gordillo, M., S.J., "La muerte de Maria madre de Dios en la tradicion de la Iglesia de Jerusalén," *Estudios Marianos*, 9 (1950), 43–62. [J]

——— "Panaghia-Kapulu," *Ephemerides Mariologicae*, 2 (1952), 359–375. [J]

Hetzenauer, M., O.M.C., "De peregrinatione B. Mariae V. in Panaghia Capuli prope Ephesum," *Verbum Domini*, 2 (1922), 246–254. [E]

Holzmeister, U., S.J., "De anno mortis Deiparae Virginis," *Marianum*, 4 (1942), 167–182.

Hümpfner, W., O.E.S.A., "Übersicht über die Literatur über A. K. Emmerick," *Theologie und Glaube*, 16 (1924), 455–482.

Jugie, M., "La Mort et l'Assomption de la Sainte Vierge dans la tradition des cinq premiers siècles," *Échos d'Orient*, 25 (1926), 5–20, 129–143, 281–307. [J]

Koch, H., "Wo ist das Grab der sel. Jungfrau Maria," *Theologische Quartalschrift*, 78 (1896), 699–702. [J]
Lagrange, M., "La Dormition de la Sainte Vierge et la Maison de Jean-Marc," *Revue Biblique*, 8 (1899), 589–600. [J]
Larson, R., "Panaya Kapulu," *Extension*, 50 (May, 1956), 17–27.
Le Hir, A., "De l'Assomption de la sainte Vierge et les livres apocryphes qui s'y rapportent," *Études bibliques*, Vol. X, Paris, 1866, 514–555.
Massignon, L., "Les fouilles archéologiques d'Éphèse et leur importance religieuse pour la Chrétienté et l'Islam," *Les Mardis de Dar-El-Salam*, 2 (1952), 3–24.
Meinertz, M., "A. K. Emmerick und das Neue Testament," *Theologische Revue*, 28 (1929), 97–104.
Neufeld, A., O.M.C., "Where did the Blessed Virgin Die?" *The Ecclesiastical Review*, 90 (1934), 164–168. [J]
Nirschl, Dr., "Das Mariengrab in Ephesus," *Der Katholik*, 74, 2 (Ser. 3, 10, 1894), 385–407. [J]
North, R., S.J., "Mary's Last Home," *The Ecclesiastical Review*, 123 (1950), 242–261. [J]
Psalty, F., "Les ruines de la maison de la Vierge Marie à Panayakapouli," *Actes du X. Congres International d'Études Byzantines*, Istanbul: Comite d'Organisation, 1957, 152–157, and *Supplément* [single page unbound summaries]. [E]
Richter, J., "The Monuments of Christian Art at Ephesus," *The Academy*, 14 (1878), 97, 98.
Rush, A., C.SS.R., "Assumption Theology in the *Transitus Mariae*," *The Ecclesiastical Review*, 123 (1950), 93–110.
Séjourné, P., "Le lieu de la Dormition de la Très Sainte Vierge," *Revue Biblique*, 8 (1899), 141–144. [J]
Senior [Descuffi, J., et al.], "Éphèse ou Jérusalem," *Marie*, 5 (1951), 12–21. [E]
—— "Our Lady's House at Ephesus," *Fatima Findings*, 10 (Aug., 1955), 1–5. [E]
Streicker, S., "Maria in Ephesus," *Schweizerische Kirchen-Zeitung*, 119 (1951), 441–443.
Stockmann, A., S.J., "Die heutige Stand der Anna Katharina Emmerick-Forschung," *Stimmen aus Maria-Laach*, 119 (1930), 292–306.
Tallon, M., S.J., "Le Culte de la Vierge Marie en Asie Mineure du Ier au XVe Siècle," *Maria, Études sur la Sainte Vierge*, Vol. IV, ed. H. du Manoir, S.J., Paris: Beauchesne et ses Fils, 1956, 887–916. [E]
Thurston, H., S.J., "The Problem of Anne Catherine Emmerich," *The Month*, 138 (1921), 237–248, 344–356, 429–439, 519–530.
—— "The Authenticity of the Emmerich Visions," *The Month*, 143 (1924), 42–52. [E]
Wright, W., "The Departure of My Lady Mary from this World," *Journal of Sacred Literature*, 7 (Apr., 1865), 129–160.

PERIODICALS

Academy, The, London, 1869–1920.
American Journal of Theology, The, Chicago, 1897–1920.
Analecta Bollandiana, Paris-Bruxelles, 1882 —
Byzantinische Zeitschrift, Leipzig, 1892 —
Byzantion, Paris, 1924 —
Columbia, New York-New Haven, 1921 —
Divus Thomas, Piacenza, 1880 —
Ecclesia, Lectures chrétiennes, Paris, 1949 —
Ecclesiastical Review, The, New York-Philadelphia, 1889 —
Échos d'Orient, Paris, 1897 —
Ephemerides Mariologicae, Madrid, 1951 —
Estudios Marianos, Madrid, 1942 —
Études, Paris, 1856 —
Extension, Chicago, 1906 —
Fatima Findings, Baltimore, 1946 —
Gregorianum, Roma, 1920 —
Journal of Sacred Literature, London, 1848 —
Katholik, Der, Mainz, 1821–1918.
Literarische Rundschau für das katholische Deutschland, Aachen-Freiburg i. Br., 1875–1914.
Mardis de Dar-El-Salam, Les, Paris, 1951 —
Marian Studies, Washington, D. C., 1950 —
Marianum, Romae, 1939 —
Marie, Nicolet, Quebec, 1947 —
Month, The, London, 1864 —
Neue kirchliche Zeitschrift, Leipzig, 1890–1933.
Revue Biblique, Paris, 1892 —
Revue Notre Dame d'Éphèse, Istanbul, 1957 —
Revue de l'Orient chrétien, Paris, 1896 —
Schweizerische Kirchen-Zeitung, Luzern, 1832 —
Stimmen aus Maria-Laach, Freiburg i. Br., 1871 —
Streven, Amsterdam, 1945 —
Theologie und Glaube, Paderborn, 1909 —
Theologische Quartalschrift, Tübingen-Ravensburg, 1819 —
Theologische Revue, Münster i. W., 1902 —
Verbum Domini, Romae, 1921 —
Zeitschrift für katholische Theologie, Innsbruck, 1877 —
Zeitschrift für wissenschaftliche Theologie, Leipzig-Frankfurt, 1858–1914.